Higher, Further, Faster

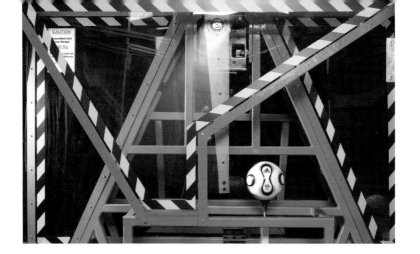

Higher, Further, Faster

Is Technology Improving Sport?

Stewart Ross

Other Wiley Editorial Offices

John Wiley & Sons Inc., 111 River Street, Hoboken, NJ 07030, USA

Jossey-Bass, 989 Market Street, San Francisco, CA 94103-1741, USA

Wiley-VCH Verlag GmbH, Boschstr. 12, D-69469 Weinheim, Germany

John Wiley & Sons Australia Ltd, 42 McDougall Street, Milton, Queensland 4064, Australia

John Wiley & Sons (Asia) Pte Ltd, 2 Clementi Loop #02-01, Jin Xing Distripark, Singapore 129809

John Wiley & Sons Ltd, 6045 Freemont Blvd, Mississauga, Ontario L5R 4J3, Canada

Wiley also publishes its books in a variety of electronic formats. Some content that appears in print may not be available in electronic books.

British Library Cataloguing in Publication Data

A catalogue record for this book is available from the British Library

ISBN 9780470516515

Typeset in 9.5 on 14 pt SM DIN by SNP Best-set Typesetter Ltd., Hong Kong
Printed and bound by Printer Trento in Italy.

Mixed Sources
Product group from well-managed
forests and other controlled sources
www.fsc.org Cert no. CQ-COC-000012
© 1996 Forest Stewardship Council

Contents

Foreword

Technology has had a massive impact in sport, particularly during the past twenty-five years, changing just about every sport in all kinds of ways. The effects of cutting edge technology have permeated most sports, as the examples that follow show. Video analysis and software programmes to analyse team and individual performance – Sportscode in rugby, ProZone in soccer, Silicon Coach / Dartfish in individual sports such as skiing, swimming and gymnastics – now assist coaches to enhance the coaching process. As computers and video cameras have become cheaper, fairly sophisticated software has become available even at lower levels of sport. Software has developed to such an extent that multi-angle views, voice activation, instant replay and recall for coaches during play are now commonplace.

Obviously, developments that help in officiating have also been extremely important; for example, the use of video replays in cricket and rugby to confirm decisions, and the Hawkeye and the Snickometer / Hot Spot technologies employed on TV for cricket matches. And you can bet your bottom dollar that the 2008 Beijing Olympics will be the most hi-tech ever – can't wait!

Moreover, it's pretty clear also that this trend is going to continue. Like it or loathe it, lovers of sport have to face up to this revolution and make up their minds about it.

That's why this book is so important.

Finding out about what's going on is not easy. The information is there, but it's tucked away in all kinds of places. There are specialist magazines, newspaper articles and supplements, websites, blogs, academic journals, books, TV and radio programmes and so on. What *Higher, Further, Faster* does is bring it all together and set it all out, for the first time, in a language that is clear and, as far as is possible in the world of sports technology, jargon-free.

Which brings us back to the vital question, Is technology improving sport? Each one of us – spectator, Sunday jogger, saloon bar pundit, enthusiastic amateur and dedicated professional – has to find his or her own answer. It is vitally important that they do, because what the public thinks will determine the way sport goes in the future.

The pages that follow give you everything necessary to make your decision. Read on – and enjoy!

Mike Ruddock OBE

Neville Southall MBE

Preface

This book is a labour of love – and a voyage of discovery.

Love first.

Sport has always played a major part in my life, from vigorous school activities to my current jogs round the hop fields and idle hours before the TV. I have been fortunate enough to have participated in just about every sport written about in the pages that follow, except ice hockey. I have skated, though.

As a teenager I played good rugby, bad football and terrible hockey. In the 1960s I won the 400-yd on a grass track, a gold medal for hammer throwing at a Hertfordshire junior games (I was the sole competitor) and broke the school shot put record. Later I refereed rugby in Sri Lanka, played soccer in Florida, coached cricket in England and swam off Saudi Arabia. Later still I watched in amazement as Massey destroyed England at Lords, Dusty Hare converted from the touchline (or so it seemed) to overcome the all-conquering Welsh and Liverpool came back from the dead to beat Milan in the Ataturk Stadium.

So when I was asked whether I'd like to write a book about technology and . . . the answer had to be yes – as long as the missing word was 'sport'.

Thus began my 18-month voyage of discovery. The further I have travelled, the more I realise how broad the sea is and what a tiny portion of it I have crossed. But I have never pretended to be an expert and I have, I hope, made some progress towards my goal: to produce a guide for people like myself – sports enthusiasts who would like to know more of the forces that are shaping their passions and their pastimes.

To my surprise, what began as a quite light-hearted exploration has turned out rather serious. Coming ashore on lands hitherto unknown to me and turning over stones there, I have uncovered some very nasty beasts indeed, creatures that need to be crushed before they get too powerful. Sport and the values and traditions that underpin it are fundamental to a free society. The ancient Greeks knew this and we in turn lose sight of it at our peril.

In sport as in society at large, technology *per se* is neutral – but how we employ it is not. There are crucial decisions to be made and this book will, I hope, be of some help in getting them right.

Glossary

Aerobic – using oxygen (usually refers to longer-lasting exercise that draws oxygen from the blood).

Anabolic – building up (usually refers to muscle and related tissue).

Anaerobic – without using oxygen (usually refers to exercise that lasts only a matter of seconds).

Androgenic – making masculine.

Binding – mechanism for fastening a ski to a boot.

Biomechanics – science concerned with the internal and external forces acting on the human body and the effects produced by these forces.

BOA – British Olympic Association.

Bobs – bobsleighs.

Carbon fibre – graphite in fibre form.

CD – controlled drug.

Ceramic – inorganic non-metallic substance formed by heat.

CFD – computational fluid dynamics – the study of fluid flow.

CFRP – carbon fibre reinforced plastic.

Chip – golf shot with a steeply angled iron club which allows the ball to drop with a minimum of roll.

CoR – Coefficient of Restitution – measurement of how efficiently the power of the striking golf club is transferred to the ball (see CT).

CRP – carbon reinforced plastic.

Cryogenic – produced at very low temperature.

CT – Characteristic Time, an improved method of measuring how efficiently the power of the striking golf club is transferred to the ball (see also CoR).

Cyclops – system of infrared beams used in tennis to help determine whether serves are in or out.

DEA – Drug Enforcement Agency (US).

DHEA – dehydroepiandrosterone (hormone).

Dissociation – switching off the brain's 'I'm-at-my-limit' mechanism.

Drag – force on a body travelling thorough fluid (includes air).

EPO – erythropoietin (hormone).

Epoxy – structure comprising oxygen and two other linked atoms, one of which is often carbon – usually found in glues and resins.

EVA – ethylene vinyl acetate, often known as simply 'acetate'.

FA – Football Association (England).

Fast twitch – muscle type used for swift movement such as sprinting.

FIBT – Fédération Internationale de Bobsleigh et de Tobogganing – world governing body for sleigh sports.

FIFA – Fédération Internationale de Football Association – world governing body for football.

FISA – Fédération Internationale des Sociétés d'Aviron (International Federation of Rowing Associations) – world governing body for rowing.

Friction – force when two things (solid, fluid, air) rub against each other.

Glycogen – substance that stores energy short-term in animal cells.

Graphite – most stable, coal-like form of carbon.

Guttie – traditional golf ball made from gutta-percha, a rubbery substance from an Asian tree.

Hawkeye – computer-camera system that tracks the path of a ball.

HGH – human growth hormone.

Hydrophilic – absorbing water.

Hydrophobic – rejecting water.

IAAF – International Association of Athletics Federations – world governing body for track and field.

ICU – International Cycle Union (Union Cycliste Internationale) – world governing body for cycling.

Irons – iron-headed golf clubs offering accuracy rather than distance.

ITF – International Tennis Federation – world governing body for tennis.

ITTF – International Table Tennis Federation – world governing body for table tennis.

Kevlar – light, strong synthetic fibre.

Kinanthropometry – using measured data to predict the body's condition and thence its performance potential.

Lactate – chemical compound produced by the body when the demand for energy is high; associated with muscle fatigue and soreness.

Lactic threshold – point during exercise when the amount of lactate in the muscles builds quicker than it can be removed.

Laminate – comprising several layers, usually of different materials.

LBW – leg before wicket (method of dismissal in cricket).

Luge – small sleigh on which one or two riders travel feet first.

MGF – mechano growth factor, a hormone that stimulates growth.

MLB – Major League Baseball (US).

Monocoque – in a single piece.

Motion analysis – acquiring highly detailed information technologically in order to analyse an athlete's performance.

MVT – Moisture Vapour Transfer.

NBA – National Basketball Association (US).

NBL – National Basketball League (US).

NFL – National Football League (US).

ODS – Overall Distance Standards (golf).

OTC – medicine available over the counter.

PCM – 'phase change' material – one that absorbs and releases heat without gaining or losing much temperature itself.

Piezoelectric – producing electricity when under stress.

Pitch – (water sports) alternate up and down movement of a boat's bow and stern.

Plyometrics – increasing power by the repeated stretching and contracting of muscles.

POM – prescription-only medicine.

Power – (in simple sporting terms) speed plus strength.

Proprioception – awareness of one's own body.

R&A – Royal and Ancient Golf Club, St Andrew's, Scotland, the body controlling the British game.

Rebound – bounce.

Reef – decreasing the area of a sail by rolling or tying it up.

Reframing – mentally breaking a protracted task, such as running a marathon, into manageable chunks.

Reverse swing – phenomenon of a worn cricket ball swinging through the air towards its polished side.

Rigger – metal structure extending the rowlock (oarlock) beyond the side of the boat.

Rowlock – fitting that holds an oar in place and allows it to pivot freely.

Shear-thickening – increasing in viscosity as the force exerted upon it grows – like honey when stirred.

Skeleton – small, single-person sleigh on which the rider lies head first.

Slalom – alpine skiing between poles.

SLE – Spring-Like Effect or trampoline effect of the face of a golf driver.

STF – shear-thickening fluids.

Sweet spot – point on a bat, racket, etc., offering best power and control when striking a ball.

Testosterone – potent steroid hormone secreted mainly by the testes.

TGH – tetrahydrogestrinone (hormone).

Transponder – wireless communications device that picks up an incoming signal and responds to it.

Trinity – electronic device that measures net vibrations to help rule on service faults in tennis.

Turn – cricket ball spinning off the pitch when bowled by a slow bowler.

USGA – United States Golf Association.

Visualisation – creating a positive mental image of an activity which one is to undertake.

VO2 – rate at which the body can absorb oxygen and use it.

Vulcanisation – technique for hardening rubber by heating and compounding it with sulphur.

WADA – World Anti-Doping Agency.

Woods – golf clubs for driving the ball long distances, originally wooden.

Acknowledgements

This book could not have been written without a great deal of help from many who have so kindly and freely given of their time, judgement and expertise. In particular, I would like to express my sincere thanks to BBC Rugby Correspondent Ian Robertson, rowing expert Richard Hooper, lawyer Tom Hawes of Tilnar Art, footballer Neville Southall, MBE, rugby man Mike Ruddock, OBE, film maker and photographer Christopher Neame, Geraint and Gethin Evans of GZ Sports Management Group, Christopher Laughton of Rocat™, Myra Cordrey of Henley Royal Regatta/PJPix, sailor Adrian Murch, cricketer Mike Wagstaffe, running back Alex Ross, hockey player Ben Hare, Brian Spence of McCready Sailboats, contacts master Charlie Ross, boxer Barry McGuigan, MBE, psychologist and omni-sportsman Dr Simon Hewson, sports medicine advisor Dr Bill Lloyd-Hughes, triathlete and Cross-Channel swimmer Dave Chisholm, school master and rugby man John Burnage, Dr Sharon J. Dixon of Exeter University's School of Sport and Health Sciences, Dr Mark King of Loughborough University's Sports Science Department, Dr Ian Swaine of Canterbury Christ Church University's Department of Sports Science, Tourism and Leisure, Dr Nick Ball, of Portsmouth University's Department of Sport and Exercise Science, my agent James Wills of Watson, Little Ltd for setting the whole thing up so efficiently and effectively and passing on useful information from time to time, to my Wiley editors Sally Tickner, Rosie Kemp and the admirably tactful and unflappable Colleen Goldring, and last but most importantly Lucy, the perfect reader, support and comforter. Despite much magnificent help, however, a book of this nature will inevitably contain errors – these, of course, are all my fault.

Introduction

The relationship between sport and technology is as old as civilisation itself. In 708 BC, the Greeks introduced a new event into their Olympic Games: a standing-start long jump. Athletes held 3-kg stone or lead weights (known as *halteres*) in either hand and swung them forward at take-off. This may sound daft – more weight means less distance, surely? – but research shows that skilfully swung halteres alter the jump trajectory in the athlete's favour, giving them around 6% extra distance.

That vital 6% – ancient Greek long jumpers gained significant extra distance by swinging forward lead halteres at take off.

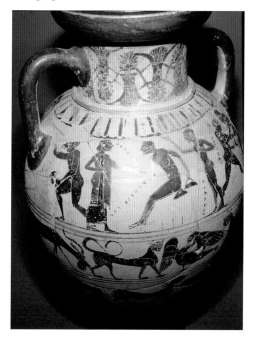

We like to believe that we have come a long way since naked Greeks strutted their stuff across the turf of ancient Olympia, yet the motivation behind the swinging weights has not changed. Today, even more than then, we will employ any device, any technology to increase our chance of winning. It is no coincidence that one of our leading manufacturers of high-tech sportswear has chosen the brand name 'Nike' – the winged goddess of victory who presided over Olympia.

The **relationship** between sport and **technology** is **as old as civilisation** itself

In modern times, two forces have wrought a revolution in the way technology is employed in sport. The most powerful of these engines is the overt professionalisation that has changed sport from a pastime into a major international business worth many billions. The second is the startling technological progress, born of the industrial revolution, which has impacted upon all areas of sporting competition, from clothing to stadiums and diet.

In the first part of the book, I will introduce this dramatic transformation by examining the impact of technology on eight spheres common to several sporting activities: bats and balls, clothing and footwear, officiating, machinery, water and air craft, surfaces and stadiums, implements and training, diet and drugs. Each chapter begins with a quick look at where we have come from, continues with an examination of current cutting-edge technology, and ends with a look at what changes may emerge in the immediate future.

The second part of the book, as the old football cliché goes, is a game of two halves. The first wonders where sport will be 75 years from now. It focuses on football (the 209th FA Cup Final), track and field athletics, tennis, cycling,

Top technology + top talent = near perfection in the form of sporting superstar Tiger Woods.

swimming (all featuring, in different ways, in the 2080 Olympics), hockey, golf, rugby and cricket, with brief comments on the Paralympics, motorsport and winter sports. In every case the conclusion is unequivocal: stimulating or just plain scary, the future will be very, very different.

The last chapter debates the question posed in the book's title, 'Is Technology Improving Sport?' The prosecution and the defence state their cases, centring around four issues that have cropped up time and again in the preceding pages. In simplest terms these involve technology's role in (i) turning sport into a profit-making industry, (ii) widening the gulf between élite performers and the rest, (iii) performance enhancement, and (iv) the escalating economic cost of world-class performance.

Having heard the evidence, I hand down a verdict. It is by no means definitive. Ultimately it is up to the entire sporting community – participants, spectators, backers and the media – to decide what sort of relationship they want sport and technology to have. The book ends with a little marriage guidance, offered in the hope that the ongoing partnership will be a happy and fruitful one.

I The Sport-Tech Revolution

1 Bat and Ball

The liaison between technology and sporting implements, like true love, rarely runs smooth. During a history that stretches back over 110 years, the ground of the Western Australian Cricket Association, affectionately known as the WACA, has seen some pretty memorable moments. None more so than what happened during the first test of the Australia and England Ashes series, 1979–1980.

During Australia's first innings, their fiery fast bowler Dennis Lillee came to the wicket carrying an extremely odd-looking bat. Looks, however, were nothing compared with the sound it made: something between a clang and a ping. This was hardly surprising as Lillee's bat, made by a friend of his who ran an avant-garde bat business, had been forged from aluminium.

Lillee drove a ball from England paceman Ian Botham and ran three runs. His captain Greg Chappell, sitting in the pavilion, believed that the blow had been stout enough to warrant a four. Blaming the bat for the shortfall, he sent a wooden replacement into the middle with instructions that Lillee was to use it. With scowls and significant gestures, he refused.

Meanwhile, the England captain Mike Brearley was complaining to the umpires that the metal bat was damaging the ball and should therefore not be allowed. It did not, though, contravene any regulation. Impasse. The game stopped for a good 10 minutes while, during a heated argument, the merits and otherwise of the new-fangled implement were discussed.

Watch the whole incident on YouTube:
http://www.youtube.com/watch?v=7Pak_OL3rhc

In the end, the umpires and Australian captain prevailed and Lillee was ordered to resume his innings with a conventional wooden bat. Furious at the enforced separation, he hurled his shiny new friend a full 35 m towards the pavilion.

Shortly afterwards, metal bats were outlawed in the laws of cricket.

From There . . .

A Bunch of Crooks

Human beings have been whacking ball-shaped objects with sticks since time immemorial. The ancient Egyptians probably had the first bash, the Romans

Human beings **have been whacking** ball-shaped **objects with sticks** since **time** immemorial

spread the idea around, the Aztecs invented the rubber ball, while Australian aborigines had their own version called dumbung. But it was not until about 1,000 years ago that we can clearly see the emergence of separate bat-and-ball games, the early precursors of cricket, golf, tennis, hockey and the range of variations that include squash, croquet, badminton and table tennis.

The first implements used in ball games were remarkably similar. Players of early golf, cricket and hockey used what was essentially a wooden shaft with an L-shaped crook at one end. Rackets, originally no more than a paddle, developed out of the need to find something a bit more powerful and less painful than a gloved hand with which to hit the ball, although the glove concept remains in fives.

> The word 'racket' or 'racquet' probably derives, via the French *raquette*, from the Arabic *rahat*, meaning the palm of the hand.

Discrete equipment for specific sports was definitely being used by the time of Henry VIII. While the king thundered about to good effect with a tennis racket, in his sister's northern kingdom of Scotland people were chipping a variety of round objects along sandy shores with wooden clubs. Irons, a later development, were used sparingly as they damaged the ball too much. Strangely, the earliest reference to a cricket bat (1624) is of a player using one to clout a fielder who was apparently trying to catch him out. The tragic consequence was not the dismissal of the batsman but of the fielder – to his grave.

Wood and Willow

The basic technology of the racket was in place by the late 19th century. It comprised sticks of ash wood carefully steamed and bent into a round or oval shape at the end of a handle. The pieces were held together with traditional animal glue made by the lengthy (and smelly) boiling of connective tissue. The proteins of the resultant soup made molecular bonds with the materials they joined. There were no worldwide regulations governing the size and construction of tennis rackets before 1979.

> Until the later 20th century, boiled-up skin, bones, tendons and hooves made the most popular glues, hide being the favoured raw material for wood adhesive.

A racket's strings were fashioned from sheep gut, with the longer and cheaper cow gut taking over after World War II. The most significant technological development until recently was the use of several woods – ash with mahogany, beech, hornbeam, sycamore and other alternatives – stuck together to form a ply of the desired weight, strength, pliability and rigidity. And there, more or less, the racket stood until the 1970s.

Golf's marriage with **technology** is **as enduring as that** of any sport

Golf's marriage with technology is as enduring as that of any sport. By the 15th century handcrafted clubs were being produced with heavy hardwood heads of holly or apple, spliced and leather-bound to shafts of ash or hazel. Metal heads first appeared in the mid-18th century and shafts of American hickory in the early 19th century. A major change followed the introduction of the gutta-percha ball ('guttie' – see below) a few years later, leading to modern-style drivers with heads

A load of kit from the garage? Maybe, but each seemingly simple piece of equipment has benefited from years of technological development.

of persimmon wood, grooved irons (1902) that gave greater grip and therefore backspin, and steel shafts that were legalised in the 1920s.

Cricket bats continued to look like hockey sticks until changes in bowling technique, first pitching then overarm, gave rise to the modern parallel-sided willow bat. In the mid-19th century, the one-piece bat was replaced by one with a spliced handle that before long was universally constructed of cane with bone then rubber springing. Similar techniques were used in the manufacture of hockey sticks, with a hardwood head spliced onto a sprung handle. Even the genteel game of croquet caught the technology bug, branching out into mallets with rubber heads and metal reinforcements.

A Load of Balls

In certain major sports – notably football, cricket, golf and tennis (baseball, too, although we do not have space to afford the coverage it warrants) – the composition and behaviour of the ball is key to the way the game is played. Consequently, ball technology is crucial.

Over the years, the golf ball has been subjected to considerable scientific investigation. Even the earliest balls – 'featheries' – were masterpieces of the technology of their day. Some sources credit the enterprising Rev. Robert Paterson with first fashioning the sap of the Malaysian sapodilla tree into the much cheaper 'guttie' (gutta-percha) ball, thereby revolutionising the game. The next step was to realise that the flight of balls with abrasions was truer than that of smooth ones, leading to balls manufactured with regular indentations.

Sewn together from three pieces of tough hide, the casing of the 'featherie' golf ball was then turned inside out, tightly stuffed with freshly boiled fowl feathers, stitched up, hammered into shape while still wet, and finally painted. The expansion of the drying feathers made the ball surprisingly hard.

Just over 100 years ago, the guttie was replaced by a 'Haskell' ball that had a solid rubber core bound with rubber thread and enclosed in a dimpled case of balata, a type of non-elastic latex. Although other designs were experimented with, including a pneumatic ball that had the unfortunate characteristic of exploding on hot days, the Haskell ball remained standard until technology again struck in the 1970s.

Unlike golf, the authorities controlling cricket, baseball and tennis resisted technological change on the balls used in their sports. By about 1700, cricket balls comprised a sewn leather outer round a hard core; the modern standard construction of a wound cork inner and stitched leather outer has remained unchanged from the later 19th century.

'Those twin orbs of the [British] empire, the cricket ball and the blackball' – Patrick Leigh Fermor

The ball used in baseball followed a similar pattern of construction and resistance to innovation. Given both sport's almost obsessive interest in individual performance statistics, the maintenance of relatively standard equipment over the years is understandable.

Lawn tennis, formally recognised as a sport in the 1870s, used vulcanised rubber balls, originally solid from the outset. The major technological innovations were the creation of a hollow pressurised ball and a wear-resistant felt cover. The exterior of Melton wool fabric was reinforced with nylon to make it harder wearing and the traditional single-piece cloverleaf construction of the rubber core was replaced by welding two hemispheres.

Football-Soccer

Makeshift games of football are as old as the human race. Although the Chinese and South Americans kicked around something akin to a sphere, elsewhere in the world the 'ball' might be anything from a human head – 'Alas, poor Yorick, he hit the crossbar!' – to an inflated animal bladder. The bladder idea caught on and by the 19th century it was customary to protect it with an outer skin of leather. Bladders, however, are not round (hence the balls used for rugby and American football) and it was not until the first rubber bladder appeared in 1862 that technology enabled football to become a serious sport. The Football Association (FA), the governing body of the sport in England, was founded in 1863 but made no regulations concerning the ball until 1872.

If you want more, try: http://www.soccerballworld.com/History.htm

Between that date and the rapid technological innovation of recent times, the soccer ball changed little. It was strengthened by adding a layer of cloth between the bladder and the leather casing, and it was more likely to retain its shape once interlocking panels had replaced the traditional 18-section exterior of stitched and tanned cowhide.

Injuries to the head and neck when heading the ball remained a serious problem. This was largely because leather balls absorbed water in damp conditions, sometimes doubling their weight. Non-porous paints offered only a partial solution. The other danger of heading – catching one's forehead on the rough lacing that sealed the hole through which the bladder was inserted and inflated – was removed by the invention of a neater valve that fitted flush with the surface of the ball. Heading the old-style leather balls was not the only danger – just kicking a mud-and-water

Injuries to the **head and neck** when **heading the ball** remained a **serious** problem

sodden rugby ball was enough to seriously damage the knee cartilage of Scotland international Ian Robertson.[1]

Heading to Death

In 2002, the coroner for South Staffordshire said that the death of West Brom and England footballer Jeff Astle at the age of 59 was probably the result of an 'industrial disease' – prolonged heading of a heavy leather football.[2] He often said heading a football was like banging your head against a 'bag of bricks'.

. . . To Where We Are Now

Clubs, Rackets and Bats

Power Drivers

Technology hit the contents of the golf bag in the late 1960s. The first part of the club to be affected was the shaft, whose weight was cut by almost 10% when

[1] In conversation with the author on 15 January 2007. I am most grateful to Mr Robertson, now BBC Rugby Correspondent, for this and other lively observations on rugby and technology.
[2] Mr Astle's official cause of death was dementia.

lightweight steel developed for the space and aero industries replaced heavier metal. Why did this matter? Well, for the average golfer like myself, for whom a perfect shot was something of a rarity, it didn't matter too much. But for top-notch players, a lighter shaft meant a quicker downswing, greater impact on the ball and therefore greater distance in the shot. It was once claimed that for such golfers, 1 mph of extra swing speed was said to equate, very roughly, to an extra 3 yd of distance, although we now know that the physics is a good deal more complicated than that.[3]

So-called 'graphite' shafts emerged in the mid-1970s, promising an even better weight-strength ratio. What is marketed as graphite is actually carbon fibre reinforced plastic (CFRP) in which the carbon (graphite) is used to strengthen an epoxy-like substance. A shaft is made by winding sheets of CFRP round a steel rod, baking the lot in an oven, then removing the rod to produce a hollow tube of CFRP that is light and strong – but also expensive. Going by different trade names such as 'Mitsubishi Rayon', by the mid-noughties CFRP appeared to have become the favoured shaft of the top professionals.

> True graphite, found in pure coal and pencil lead, would be worse than useless in a golf club.

The technology of the clubhead, notably of drivers, entered new territory in the 1970s when hollow metal clubheads began to replace the traditional persimmon woods. This led to the analysis of a phenomenon known as the Spring-Like Effect

---

[3] See US Golf Association on the subject: http://www.usga.org/news/2006/april/distance.html

(SLE). What happened was this: to maximise the size of a driver's 'sweet spot', the size of the clubhead was increased and, surprisingly, it was found that the ball travelled further. The broad club face, now made of titanium, was acting like a trampoline when it came into contact with the ball, adding 'bounce' to the force of the strike. Once this was realised, clubheads were made even bigger, rising from 250 cc of volume to today's maximum of 460 cc.

> The 'sweet spot' is the point on a bat, racket, etc., that offers the best power and control when striking a ball. More specifically, it is a combination of three points: one that gives the best bounce, one with the least vibration and a third known as the 'centre of percussion'.

Governing bodies quickly stepped in to prevent technology rendering all existing golf courses obsolete. The measurement they used was the rather technical-sounding Coefficient of Restitution (CoR). The CoR of a wooden club, with no SLE and using a normal ball, is about 0.78. The CoR of a 'trampolining' giant titanium-faced club is limited to 0.83, although, if there were a market for them, manufacturers could make clubs with an even higher CoR. In a further effort to tighten the regulations, CoR was recently replaced by a new and more accurate measurement of the SLE known as Characteristic Time (CT).

> In layman's terms, CoR quantifies the amount of energy lost when an object (the club) collides with another (the ball) – in other words, how efficiently the power of the striking club is transferred to the ball. A CoR of one would mean no loss of energy.

It has been suggested that in major tournaments **all players use identical clubs**. But **which** clubs? There's **the rub**.

All this toing and froing between administrators and manufacturers harms the good name of the sport because there is always a sneaking feeling that, as in motor racing, a winning performance might be due to technology rather than skill. In an effort to stop the suspicion of technology triumphing over talent, it has been suggested that in major tournaments all players use identical clubs. But which clubs? There's the rub.

Dangerous driving . . . Unregulated technological development would render obsolete every golf course in the world.

▌▌ [The rules outlaw] any device . . . **to change deliberately** any physical **property** which may affect the performance **of the racket** ▌▌

Creating a Racket

Technology's impact on the modern tennis game is not dissimilar to that on golf, increasing the power of shots to the extent that the viability of the game at the top level has been threatened. To a great extent, this has been solved by altering the balls and tighter regulations over racket specifications, stipulating a maximum size and outlawing 'any device . . . to change deliberately any physical property which may affect the performance of the racket.'[4]

Wooden rackets are now for collectors and sentimentalists. Metal rackets, made of varieties of aluminium and steel, were in widespread use by the 1970s and today offer the best value for money. Oversized heads appeared at the same time, offering the player a larger 'sweet spot'. When it was found that large-headed metal rackets had a tendency to deform considerably when the ball was hit off-centre, sending it flying off at an embarrassing angle, graphite (see above) became the favoured material for top-of-the-range players. Frames of varying thickness soon followed.

Compared with a traditional wooden racket, a modern one with a composite frame (in which the graphite is combined with a number of materials, including ceramics, boron and Kevlar) has a 40% larger head, is three times stiffer and 30% lighter.

[4] ITF Rules of Tennis, 2007 on http://www.itftennis.com/shared/medialibrary/pdf/original/IO_23865_original.PDF

Lighter rackets may mean fewer injuries (e.g. tennis elbow), certainly among amateurs. Less weight is not necessarily an advantage; however, former world no 1 Pete Sampras reputedly added lead weights to his rackets to produce a 'heavier' serve. The real advantage of the modern graphite racket is in its greater stiffness, which gives the player greater control because the head distorts less as it makes contact with the ball.

Developments at the cutting edge include the incorporation of piezoelectric technology into rackets. Piezoelectric crystals, which produce electricity when under stress, are incorporated into the frame. The current generated by a ball hitting the strings is sent to the handle, amplified and returned to the ceramic composites in the frame, causing them to stiffen. The claimed result is greater power and 50% less vibration. We have come a heck of a long way since, barely 20 years ago, Bjorn Borg was winning Grand Slams with a racket of plain old wood!

For more on piezoelectronics (pretty technical), try: http://www.sem.org/ PDF/kistler_PiezoStar.pdf

Bats and Sticks

The regulators of cricket and field hockey have resisted technology-led change in bats and sticks more fiercely than those of golf and tennis. Perhaps this is no surprise. The latter sports are massively influenced by the USA, where dollars, especially those of sports gear manufacturers, give innovation a momentum that is difficult to resist. Every change, every well-marketed development, sends thousands of opulent enthusiasts off to the shops, virtual or otherwise, to bring their equipment up-to-date.

The length and width of a cricket bat are laid down in the laws of the game (Law 6). So too is the composition of the wooden blade, which may be covered with a material no more than 1.56 mm thick. The stipulation of a wooden blade followed the famous incident, featured at the beginning of this chapter, when Dennis Lillee came to the wicket with an aluminium bat: the din it made when striking the ball was drowned only by the cacophony of complaints.

The post-Lillee laws leave two areas of flexibility: the bat's handle and its weight. In the latest bats, the traditional cane and rubber handle is replaced by one of carbon fibre with a polymer insert. There is even talk of incorporating piezoelectric technology to dampen vibrations, as tried in tennis rackets. Experiments have also been made with the different coverings on the blade, but results have been inconclusive. The main distinguishing feature of the modern bat is not so much its composition as the increased power that comes with greater weight, principally lower down the blade. [The weight of willow wielded by today's big hitters (over 3 lbs, or 1.4 kg) can be as much as one third greater than that of the slim bats with which the greatest batsman of all, Sir Donald Bradman, stroked and nurdled the ball around the field.]

As one might expect, from the 1970s onwards graphite and composite materials have appeared in both field and ice hockey sticks. Metal was tried, then banned on safety grounds: a broken stick became a lethal spear. Carbon fibre and Kevlar are currently the favoured man-made materials, although in both sports there are first-class players who still prefer the traditional wooden stick. As with cricket bats, hockey sticks now come in a variety of lengths and weights to suit individual players and their roles during the game.

More Balls

Spins and Scoops

A perfectly smooth and spherical ball hit at precisely 90 degrees and travelling through tranquil air would fly in a dead straight line. Sport, however, is not like that. For a variety of reasons, such as the uneven surface of the ball or because it is spinning, air invariably passes more easily over one side of the ball than the other. This introduces two effects (physics-o-phobes look aside now): (i) Bernoulli's Principle that as the velocity of a fluid (this includes air) increases, the pressure it exerts decreases, and (ii) the Magnus Effect, which is that an object spinning in air or liquid creates a whirlpool about itself.

The practical effect of all this is that when a ball spins, air moves quicker past the side that is going with the spin than against it. At speed, air pressure builds up on the side going against the spin while it decreases on the other side because it can flow by more easily. The ball then moves (is drawn) into the area of lower pressure, swerving up, down or sideways as it passes through the air.

The spin effect applies to footballs, tennis balls and, to some extent, cricket balls. Actually, faster bowlers prefer to use the raised seam that joins the two halves of the ball together. If the ball is delivered so that the seam, running vertically, faces more to one side than the other, then the air passes more swiftly over the side without the seam, causing the ball to swerve in the air.

If you want to know about the physics of swing, start here: http://www.geocities.com/k_achutarao/MAGNUS/magnus

A golf ball's dimples give it characteristics all of its own. Like balls used in other sports, a golf ball with backspin will travel a greater distance because the air on top is moving in the same direction as the spin, and therefore more easily. As a consequence, the more pressured air below, going against the spin, forces the ball higher and, if it is launched at the right angle, further. However, a dimpled ball goes even further because its inundations act like spinning scoops, pushing the air backwards. This reduces drag (explained in the 'Ply to Plastics' section of Chapter 5) as it helps level the pressure behind the ball with that in front.

Beautiful dimples: a dimpled ball with backspin travels further than a plain sphere because air flows more easily over the top than the bottom.

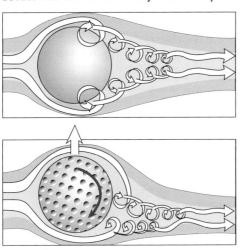

Flying High

Aware of the physics of golf ball flight, modern manufacturers have sought to use its principles to give the players maximum distance and control. A standard ball size and weight were first introduced in the 1930s but by the 1970s, when the behaviour of a ball was better understood, it became clear that these limits were insufficient. The result was a sort of 'hittability' test, known as Overall Distance Standard (ODS), which stipulated the maximum distance a ball might travel when launched with a specific force.

In 2002, the ODS was raised from 296 yd to 320 yd (golf measurements are traditionally imperial, not metric), although most professionals reckon that the chief benefit of modern balls is consistently straight flight rather than added distance. The extra yardage was obtained by working out the optimum placing, number and size of the dimples, and improving the ball's CoR (see above) with a harder core. By now a three-layer ball with a polyurethane exterior was in production, low-flying and slow spinning when hit off the tee but fast spinning and high-flying when struck with an iron.

We are nearing **something** of a **performance plateau** with the average driven distance increasing by **less than** a **yard** a year

By the early noughties, the combination of ball and club technology was threatening to make even the best courses too short – the mighty Masters course at Augusta, Georgia, had to be lengthened by 500 yd. Fortunately, however, it now seems that we are nearing something of a performance plateau with the average driven distance increasing by less than a yard a year.

Bending It like Beckham

As the physicists got to work on the football, FIFA (the body controlling the world game) established a standard size, pressure, air and shape retention, bounce and weight, and also regulated the materials from which it could be made. Coloured balls were permitted for the benefit of TV and the first synthetic (polyurethane) World Cup match ball was used in 1986. Since then, the aim has been to produce balls that remain consistent in weight whatever the weather – the 2006 World Cup ball was said to gain no more than 0.1% of its weight in the wet when the maximum permitted weight gain is 10%. The improved water resistance is achieved by replacing traditional stitching of the panels with thermal bonding.

The number of panels has also been reduced from 32 to 14. Their shape has been altered, too. Together with a multi-layered construction (including polystyrene foam) and the use of high-tech materials, the modern first-class football is more round, durable, consistent and comfortable to play with than anything used in the past. With fewer interruptions on the surface and a shell designed to maximise friction between itself and a boot, the ball is easier to control. These characteristics enable a good many more players than hitherto to enjoy bending it like Beckham.

The football used at the 2006 World Cup was capable of movement through the air impossible in previous generations.

These **characteristics** enable a **good many** more players than hitherto to enjoy **bending it like** Beckham

For the science of ball swerve, start here: http://plus.maths.org/issue40 /features/bray

Technology Rules

The basic technology of the tennis ball has changed little in recent years. Sadly, however, the variety of court surfaces and the increased power of rackets and of players had led to so simple an object as a ball being the subject of three pages of closely typed regulations and a multitude of complex tests. The result is a game which at the top level is played with four types of ball, each subject to five tests. This makes professional tennis awkwardly technology-dependent, which is confusing for the fan and perhaps even off-putting for young sportspeople thinking of taking it up.

The four types of tournament ball (Types 1–3 and High Altitude) are all the same weight. Where they differ is in size, their rebound (bounce) capacity and two aspects of deformation under pressure as measured by a modified Stevens machine. Certain balls are deemed appropriate for specific conditions, these being a combination of the court's surface and altitude. The pace of a court (the amount by which a ball slows when it strikes the surface) ranges from slow (clay, as at Roland Garros, the French Open) to fast (grass, as at the All England Championships, Wimbledon) and is allocated an International Tennis Federation (ITF)

This makes professional **tennis** awkwardly technology-dependent, which is **confusing** for the **fan** and perhaps **even off-putting for young** sportspeople thinking of taking it up

Surface Pace Rating of between 0 and 40+. The aim of officials is to make all conditions – the variety of court pace and altitude – as equal as possible by varying the ball type. Thus, in an attempt to stop Wimbledon being dominated by big servers who thrive on a fast court, for that tournament the balls are larger than those used at Roland Garros.

The original Stevens Machine, named after its inventor, was a simple mechanical device that squashed a tennis ball between two plates and measured the amount of deformation under a known force. Modern versions of the machine conduct the whole operation automatically.

Steady as She Goes

Unlike golf, football and tennis, the bodies regulating most other sports have striven to keep technology's influence on the ball to a minimum. As already intimated, they have been considerably helped by the fact that generally their sports are not multibillion-dollar businesses subject to enormous pressure from giant corporations. Furthermore in several sports, the degree to which ball technology can influence a game is limited. Once the shape, weight and bias of a ball used in lawn bowls are established, for instance, there is not a lot technology can add. The story is similar in basketball, where the official ball has changed only once in the last 35 years – the latest version, replacing leather with a composite material, promises greater consistency, grip and, with an almost inevitable touch of marketing gobbledegook, 'moisture control'.

Table tennis has kept a grip on innovation by regulating both bat and ball tightly, maintaining the traditional celluloid ball and keeping bats (or 'rackets' as they are known officially) of largely wooden construction. The primary influence of technology has not been on ball or bat but indirectly through TV: the size of the ball has been increased in order to slow the game down and so make it more telly-friendly. The International Hockey Federation has made no such compromise for field hockey, leaving its supporters complaining loudly that it is not seen often enough on TV.

Luck of the bounce? Not any more. Stick, ball and surface technology enable hockey skills to be displayed as never before.

©NICHOLAS RJABOW/SHUTTERSTOCK

While baseballs come in various types, those used for professional adult competition, notably the US Major League Baseball (MLB), are tightly regulated, as is the bat, which must be made from 'one piece of solid wood'. Cricket has retained its traditional ball, although for certain limited-overs games a white ball is used in place of the better-known red one. There is now talk of replacing that with a pink one. 'As well as overcoming the problems with the deterioration of the ball, we anticipate that batsmen will find the pink ball easier to see, particularly in poor light', said MCC's John Stephenson in 2007.[5] To the bemusement and even amusement of outsiders, about the performance of different coloured balls cricketers argue till they are red (or white or even pink) in the face.

When a number of star players, including England's Jonny Wilkinson, began missing an unusually high proportion of kicks at goal during the 2007 Rugby World Cup, the ball was inevitably called into question. The cause of the problem was eventually identified as the provision of a different type of ball for training and for matches.

Like footballs, the balls used in rugby have changed from leather to composite exteriors. The application of technology to design and construction means that the modern ball is easier to handle and kick, absorbs hardly any water, and retains its shape during the stresses and strains of a match. Fortunately to date there is no call for a rugby ball to swerve in the air like a football – but it may well come, and if it does the manufacturers will no doubt oblige and claim that the game is thereby all the better.

[5] Reported on http://news.bbc.co.uk/sport1/hi/cricket/7092114.stm

What Next?

The Power of the Market

The future impact of technology on the bats and balls with which we play sport will probably be decided not by the sports themselves but by their paymasters. Ultimately these are the supporting sporting public who play, watch and follow. At the professional level, which most concerns us here, popular opinion is expressed by choosing to watch an event live or on TV. This means that if a technological change – a cricket bat capable of hitting more sixes, say – wins the approval of the crowd, then it is likely that it will eventually be incorporated into the game.

Is this **the way we want** to go, with the **nature** of our sport **dictated not** by those who **play** but by those who **pay**?

A good example of this, in reverse, occurred in tennis when racket technology made the game on fast surfaces more fragmented, predictable and boring. Both players and supporters began to turn off. The organisers' reaction was to slow the game down by adopting balls of a larger circumference. This was an interesting decision because it actually *increased* manufacturers' opportunities for making money as they now could sell a range of balls, rather than putting limits on rackets, which would have *reduced* marketing opportunities. Is this the way we want to go, with the nature of our sport dictated not by those who play but by those who pay?

Power player: all-time great Pete Sampras reputedly added weight to his racket to increase the power of his serves.

Razzmatazz and Records

Technological innovation may take sport along the high road already mapped by modern culture. We live in a society of instant gratification and decreasing attention spans. We bore easily, demanding fresh stimulation, new highlights at shorter and shorter intervals. Our news is packaged in 1-minute bites on TV or arrives over the internet in the form of picture and simple caption. Movies are faster-paced, ever more action-packed. Music is a 3-minute jingle, an examination is a quick tick-the-box exercise, a written message is a txt. Sport, inevitably, has moved with the mood and technology has enabled it to do so. In all likelihood, the trend will continue. Crowds, real and virtual, love excitement, record breaking and new experiences. If technology can facilitate such delights, bring it on!

Crowds, real and virtual, love excitement, **record breaking** and new **experiences**. If technology can facilitate **such delights**, bring it **on!**

The bats and balls of the future will certainly be capable of providing more spectacular performances at the top level, but does spectacular necessarily mean better? Take football. One of the perceived problems of the modern professional game is that there are not enough goals to satisfy the non-aficionado spectator, especially in the USA. Defences are tightly organised, players so fit and skilful that in most major tournaments a large proportion of games end up with a score of 1-0, 1-1 or 2-1. It should be possible over the next 50 years for technology to come to the rescue: what about a ball whose 'flying' and swerving characteristics are twice as acute as those of today? We have been seriously applying science to footballs for only about 25 years – just imagine where we might be half a century from now: a ball that could turn at 90 degrees or even boomerang? A ball that might fly in an 'S' shape, first one way then another? There wouldn't be too many bore draws with one of those. But would it still be football?

The opportunities in golf could be equally revolutionary. By limiting the power of modern clubs and the flight capabilities of the modern ball, traditionalists have

Commercial considerations have obliged the Royal and Ancient Golf Club of St Andrew's, the sport's spiritual home, to combine its rigid traditions with a more accommodating attitude towards technological innovation.

defended the status quo. More than most other sports, golf is run by ex-players who cherish memories of the version of the game at which they excelled. To break the mould, an enterprising individual or organisation might build new, super-long courses on which players were permitted to use any combination of club and ball they wanted: monster-headed, lightweight drivers of titanium and balls designed to fly like a bird. At the same time, lavish payments could attract the top players to the new, free enterprise system. Once it was established, who would choose to return to our game when the alternative power golf offered Tiger Woods III booming 500 yd drives and sliding in dead accurate chips from 200 yd out?

More than most other **sports**, **golf** is **run** by **ex-players who cherish memories** of the version of the game at which they **excelled**

There is potential for something like this in cricket, too. What the majority of a modern crowd like is big hitting and dramatic dismissals, and over the next 50 years, technology will be able to produce more of both. As we learn about how a cricket ball behaves off the pitch and in the air (even today the physics of 'reverse swing' is disputed), so we will be able to produce balls that exhibit these characteristics increasingly vividly. Swing and reverse swing will become more pronounced, turn off the pitch sharper. At the other end, the batsman, fitter and stronger than now, will wield vibration-free, super-spring bats capable of sending the ball over the boundary with a flick of the wrists. Wickets tumble, 4s and 6s pepper the boundary – and spectators enjoy every minute of it.

Similar sensational changes may be envisioned in other sports: a rugby ball that sticks to the hands and penalties that fly through the posts from deep inside one's own half, self-adjusting tennis rackets that compensate for bad shots, hockey balls that swing and dip like footballs . . . they may all be reality one day. Progress – or decline?

The Other Way

There are, of course, alternative approaches. One is a freeze on all development and change in equipment. This would mean tightening rules still further, fossilising a sport at a certain stage of its technological development. In some aspects of sports like table tennis, baseball and cricket, this has already happened. But refusing to admit change risks turning a sport into a museum piece; besides,

In the end, technology must be our servant, not our master

outlawing further development is a sure way to kill the vital sponsorship of manu-facturers. It might also encourage clandestine technology.

Another way of handling the potentially anarchic forces of technological develop-ment is to allow widespread innovation and experimentation in all tournaments and competitions except the very highest – the world cups and the like. Then, at a specified distance in time before a major competition, its organisers decree what equipment they will permit. Not only that, but they also specify the identical equip-ment to be used by all competitors.

The NBL currently authorises just one ball from a specific manufacturer and FIFA does the same with the ball used in the football World Cup. The next step is for bodies like the United States Golf Association (USGA, the body regulating the sport in the USA and Mexico) and the Royal and Ancient Golf Club, St Andrews (R&A, the body regulating the sport everywhere else in the world) to select a ball and one set of clubs to be used in the major tournaments each year. The International Tennis Federation (ITF) could do the same with tennis, the International Table Tennis Federation (ITTF) with table tennis and so on.

The introduction of some such system would allow bat and ball innovation to continue – and might even boost it as manufacturers strive to be the 'chosen one' – while the anarchy of free-for-all and unfair technological advantage would be eliminated. At first, the players might well kick up a fuss at having to surrender their favourite driver, their tailor-made cricket bat. Tough. In the end, technology must be our servant, not our master.

2 Tracksuits and Trainers

'Run like you've never run before,' went the strap line for Nike sports shoes. The implication, of course, was that shod with Nike you would bounce along to new personal bests and beyond. Yet barely a quarter of a century ago, a teenage runner was taking the world by storm, breaking the women's 5,000 m record by a full 10 seconds – and doing it in bare feet.

Her name was Zola Budd. Raised in South Africa's apartheid regime and therefore banned from international competition, Budd was hastily brought to Britain and given the citizenship that allowed her to compete in the 1986 Los Angeles Olympics. If that move was controversial, it was nothing compared with what followed. The women's 3,000 m was billed as a head-to-head between Budd and the flashy American blonde, Mary Decker.

Kenyan distance runner Tegla Loroupe began her remarkable career by competing barefoot. Regarded by Athletic Kenya as too slight to be taken seriously, only after winning a cross-country race in 1988 was she able to afford her first pair of running shoes.

Breaking the **women's** 5,000 metre record by **a full 10 seconds** – and **doing** it in **bare** feet

With three laps to go, the two women collided. Decker staggered, grabbed the number from her rival's back and fell off the track in floods of tears. She was unable to continue. Tears streamed down Budd's face, too, as she struggled with the double handicap of a spike wound inflicted by Decker's shoe and a cacophony

High performance, low-tech: Zola Budd (front left), the outstanding South African-British runner whose barefoot career was dogged by controversy.

of boos and catcalls from the partisan American crowd. She faded badly at the end and finished seventh.

Would all this have happened if Budd had been wearing Nikes – or any other running shoe? Who knows. But since then, no other barefoot athlete has been seen competing on the track at the highest level.

In this area at least, the triumph of technology is total. Looking back on her career, even Zola Budd concluded, 'as I got older I had injuries to my hamstring. I found that wearing shoes gives me more support and protection from injuries.'

From There . . .

Nothing to Boast of

The current consensus is that athletes in the ancient Olympics competed stark naked. Some claim that the portrayal of nude athletes in artwork is simply artistic license, done to illustrate splendid physiques rather than be true representations of actual sporting events. The majority of scholars reject this position. Naked the Greek runners and jumpers were, and naked they are shown – and an awful lot of fuss and bother it saved too.

Fashions changed and at the close of the Graeco-Roman era organised sport entered a fragmented phase of its history. Where sport took place in its haphazard, amateur way, the participants generally wore whatever items of everyday apparel seemed most appropriate, be this a loincloth in Central America or muddy doublets in medieval Europe. There is evidence, however, that Italian teams playing 'football' (a wild mix of soccer, rugby, wrestling and anything else that came to mind) in the late 15th century wore distinctive uniforms, rather like

The adoption of the original Olympics' dress code might well boost athletics' declining TV viewing figures.

soldiers on the battlefield, to distinguish friend from foe. Perhaps horse racing – relatively well organised by the early 18th century – was the first sport to apply basic technology to a participant's clothing, although this was no more than lightweight and distinctive jerseys for the jockeys.

Naked the Greek runners and jumpers **were,** and naked they are **shown** – and an **awful lot of fuss and bother** it saved too

Victorian Legacy

The revolution really took off in the 19th century. Industrialisation, urbanisation and greater wealth, coupled to a British passion for organising and regulating sports and games (along with everything else), produced an explosion of sporting activities for both participants and spectators. Business people and scientific entrepreneurs were not slow to realise that here was a fresh market for a new range of clothing. Feet led the way. It began with the discovery of vulcanisation, the process of curing rubber by the addition of sulphur. A torrent of sporting footwear followed: heel-less cycling shoes, studded football boots, spiked running shoes and a variety of light, canvas-rubber 'plimsolls' or 'sneakers'. With the addition of Adi Dassler's (guess the name of the company he founded?) screw-in studs, this is more or less where the application of technology to sports shoes remained until the 1960s.

Surprisingly, a quintessentially amateur sport was the first to benefit when lace-up croquet shoes with rubber soles and canvas uppers went on sale in the 1860s.

Meanwhile, the sport-tech revolution had been moving its way up the body, albeit slowly. Protective wear was a rare area of significant technological development before 1945. It applied principally to sports in which there was a serious chance of physical injury, although not to all of them. Until quite recently, rugby players were shielded by nothing more sophisticated than a 'scrum' cap, for example, and the heads of cyclists, motorcyclists and racing car drivers were protected by padded leather caps of pretty basic design.

First-class **wicketkeepers** laced the **insides** of their gloves **with meat** to protect their hands

The name 'plimsoll' comes from MP Samuel Plimsoll and his wife Eliza, passionate crusaders for safer merchant ships. As well as sporting footwear, the Victorian couple gave us the mark on ships' hulls showing how heavily they may be loaded.

Cricketers were better looked after. The introduction of overarm bowling in the 19th century necessitated batsmen wearing leg guards ('pads') and wicketkeepers donning gloves. The technology remained basic, using canvas, wood, leather and horsehair, cotton padding – and even raw steak: first-class wicketkeepers laced the insides of their gloves with meat to protect their hands. That, with the addition of a 'box' (or 'abdominal protector'), was a (male) cricketer's lot. What was arguably the most precious area of all, the skull, went unguarded, as England batsman Derek Randall ironically noted after being hit on the head by a ball from Dennis Lillee in 1977: 'No good hitting me there mate. Nothing to damage.' Some of this protection was taken up by other sports, notably field and ice hockey. Footballers took to wearing shin pads, too.

As today, the most spectacular (and expensive) protective clothing was reserved for players of American football. Helmets, worn by some since the 1890s, became compulsory in the 1930s as protection for other parts of the body burgeoned. Finally, there was the delicate but vital issue of 'internal protection': the mass production of tampons from the 1930s onwards freed millions of women for sporting activity unimaginable to their forebears.

'Hockey is a sport for white men. Basketball is a sport for black men. Golf is a sport for white men dressed like black pimps.' – Tiger Woods

. . . To Where We Are Now

Weight and See

Modern sporting apparel owes much to man-made fabrics, the majority of which appeared for the first time after World War II. Rayon (1891) and nylon (1939) paved the way for acrylic (1950), polyester (1953), spandex (1959) and, more recently, the environmentally friendly lyocell (1992). As a result, it is rare to find a modern sportsperson wearing anything in pure cotton, let alone pure wool.

Wet fabric, such as **a soaking cotton soccer** shirt, conducts heat **25** times faster **than a dry** one

The first advantage of technology-produced fabrics is weight, especially when wet. Polyester, for example, which is a main ingredient of most modern sports garments, is hydrophobic (it does not absorb water), unlike hydrophilic wool, cotton and even nylon. An old-fashioned rugby shirt, whose strength came from the thickness of the weave, might absorb almost 3 kg of water and mud by the end of a game played in heavy rain on a waterlogged pitch – no great problem for a 17-stone forward but a considerable handicap for a twinkle-toed winger (although he rarely received the ball in such conditions).

Wet fabric, such as a soaking cotton soccer shirt, conducts heat 25 times faster than a dry one. This has serious implications. First, it can involve a high-performance athlete burning off precious energy simply to maintain body temperature. Second, it can lead to hypothermia when the body is unable to generate sufficient warmth to compensate for that being lost.

However, polyester's hydrophobia is a clear disadvantage in hot conditions because an athlete's sweat evaporates less easily, leading to a build-up in body temperature and loss of performance or even illness. One answer is simply to wear less (back to the Greeks again!), hence the near-bikini outfits of many of today's female track athletes. Yet this is unacceptable for competitors from more puritanically-minded societies. It can also lead to sunburn and – that most mundane yet perennial of problems – where does one attach one's number?

'I'm Muslim, so I will try to wear clothes that cover all my body . . . I will wear long trousers to cover all of my legs, but my sleeves will be short.'
– Robina Muqimyar, Afghanistan's first female Olympic athlete, 2004

Breathing and Wicking

Wearing less is not an option in sports where clothing is essential for protection, as in rugby or sailing, or identification, as in almost all team sports. Here technology has pursued two similar options, 'breathing' fabrics and improved wicking. To date we have yet to devise a way of enabling inanimate cloth literally to breathe: breathing fabric is just promotion-speak for a material that is impervious to rain on one side but allows moisture (sweat) to pass through from the other. Sold under names such as Gore-Tex and PB2, the cloth was developed for babies' nappies as well as walkers and climbers, and is increasingly featuring in other sportswear. Its effectiveness at shifting moisture from inside to out is measured as MVT (Moisture Vapour Transfer). A good MVT reading is said to be about 20%.

Wicking is **the ability of a material** to soak up **sweat**, as a candlewick **draws up molten wax**, and move it away from the **body**

Wicking is the ability of a material to soak up sweat, as a candlewick draws up molten wax, and move it away from the body. It leaves the athlete not only feeling more comfortable but also saves using up energy on maintaining skin temperature. All kinds of fabrics have been devised to do this, most mixing cotton with man-made fibres. The American football industry – it is indeed an industry – was particularly keen to find a way of keeping its players cool and comfortable under their shell of protection.

Several answers emerged, one of the most popular being marketed with the name Under Armour. The best are complex and expensive garments, usually incorporating a highly hydrophilic fibre like Ingeo and/or a very hydrophobic one like olefin. Worn next to the skin, they help keep the body at a constant temperature: cool in hot conditions and warm in cold conditions. The most advanced incorporate 'phase change' materials (PCMs). These remarkable substances start off as a gel. When they reach the temperature at which they change phase (i.e. melt), they absorb a great deal of heat without themselves gaining much temperature. Then, when the temperature around them falls, they release their stored heat as they return to the gel state. The use in sportswear of a PCM that changes state around the optimum body heat is obvious.

'Being short and slow, I was looking for every ounce I could spare.' Kevin Plank, inventor of Under Armour. More on http://www.underarmour.co.uk

The idea of temperature-sustaining garments caught on quickly and in a couple of years spread around the sporting world, so that high-performance athletes in a range of sports were seen stepping out in the latest high-tech version of the string vest. Footballers' tops are fashioned from a wool-polyester mix, 'sport wool', in which the natural material is closest to the skin in order to wick away the sweat.

High-performance athletes in a range of sports were **seen stepping out** in the latest high-tech version of the **string vest**

Stretch and Support

The benefits of artificial fibres stretch way beyond weight and temperature. Take the humble (and once-smelly) sock, for instance. The modern version – quick-wicking and waterproof, of course – has not only built-in odour suppressants but also boasts an anti-microbial element to combat the fungi that cause athletes' foot and other fungal infections. Equally comforting, the latest sport socks are designed for optimum support without impediment and even feature an anti-blister construction. The material on the outside of the sock is chosen for the way it adheres to the boot or shoe, while that on the inside is chosen for its capacity to grip the skin of the athlete. This means that the friction inevitably arising when a foot moves within a shoe is absorbed by the sock and not by rubbing against the skin of the foot. That is, unless one puts the socks on inside out . . .

Suzanne Lenglen, the French tennis star of the 1920s, shocked many by playing at Wimbledon in a simple calf-length cotton dress . . . No corset or petticoats? Zut alors!

The neat fit of the sock brings us to stretch, and that means spandex, invented by the DuPont chemist Joseph Shivers in 1959. But today nobody talks of spandex and certainly not of elastane, its alternative name. Instead, the word on most people's lips and the material on most sporting bodies is Lycra, the trade name of Invista's highly successful version of the product.

Spandex is a form of polymer, basically a substance made up of large molecules that are arranged in repeating structures. Perhaps the best-known polymer is DNA. The trick with spandex is that it combines the toughness of polyurethane with a rubbery stretchability due to segments of a substance known as polyethylene glycol. Polyurethane is well known for its everyday use in varnishes, furniture and so forth. Polyethylene glycol is less well known, although nearly everyone comes across it in toothpaste, and significant numbers are grateful for its use as a laxative and sexual lubricant. It is one of the wonders of modern technology that

Dubbed 'the Goddess' by the American media, Suzanne Lenglen took the staid tennis world by storm with her calf-length dresses and her habit of sipping brandy between sets.

polyurethane and polyethylene glycol combine in the manufacture of bras, swim-suits, bandages and seductive sportswear.

Lycra Louts

'David Cameron [leader of the Conservative Party] has been accused of joining cycling's growing army of "Lycra louts" who openly flout the rules of the road after he was snapped riding through a red light.' *Daily Mail*, 21 July 2007

Rip to Slip

Manufactured fibres bring enormous strength to garments that have to endure constant stresses and strains. We are here mainly talking about contact sports such as American football, rugby, ice hockey, Gaelic football and Aussie rules, although the toughness principle also applies to many winter sports, waterskiing, surfing, wrestling and other martial arts. Not so long ago a serious rugby jersey was a massive affair of thick weave cotton doubled or trebled in the shoulder area. Nor was it uncommon for a game to be stopped while a team formed a huddle around a player while he changed his ripped cotton shorts.

Torn clothing is now comparatively rare, even in the fiercest of contests (although England suffered some embarrassing rips at the start of their 2003 Rugby World Cup campaign), and the old suit-of-armour jerseys have been replaced by high-tech, figure-hugging garments fashioned from polyester, spandex and nylon. Experiments have been made with non-slip panels on the front to facilitate catch-ing the ball. The tight fit, collarless design and shiny finish of the surface make it much harder for a player to be grabbed by the jersey.

> When I played rugby, back in the Neolithic past, the shirts were akin to the padded armour worn by Genghis Khan. In winter they were delightfully warm for pre-match formalities but acted like sponges when it rained – and in the heat they were like wearing an electric blanket.

Spandex undergarments (the 'base layer'), such as cycling shorts, are also supposed to help remove lactic acid from the muscles, facilitate blood flow, dampen muscle vibration and even improve proprioception. The latter is a technical term for awareness of one's own body: the greater one's awareness, the sharper one's skill. In other words, the technology of clothing can impact upon the skill of a player. Quite a claim.

For more on proprioception, try:
http://serendip.brynmawr.edu/bb/neuro/neuro02/web2/slee.html

Recently spandex has been added to football jerseys, and not just for a closer fit. One of the most difficult fouls for a referee to spot is when a defender, whose body may well be blocking the referee's line of sight, grabs the shirt of an opponent in order to pull him back. If that shirt stretches (straight spandex can expand 600%) as the attacker carries on running away from the defender, the chances of the referee seeing the offence are significantly increased. So the technology of sports clothing aids fair play. Another remarkable claim.

Shark Skin

Swimmers competing at the highest level are not quite sure what they should wear. For a long time it was simple: close-fitting briefs for men and an all-in-one

The trouble is, although swimming **records are** broken by **swimmers** wearing the new-style suits, **there is no way to show** the **extent** that this is **due to their** costumes

suit for women, both fashioned from material that contained a high proportion of spandex. This was challenged around the turn of the century when the British firm Speedo International came up with a fabric it called 'Fastskin'.

For more on Fastskin try:
http://www.speedo.co.uk/index2.php

Reputedly developed in conjunction with London's Natural History Museum, the new material was modelled on the skin of a shark. Minute teeth channelled the water over the skin, thereby reducing drag (explained in Chapter 5). It was claimed that this enabled swimmers to improve their time by around 3%. Since this was more than the difference between the first and last in an average race, the effect could be marked. The trouble is, although swimming records are broken by swimmers wearing the new-style suits, there is no way to show the extent that this is due to their costumes.

More recently, Speedo have brought out newer versions of their suits and other firms have developed their own. The materials, all of which go by special names and trademarks (e.g. Fastskin and Flexskin), are ultra-light and have water-repellent qualities that reduce surface drag and skin friction in the water. Some firms offer special drag-reducing caps too. Manufacturers also suggest that the tightness of the suits increases 'core stability' (the ability of the swimmer to maintain a constant shape during a race) and cuts muscle oscillation that might reduce power.

Not everyone is enamoured of the new suits, but by 2008 there was growing evidence that they really were enabling their wearers to achieve faster times. For example, Speedo pointed out that swimmers in their very latest skin-tight Fastskin FS Pro (introduced March 2007) broke 21 world records in less than a year. This persuaded US head coach Mark Schubert to suggest that the kit was 'probably the biggest jump in [swimwear] technology since the mid-1970s.'[1]

Interestingly, the jury also appears to be out on all-in-one body suits for track athletes. They made a spectacular debut at the 1988 Olympics, when sprinter Florence Griffiths-Joyner turned heads with a stunning Lycra outfit.[2] Cathy Freeman won the woman's 400 m wearing one at the 2000 Sydney Olympics, too. Like the all-in-one swimsuit, the track bodysuit is supposed to reduce drag and muscle vibration. The tightness of the suit is said to stem from NASA research showing that blood passes more quickly through muscles when they are compressed, increasing efficiency and cutting unnecessary movement. Again, like the all-in-one swimsuit, the bodysuit has yet to become universal among élite athletes.

See Flo Jo in Olympic action on:
http://www.youtube.com/watch?v = m0eXOXO5fjM

[1] *Washington Post*, 31 July 2007.
[2] For more on the famous 'Flo-Jo', see Chapter 8.

Skiing or Flying?

To a greater or lesser extent, costume affects performance in all sports, and this inevitably stimulates technological analysis and innovation. We have looked at general trends common across activities and there is not the space here to go into all the specialities, nor is it our intention to get too anoraky – analysis of the suits worn by current F1 drivers, for example, would fill a book by itself. So let's conclude with a quick look at one further pursuit where apparel has the potential to change the nature of sport entirely: ski jumping.

Athletes could be given the ability to sail like a kite

Technology impacts upon this most spectacular of winter sports in many ways, from physical preparation to ski design and body position (see Chapter 4). What the jumper wears is even more crucial. Taking off at 100 kph, they fly 120 m through the air before landing. 'Fly' is the keyword. Scientists looking closely at ski jumping realised that with careful attention to the aerodynamics of their

Now you see him . . . Soon you won't . . . Michael Schumacher in Ferrari's F2007 car. Once in action, today's helmeted F1 drivers are as anonymous as Darth Vader.

clothing, athletes could be given the ability to sail like a kite. Ski jackets appeared with extra fabric between the arms and body that acted like a wing. Technology, it seemed, would enable jumpers to soar enormous distances. Seeing what was happening and how dangerous it was, the regulators intervened.

Today, to reduce gliding, a ski jump suit may be no more than 5 mm thick. Furthermore, measurements of its circumferences may be no more than 60 mm greater than that of the corresponding parts of the body it encases. Even so, there are rumours of athletes finding their way round the regulations. One is to open up the collar area; another is to take liberties with the crotch (always a tricky area to regulate). By allowing it to sag downwards, in the modern street fashion, the jumper begins to look a bit like a flying squirrel – which, of course, is just what is intended.

> 'All portions of the ski jumping suit must be made of the same material and must show a certain air permeability and have a certain thickness as a maximum. The size of the suit must conform to the body shape in an upright position with certain tolerances.' Simplified regulations from www.olympic.org

Protection

Technological development in sport feeds off itself. As one branch of science builds up athletes' speed and power, another strives to give better protection to those who may suffer as a consequence. We are not just talking about the contact and hardball sports, either. There is a whole range of other activities, particularly winter sports, where collision is a very real danger. Furthermore, safety is of far greater concern than previously, increasing the demand for more and better protection for athletes.

For the purposes of this overview, we will divide protective technology into three areas, (i) helmets and headgear; (ii) additional body padding and protection; and (iii) protective clothing.

Helmets and Headgear

The requirements of all sporting head protectors are essentially fourfold: they need to combine strength, lightness, comfort and practicability. This is another area where artificial materials have come into their own. Strength comes from the use of composite materials. These are generally petroleum-based thermoset (remaining rigid once set) polymer plastics reinforced with carbon fibre – CFRP or CRP. Sometimes manufacturers talk of graphite reinforcement because it sounds more cutting-edge. Where even more strength is needed, as in motor racing for example, the super-strong Kevlar – the principal material for the manufacture of bulletproof vests – is added to the composite construction. None of these helmets comes cheap (£30 to £100+ for a cricket helmet at 2007 prices), which is all the harder to bear when most cease to be effective after sustaining a heavy blow.

The personalised helmets of Michael Schumacher, each weighing 1,350 grams, cost some $2,000 each

Comfort is often a matter of price because for those who can afford it, helmets are made to measure. In 2006, for example, the personalised helmets of Michael Schumacher, each weighing 1,350 grams, cost some $2,000 each. The F1 champion got through about twenty a year. To get round the price problem, some American football helmets have padding that inflates to give the perfect fit around every head shape. Comfort also comes from including washable, anti-bacterial interior padding and a design that prevents the build-up of sweat.

Protect or perish – the introduction of the helmet in American football has saved hundreds from serious head injury.

Many high-performance helmets are computer-designed using the results of wind tunnel and anti-drag tests. Recently two types of cycle helmet revealed startling results: it was shown that simply by changing helmet from a modern yet imper-fectly aerodynamic one to an 'aero helmet' gave the rider a 4% improvement in performance. This equated to 1,614 m (1.002 miles) further in an hour using the same energy expenditure. No wonder one competitor labelled his new helmet his 'happy hat'!

For interesting research on the different shaped heads of various ethnic groups see:
http://www.newscientist.com/article/mg19526226.000-end-of-one-shape-fits-all-cycle-helmets.html

Practicability means doing the job properly. To this end, tougher tungsten has replaced steel in the visors of top-range helmets used in cricket, American football and other sports. Because there is so much money in it and because it is so dangerous, American football is at the forefront of protective technology, especially in the sphere of headgear. As Frank Gifford, the celebrated American football player and broadcaster, quipped, 'Pro football is like nuclear warfare. There are no winners, only survivors.'

The year 2006 saw the introduction of helmets specifically designed to reduce concussion on collision, an ever-present worry for American football players. Over 4 years of research and development, the manufacturers noticed that side impact was as responsible for concussion as was head-on collision. To take account of this, the helmet was extended to cover the side of the head and jaw, and the distance between the skull and the helmet's outer shell was increased. The same technology will no doubt quickly filter through to other sports, as has the use of aircell mouthguards.

❝ **Pro football** is like nuclear warfare. **There are no winners**, only survivors ❞

In 2003, the revenue of the US National Football League – NFL – was a staggering $5.3 billion.

Pads and Gloves

The technology of protective apparatus worn by sportsmen and women is largely covered by topics already mentioned. It incorporates a variety of man-made fibres such as Lycra, moulded closed-cell high-density foam, sometimes with varying density and a vinyl coating, and other super-tough yet light materials. Gloves, pads and items such as chest protectors in cricket have all kinds of ingenious designs and devices to prevent the player overheating and the accumulation of moisture. Strapping features Velcro and other ways of eliminating cumbersome straps and buckles. The consequence of all this is that American footballers cover themselves in a high-tech welter of foam, plastic, Lycra, steel, Kevlar and CRP that would make Sir Galahad jealous.

> Every surface of the goalie pads worn in America's National [Ice] Hockey League 'is designed to deflect the puck in a certain way, depending on the goaltenders' style.'[3]

Interestingly, rugby gloves shy away from artificial fibres and opt instead for kangaroo skin. Boxing gloves stick to natural materials, too. The outer layers of the best are made of goat skin, although they now have water-resistant linings to prevent the padding from absorbing sweat and therefore becoming heavier. Another change has seen the thumb attached to the rest of the glove to prevent it being used for jabbing or gouging.[4] More importantly, in amateur boxing the amount of closed cell foam padding on the knuckle area of the compulsory 10-oz glove has increased to the point where it is now significantly more difficult to deliver a knockout blow. The introduction of headguards at the 1984 Los Angeles Olympics and of so-called 'computerised scoring' (see Chapter 3) at the 1992 Barcelona Olympics compounded the situation.

[3] http://entertainment.howstuffworkscom.hockey4.com
[4] For much of the information on boxing, both here and in the next chapter, I am deeply indebted to Barry McGuigan, MBE, former WBA World Featherweight Champion and BBC Sports Personality of the Year (1985), who gave most generously of his time and expertise.

These technological developments have impacted on the way amateur boxers fight, obliging them to behave more like fencers. The amateurs' tactic now comprises a swift move forward, a quick blow or two on the target area, then immediate withdrawal. Multiple combinations of punches and wearing one's opponent down with body blows (particularly now that rounds are 2 rather than 3 minutes) have been rendered unprofitable in a new jabbing style of fighting which many consider boring compared with the more varied and tougher variety of the

Pit-a-pat padding – technology intended to make amateur boxing safer has also made it more boring.

sport. Furthermore, amateurs raised in the 'tap-and-go' era find it difficult to adapt to the professional game – Olympic Heavyweight Audley Harrison being a good recent example.

Clothing

Protective clothing ranges from wetsuits to winter sports suits and hikers' outfits. The basic wetsuit is made from a form of neoprene, a synthetic rubber based on the polymer polychloroprene. The degree of insulation depends on the thickness of the suit. More interesting from a technological point of view is the development of SmartSkin, originally for ocean diving. This ingenious new material works by automatically controlling the amount of water flowing through the wetsuit's inner layer, thereby regulating the amount of heat lost by convection. Remarkably, this maintains the suit at body temperature regardless of the material's thickness.

The most exciting **development** in the **technology of protection** in years: the potentially **revolutionary** d3o

Protective ski clothing – which the manufacturers call 'laminated polyester stretch fabric' combines much of the technology already covered, including tough nylon exteriors, Lycra and pads of carbon fibre and Kevlar. The very latest ski suits, however, are starting to feature the most exciting development in the technology of protection in years: the potentially revolutionary d3o[5].

---

[5] Pronounced 'dee-three-oh'.

For more on d3o try: http://d3olab.com

The science of d3o is pretty complex. In essence it is a shear-thickening material in a soft foam matrix (base). So what is 'shear-thickening'? We start with 'viscosity', which is the resistance of a liquid to a force acting upon it: water has a low viscosity, for example, while honey has a high one. In other words, it's easier to stir water than honey. However, the viscosity of some liquids gets higher the more force is applied – the harder you stir, the more difficult it gets. These are called 'shear-thickening fluids' (STFs).

The crafty trick of d3o's inventors is to incorporate their special sheer-thickening substance into a material. The greater the force acting upon this material, the more solid it becomes. The change happens very quickly, in 1/100th of a second. Under normal conditions the material is as soft and pliable as conventional fabric, but when subjected to a great force – impact, for example – it suddenly hardens. Hey presto! Instant armour, padding with no pads.

Remarkably, too, d3o reverts to its normal state as soon as the force stops. The scope for the use of this material or something like it in the sporting world is endless: jerseys with shoulder-pad capacity, socks that become shin pads, ski suits that turn into armour plating the moment of a crash, or even soft hats that harden with impact. Similar research in the USA has impregnated Kevlar with STF to produce flexible body armour.

Footwear

Despite the promotional hype of the big-name manufacturers, athletic footwear has not undergone quite the technological revolution one might have anticipated.

What does distinguish the present-day situation, however, is the huge variety of specialised footwear and the crossover between sportswear and fashion. The main developments have been in the running shoe (the ubiquitous 'trainer') in all its roary varieties and in football boots.

For all our technological advance, it seems, we are **not yet able** to match **kanga's** super-strong, **ultra-stretchy** qualities

Sports shoes feature a range of man-made fibres and materials, from polyurethane soles to ethylene vinyl acetate (EVA) cushioning and Kevlar reinforcement. The better (more expensive!) shoes also incorporate the latest wicking and breathability technology. The result is a piece of equipment that is both stronger and lighter than anything used previously. Interestingly, the most fashionable material for the best football boots is not artificial but the skin of the enigmatic kangaroo. For all our technological advance, it seems, we are not yet able to match kanga's super-strong, ultra-stretchy qualities.

Other technology has focused on the three areas of overall shoe design, grips and protection against injury. About 30 years ago, sports technologists discovered that we run in one of three different ways: one (neutral) where the foot hits the ground in a straight line from where the heel impacted, two (pronation) where the foot rolls inward from the heel strike, and three (supenation) where the foot rolls outward from the heel strike. This revelation has led to top-flight athletes having shoes individually made to suit their running style. For the rest of us, it means manufacturers have redesigned shoes to incorporate padding and strengthening that best supports all three running styles.

Grip might seem straightforward – the better the grip, the better the shoe or boot. This is not necessarily true. A shot-putter, for instance, requires footwear that will glide over the surface of the circle and allow the foot to spin easily. This is done by fitting throw shoes with circular grooves on the balls of the feet. Similarly, a javelin thrower's shoes have spikes in the heel to prevent slipping in the delivery

Lab testing the 'bounce' of a sports shoe at Exeter University.

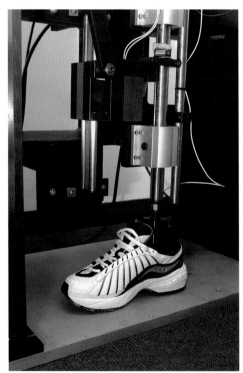

©EXETER UNIVERSITY, PRESS DEPARTMENT

stride, while a sprinter's have spikes at the precise points where the front of the foot hits the ground.

Even more research has gone into the grips of boots worn by footballers and others playing on grass pitches. This arose partly from the number of non-contact knee injuries (particularly to the anterior cruciate ligament) professional players were suffering. The fate of the England star Michael Owen in the 2006 FIFA World Cup was a classic example. One reason suggested for such injuries was that boots were providing too good a grip, so that the forces of twist and turn were passed on to the knee joint rather than being partly dissipated at the point where the foot made contact with the pitch. Better pitches (see Chapter 6) were also believed to be part of the problem.

Hot Topic

'Do blades cause more injuries to players due to the way they grip the turf? The argument is that once a blade has gripped, it cannot swivel as freely as a stud whilst in the ground. This therefore could leave your foot embedded in the turf whilst your body countermeasures an impact from a tackle or fall.' The blog of a Spurs fan (2007) on http://theshelf.co.uk/2007

All kinds of ways of dealing with the situation were tried, including changing the stud pattern, length and circumference, and replacing studs with 'blades'. Nothing really solved the problem of providing perfect grip for the foot that was in contact with the ground when the other was kicking the ball, yet relaxing that grip when the player needed to swivel or turn quickly.

Bounce and Cheques

By the 1970s, there was growing concern at the damage done to athletes pounding the ground day after day, week after week, year after year. Stress fractures (hairline cracks) of the tibia were especially common. The result was a shoe with an air cushion in the heel, pioneered by Nike. Experiments were even made with basketball shoes that came with a valve and pump to re-inflate the air bag!

Cushioning shoes, giving the user extra bounce, raises some interesting questions. The International Association of Athletics Federations (IAAF), the body that regulates international athletics, states that athletes' shoes must be for the purpose of 'protection and stability to the feet' only and they may not 'be constructed so as to give an athlete any unfair additional assistance, including by the incorporation of any technology which will give the wearer any unfair advantage.' (Rule 143.2)

This asks as many questions as it answers. What sort of advantage is 'unfair'? Is it 'unfair' that a runner from a developed nation may be able to afford a pair of handcrafted, high-tech shoes that give added spring while a competitor from a developing nation can afford only a pair of souped-up plimsolls? Perhaps the technology of footwear has reached the state – as some suggest for F1 motorsport – where the only way to get a fair race is to give all athletes the same shoes?

❞ [The shoes may not] be constructed so as to give an athlete any unfair additional assistance, including by the incorporation of any technology which will give the wearer any unfair advantage. ❞

Superb 'kicking machines' modern boots may be, but they have been criticised for sacrificing protection

Football aficionados raise similar issues. The latest boots not only have the laces offset to the outside to give an uninterrupted surface for kicking the ball, but they also have interchangeable soles, a high-friction pad on the kicking area (supposedly to enable the ball to be spun more easily – see Chapter 1) and a design that moves the mass to the front of the shoe to optimise the power transfer from foot to shoe. The British company P2L even makes boots through 'laser sintering', enabling them to be not just the right size but personalised to accommodate an individual's movements. Superb 'kicking machines' modern boots may be, but they have been criticised for sacrificing protection. The fact that England's star striker Wayne Rooney broke a metatarsal bone in his foot three times in as many years may be simply misfortune, but many frustrated fans in the stands blame his skimpy boots.

> There is a school of thought, backed by respectable research at university level, that contrary to what footwear manufacturers tell us, cushioning in the sole of a sports shoe can do more harm than good because it alters the way athletes run.

It's worth remembering that close analysis of boot technology is of little relevance to the average player. Indeed, on many feet, super-tech boots are probably more of a hindrance than a help because they send the ball powerfully and precisely where the kicker's foot directs it: as a stalwart but none too talented left back of the Pig and Whistle Sunday Morning 2nd XI, my lusty clearances might well veer

Studs or blades? The injury to England forward Michael Owen during the 2006 World Cup added to the controversy over what style of footwear was best for footballers.

©ACTION IMAGES/ALEX MORTON

into the nearby river instead of lobbing in the general direction of the opponents' goal. On more talented feet, however, the latest boots give considerable advantage – as long as the possessor of those feet can afford a pair.

What Next?

Supercloth

The most obvious development in athletic clothing will be a single composite fibre that does everything currently achieved by a range of materials. What we are looking at is a stretchy, light and steel-tough material that wicks away sweat, insulates in such a manner as to maintain a constant body temperature, is rainproof, perhaps fireproof, and has the instant-armour properties of d3o. A tall order? Maybe by present standards, but we are still in the infancy of fabric technology.

The creation of such a material would obviate the need for all bulky clothing, padding, etc., keeping the athlete light, cool and fully able to concentrate on their game. Incidentally, cricket batters without pads would be a lot easier to bowl out than at present, so maybe pads would need to be retained as 'functional anach-ronisms'! Perhaps to our supercloth we might add slip or stick properties as required – slippery qualities for a rugby jersey to make tackling harder and sticky properties for gloves worn by cricketers, baseball players, goalkeepers and all others who need to catch.

The most **obvious** development in athletic clothing will be **a single composite fibre** that does everything

And just before we go into production, let's add one final quality, 'ionising'. The 2007 Rugby World Cup saw players experimenting with Ionx-impregnated undergarments that were said to give extra performance (2.7%, according to Loughborough University scientists) by stimulating blood flow by means of elec-tromagnetism. The initial response of the World Anti-Doping Agency was that nothing was amiss . . . Watch this space.

Superlens

What about playing in all light conditions? Currently cricketers wear sunglasses (shades) that cut out ultraviolet (UV) rays, glare (polaroid lenses) and enhance the light in dark conditions, making the ball easier to see. The problem is that although such glasses may present a cool image, the lenses get dirty, their presence is a safety hazard and they can be worn only in relatively slow-moving sports such as cricket and baseball.

The answer is to develop a form of contact lens that does everything currently done by sunglasses. To be acceptable it has to be light, easily inserted by someone not used to wearing contact lenses, virtually unnoticeable when worn and able to retain its position whatever stresses and strains are put on the surrounding tissue. It also has to be easily removed at the end of the game, and disposable. There's a challenge – and a fortune to be made by whoever gets it right!

Superhat

The safety helmets of the future will be wholly breathable, far less bulky than today thanks to d3o-type materials, packed with microchip technology and personalised by the wearer the moment they are put on. The last point first. Today a player can buy an off-the-shelf mouthguard, heat it and press it into the shape of their mouth the first time of use. The same idea will come with safety helmets. They will arrive flexible, be put on the head and adjusted. When the wearer is comfortable and the fit is exact, the material will be permanently hardened. Perfect fit guaranteed.

Superknickers

During the first Gulf War, US military medics were surprised and alarmed to find that more casualties came from bacterial infection than enemy fire, friendly fire and accident. Bugs not bombs brought the soldiers to their knees. Sweating

Bugs not **bombs** brought the soldiers to their knees

around in the desert for days on end without an opportunity to change pants, nasty itches and infections were hardly a surprising outcome. The answer? Self-cleaning cloth.

The new fabric is produced by using microwaves to attach nanoparticles to a fabric. The nanoparticles become effective when they are bound with chemicals designed to do a variety of tasks, such as repel water and kill bacteria. As a result, liquids that come into contact with the fabric run off as beads and harmful bacteria are zapped. Apparently, soldiers wearing underwear made from the new material were able to wear the same pants for weeks on end without being mistaken for skunks. The material can be washed, too, and regains its pong-free properties simply by soaking in a special chemical solution.

For more on self-cleaning cloth see:
http://www.eurekalert.org/pub_releases/2004-11/acs-sm111904.php

The benefits for athletes of the new material are numerous. Most obviously, it is wholly waterproof. The fabric's anti-bacterial properties replace smell with sweet-ness: no more 'scrum pox' for rugby players, marathon runners and triathletes will remain as fresh as the second they set out, parents won't have to wash muddy football shorts every day, socks will be happily left on the kitchen table after use . . .

Supershoes

The shoes of the future will be even more sport-specific than they are now. With football boots, the aim must be to let the players feel as if they are playing in bare feet, with as little as possible between their skin and the ball.[6] This will benefit the most skilful players. Some form of shear-thickening material, at least on the part of the boot that makes contact with the ball, would seem to be the solution.

The two other requirements of a boot – support and grip – might be met by 'intelligent' fabrics and materials: an ankle support that remained fully flexible until twisted to an unacceptable angle, for example, or sole grips that self-adjust to the requirements of the pitch and conditions – and even, perhaps, to the needs of an individual player. What about a pair of boots that a player 'wore in' with a full range of normal movements during a game, then fixed to permit those movements but no more?

Football boots are an exception because they play such a crucial role in the game, like a bat in cricket. Nevertheless, the future for other sports footwear is likely to follow a similar path. Cushioning will improve so that hairline fractures – even in fast bowlers – become extremely rare. Intelligent surface grip will become universal, as will intelligent support. Self-cleaning goes without saying, too. Before all that, within only a short space of time it will be possible, using the internet, to allow everyone to order a pair of sports shoes or boots tailor-made for his or her feet alone. It is already possible to buy ski boots that are hot moulded in the shop for a perfect fit.

With running shoes, unless we return to performing in bare feet, the question of 'springing' – when protection becomes performance-enhancing – is likely to

[6] See Chapter 9.

rumble on.[7] Then there is the SMART shoe that records your movements or, more embarrassing, feeds them back to a coach (see Chapter 7) . . . bringing a whole new meaning to the word 'sneakers'!

Superspray

Spray-on clothing is already here, although it has yet to be exploited for sport. Imagine a swift modesty spray before going out for a jog? Quick, disposable, a perfect fit, unlimited choice of colours and finishes and, on the right body, enormously sexy.

Imagine a swift modesty spray before going out for a jog

Then there's the question of numbers and names on shirts. The present system is expensive and wasteful because each shirt can carry only one set of imprints. With a panel of electrochromatic polymers or some other colour-changing material, each top could be individually set up for a specific occasion. What about one sponsor for the first half of a game and another for the second half, or a message that tells the spectator and viewer that the goal, try or point they have just seen was sponsored by a particular brand? Fanciful, fun – and perhaps not just a weird dream?

Going further, with a screen-like space on the chest and back of a player performing before a TV audience of billions, the opportunities are infinite: two

[7] See also the 'Real Olympics' idea in Chapter 9.

sets all, tie-break, you are serving for the match ... in a desperate effort to break your opponent's concentration, your coach beams an alluring striptease on to the front of your shirt ... Game, set and match – and one hell of a controversy!

Finally, there is the possibility of more aerodynamic clothing. To some extent this is already here as scientists have ascertained that by taking measures such as wearing tight-fitting, smooth-surface outfits of, say, polyester or Lycra and removing excess body hair, drag can be reduced by up to 6%. Even so, the basic problem remains: the human body running in an upright position – flat at the back and flat (gender variations are minimal in sport) at the front – is an aerodynamic nightmare because its drag coefficient (resistance) is so high. We have only to compare

Appearance matters – carefully designed clothing can reduce an athlete's drag by at least 5%.

©ISTOCKPHOTO.COM/TROTSCHE

ourselves with a modern car, train or aeroplane, or even a cheetah, to realise how poorly designed we are for speed.

One answer might be vests, shirts and even shorts or bodysuits that adopted a more aerodynamic shape as the runner's speed increased, thereby cutting down drag. The IAAF would probably not approve of 100 m runners thundering down the track looking like Eurostar trains, but there is nothing in the regulations to prevent it. The only stipulation at present is that athletic clothing has to be clean, 'non-objectionable', the same colour back and front, and, as with swimmers, not transparent 'even if wet'. Morality before medals, obviously.

Superbudget

The more high tech sports clothing, especially footwear, becomes, the further out of the reach of the less well-off athletes it gets. Either hard-up sportsmen and women move to richer, developed states, as happens today, or the advantages remain with competitors native to those countries. The result is the same either way: the medals, cups and trophies remain an almost exclusive province of the well-heeled – literally and metaphorically. Given the comparatively small market for professional sportsgear compared with, say, computers, it is unlikely we will see falling prices due to exponentially growing turnover.

▟▟ 'An African nation will **win** the **World Cup** before the **year 2000**,' predicted Pelé on several occasions **▟▟**

'An African nation will win the World Cup before the year 2000' predicted Pelé on several occasions. He was wrong, and with every year that passes the chances of it happening grow more remote. As African soccer writer Lungile Madywabe admitted in *Mail & Guardian Online*, 9 June 2006: 'Although we are always capable of springing the odd surprise, no one seriously believes that an African nation can win the cup.'

Madywabe explained his reasoning further: 'There is a plethora of reasons for Africa's failures, varying from ongoing conflicts, to corruption and competition for funding. How can you give money to sport when there is endless poverty? What comes first, attention to rising levels of infant mortality, or training facilities? Can governments ignore pandemic diseases and give preference to soccer?'

One answer, explored further in Part II, is to go back to where it all started and insist on athletes competing naked. After all, track and field and swimming in the nude would not be so different from what we have today. Stripped-off rugby, on the other hand, would be something else. The idea might or might not please the spectators, but at least everyone would compete on equal terms.

Or would they?

3 **Hey Ref!**

What the Eye Doesn't See . . .

The 2007 English FA Cup Final was a tough, relentless battle between the two best teams in the country. Manchester United had more possession, Chelsea, when they had the ball, looked more dangerous. After 45 minutes neither side had scored.

The second half started brightly, but still the deadlock remained unbroken when the 90 minutes were up. Finally, just before the end of the first period of extra time, United's Wayne Rooney found himself in space on the right and delivered a neat cross. Two players advanced to make the ball theirs: the Chelsea goalkeeper, Petr Cech, and the red-shirted Ryan Giggs.

Cech got there first and went down on the ball, hugging it to his chest. Giggs' boots made contact with the ball half a second later. In the mêlée that followed, the forward's momentum carried himself, Cech and the ball towards the goal line. Giggs believed the ball actually crossed the line and claimed a goal. The Chelsea players said their keeper had been fouled. The referee disagreed with both parties and the game continued. Chelsea eventually won with a goal scored close to the end of the second period of extra time.

The 2007 English FA Cup **Final** was a **tough**, **relentless battle between** the two best teams in the **country**

TV replays showed that Cech had indeed carried the ball over his own line. As the referee had not blown for a foul, it should have been a goal. A piece of technology as simple as TV replay, as used in rugby, could have sorted the matter out almost instantaneously. But no . . . Clinging to its belief that wrong decisions are 'all part of the game', football refuses to allow its referees technological assistance. Few other aspects of the relationship between sport and technology are so contentious.

'I've never been an advocate of technology but sooner rather than later they should bring it in . . . When huge decisions at the top level have an impact on teams, management and players

then something has to be done.' – Mark Hughes, manager of Blackburn Rovers, 2007

From There . . .

Keeping the Peace

As far as we know, cricket was the first modern sport to insist on the presence of an official to mediate between opponents, although before that, the ancient Greeks had employed judges for athletics events and in early modern times some relatively impartial party had probably been given the task of deciding the winner in horse races. The reason for cricket taking the lead in this matter was its growing complexity: 'leg before wicket' (LBW), for example, which appeared in the 1809 laws as a method of dismissal, could be decided only by an umpire. Other sports were self-regulating, and their scoring more obvious. As there were no soft victories on points in the early days, bare-knuckle boxers fighting over an unlimited number of rounds triumphed when their opponent was unable to fight on, a decision for which no referee was needed. Early football was won by the side scoring the most goals – again, no third party was required to do the counting.

By **the outbreak of** World War I, **virtually** all sporting events of any consequence **employed** umpires, referees or **judges**

Want to know why an umpire was needed to decide on LBW decisions? Well, here's the (modern) law:

'Out LBW

The striker shall be out LBW in the circumstances set out below:

(a) Striker attempting to play the ball

The striker shall be out lbw if he first intercepts with any part of his person, dress or equipment a fair ball which would have hit the wicket and which has not previously touched his bat or a hand holding the bat, provided that:

> (i) the ball pitched in a straight line between wicket and wicket or on the off side of the striker's wicket, or was intercepted full pitch; and
>
> (ii) the point of impact is in a straight line between wicket and wicket, even if above the level of the bails.

(b) Striker making no attempt to play the ball

The striker shall be out LBW even if the ball is intercepted outside the line of the off stump if, in the opinion of the umpire, he has made no genuine attempt to play the ball with his bat, but has intercepted the ball with some part of his person and if the other circumstances set out in (a) above apply.'

Fat chance highly competitive, professional players sorting that out on their own!

The need for neutral officials in sports other than cricket and racing came when participants could no longer settle their own disagreements. This arose in the 19th century as sport became more organised and serious. With cups to be acquired, fame to be won, bets to be pocketed and pay to be earned by the growing number of professional players, disputes grew acrimonious and the need for a neutral arbitrator inescapable. Football teams appointed referees in the mid-19th century, in 1878 gave them the simplest of technology, a whistle, and in 1891 allowed them on to the pitch. By the outbreak of World War I, virtually all sporting events of any consequence employed umpires, referees or judges.

A Matter of Timing

Timepieces were first used simply to determine the start and finish of a match. Then came the timing of races, starting around 1860. In 1865, England's Richard Webster is said to have set a world mile record of 4 minutes 36.5 seconds, the earliest recorded timing of a race. This was a dramatic technological innovation, opening up a whole new vista for track and field athletics: winning a race was no longer the ultimate quest; now there were records – personal, national, meeting and world – to beat. Webster's timing is also interesting for the 0.5 second accredited to him. As the stopwatch was not patented until 1869, one wonders where that odd half second came from.

At the 1912 Stockholm Olympics, a hand-cranked camera was set up at the finishing line to enable athletes to be separated by photo finishes, although developing the film took many times longer than the race itself. Some sort of electronic timing was also available although it was not used officially. Twenty years later, at the 1932 Los Angeles Olympics, the judging process became still more sophisticated with a camera linked to a chronometer so that each photo frame came time-stamped. Within another 20 years, accuracy was down to 1/100th of a second.

Such accuracy did not become official, however, until 1972. By now the start time was triggered by the starting gun, contact plates were being used in swimming for timing and the separation of places and times were being shown live on TV.

You can get some idea of how imprecise photo technology was at the 1912 Olympics from YouTube:
http://www.youtube.com/watch?v=wlFgfh2CplQ

Video Nasty

Until the 1950s, nearly all non-racing sports were in the hands of officials equipped with nothing more than a pair of eyes and a whistle. All this ended in 1955. The ongoing revolution began when the Canadian Broadcasting Corporation, in its enormously popular Hockey Night in Canada, used instant TV replay for the first time. At a stroke, the authority of the officiating personnel was dramatically undermined. After that moment, slowly, painfully slowly, the sporting world came to realise that, if it really wanted the truth, technology was able to provide it better than fallible human beings.

In 1996, rugby league first allowed referees to ask a 'Fourth Official' whether a try had been scored and light meters became a feature of major cricket matches. In the USA, the National [American] Football League (NFL), basketball and ice hockey introduced TV replays to assist in decisions and appeals. The same technology was gradually rolled out worldwide across a broad range of sports as a way of identifying foul play. Increasingly, referees on the pitch were put in live radio contact with other officials and even with the broadcasting media. In 1980, an electronic device not dissimilar to a burglar alarm was installed at Wimbledon to rule whether a serve was in or out. Another electronic device bleeped if a service ball touched the top of the net.

Then came Hawk-Eye . . .

. . . To Where We Are Now

Half a Mo!

The human and electronic judges at the end of a race – be it running, swimming, cycling or any other sport – have two tasks: to place the finishers in order and to record their times. Except in swimming, positions in the most important meetings are determined by high-speed video cameras that scan an 8-mm finishing line 2,000 times a second. All matter, human or mechanical, that crosses this line is photographed in miniscule sections which, if necessary, can be as tiny as a human hair. These sectional pictures are then assembled electronically to produce an unrealistic but super-accurate photo-finish image.

Enraged competitors **threatened to beat up** the **timekeepers** because they **did not** believe the technology was accurate. **It was**

Because visual differentiation is difficult in water, swimmers are separated and timed electronically. Sensors in the starting blocks record when a swimmer leaves, and touching a plastic pad on the end wall determines their finish – and therefore their race time. Video cameras are run as backup. At the 1987

Not even by a hair's breadth? As far as the judges of Race 1 at Hollywood Park on 19 December 2005 were concerned, this was a dead heat. Agree?

Commonwealth Games, the first major competition to employ electronic timing, enraged competitors threatened to beat up the timekeepers because they did not believe the technology was accurate. It was.

Beams and Chips

Technology derived from swimming's starting and finishing pads is also now employed in the starting blocks used by sprint athletes. The race time is begun by the firing of the starting gun. But athletes who put undue pressure on their starting blocks (i.e. set off) less than 0.110 of a second later are deemed to have false started. This is because tests have revealed that no one can react in less than 0.110 seconds after hearing the gun. A light now appears automatically in the lane of the sprinter who is too quick off the mark, informing the officials, the athlete and the spectators.

Off the track, electronics have also replaced the tape measure. In throwing events, a reflector is placed in the ground at the precise point where the shot, discus or javelin lands. By bouncing a laser beam off the reflector, the distance from the front of the circle is measured immediately and automatically relayed to an electronic scoreboard. Similarly, at the most prestigious events the height of the bar in pole vault and high jump is checked electronically.

The timing and positioning of competitors in mass events with uneven or staggered starts, like a city marathon or the Tour de France, require special technology. Enter 'transponders', wireless communications devices that pick up an incoming signal and respond to it.

A 'passive' transponder, as in the 'chip' on a credit card, releases its coded information when triggered by a sensor up to a metre or two distant. An 'active' transponder operates over much greater distances, even thousands of miles, sending out a coded signal when prompted, thereby allowing itself to be tracked. Navigation systems are an obvious use of active transponders.

Passive transponders are now being used in marathons, attached to the laces of a competitor's running shoe and read by mats placed at 5 k intervals around the course. The information is relayed by a computer program that identifies the time

Although **his torso** had **crossed** the line, **his chipped lace** had not. Electronically, he **had not finished** the race.

and position of all athletes at any given moment and is able to pass this on to the waiting media in graphic form. A brilliant system, maybe, but one that is not yet foolproof. While leading the 2006 Chicago marathon, Kenyan Robert Cheruiyot tripped on a sponsor's mat placed just before the finishing line, fell forward and knocked himself out. Although his torso had crossed the line, his chipped lace had not. Electronically, he had not finished the race. Happily, the first 15 runners were also being timed by stopwatch – just in case – and the referee declared Cheruiyot the winner because his chest, if not his feet, had come home first.

The Tour de France has gone one better. In 2006, a selection of cyclists on certain stages of the Tour were fitted with high-tech, 95 gm active transponders that allowed them to be tracked by satellite. Their progress, presented graphically, was electronically represented on screen with the relevant sector of Google Earth. This intensely sophisticated system, using technology devised by the European Space Agency, claims to be accurate to within 1 or 2 m, comparing favourably with the 15 to 20 m accuracy of the more familiar GPS used in vehicle Sat Nav systems.

The Wikipedia article on GPS is one of its more reliable ones:
http://en.wikipedia.org/wiki/Global_Positioning_System

" And **why pretend** to be punched, when in **30 seconds'** time you'd **be receiving red** for play-acting? **"**

Going Upstairs

Video recording has been available for years but it was only with the development of instant digital review – recording images on disc using the same technology as a computer – that it began seriously to influence sport. The impact was enormous. Within just a few years it was impossible to imagine a top-level tennis or cricket match without it and sports that had rejected it – notably football and baseball – were continually having to justify their position. 'Introduce [instant replay] and immediately the risk v reward debate which zips around a player's head changes', explained the *Guardian* on 4 May 2006. It went on to explain, 'there'd be no incentive to dive when someone in the stands can alert the referee, who would soon be waving yellow in your direction.' 'And why pretend to be punched, when in 30 seconds' time you'd be receiving red for play-acting?'

Top rugby league ref Stuart Cummings said he felt the presence of technology made him a better official: 'I always enjoyed the game better from my point of view when the video referee was in place.'[1]

[1] On www.sportandtechnology.com, August 2007.

Rugby league, rugby union and American football, all stop-start games, have embraced video technology, but in very different ways. In the two rugbys, it is used to support and assist the referee, allowing him to 'go upstairs' – i.e. talk with a video ref presumed to be seated in an office somewhere in the stands – asking a specific question relating to the scoring of a try. 'Was the ball knocked on?' for example, or 'Is there any reason why I may not award a try?' The fourth official then views the incident from as many different viewpoints as are available and radios back his verdict to the ref on the pitch. At the same time, 'Try!' or 'No Try' is flashed up on the electronic scoreboard. New drama, better decisions . . . An improved game all round, surely?

Try or no try? Mark Cueto does or does not score for England in the final of the 2007 RWC. The decision (no try) raised the question of the relationship between the video ref and the editor of the TV programme being broadcast.

©ACTION IMAGES

There are those who argue that rugby could go even further in its use of replay evidence. Writing in the *Guardian* (November 2007), Wasps and Wales coach Shaun Edwards declared that 'If we have the technology it should be used properly and, no matter what the television director wants, the official making the decision should have the first say on the angles he wants repeated and how many times they are shown.' This raises interesting and important questions about ownership of replay material. Officially it is the broadcaster's, who allow the sport to use it for their own benefit. If the way this is done is not to the sport's liking, then they need to set up their own network of cameras and back-up computers. Easier said than done – which European sport, except perhaps for Premiership football, could afford such an outlay? So using replay technology leaves sports even more beholden to their media paymasters . . .

Recordings of a game are also used by disciplinary panels investigating incidents such as an allegation of foul play. There is no question of replay ever being officially used to contradict a referee's decision. To do so, the games' authorities believe, would be to undermine fatally the authority of the officials and push the sport on a dangerous downhill slide towards anarchy. Referee-initiated replays in ice hockey are based on a similar philosophy.

Not so in America's National Football League (NFL), the sport's only fully professional league. After an unsuccessful flirtation with videotape replays between 1986 and 1991, in 1999 the NFL introduced digital replay and a complex set of rules by which it might be used to influence a game. Essentially, trying not to oversimplify, the arrangement is this: having watched a recording of a 'play' (the game is divided into a series of self-contained plays), a coach may, at the risk of a penalty if his plea is rejected, challenge a refereeing decision during the previous play; the challenge is upheld only if referees decide that there is indisputable evidence for a decision to be reversed.

The NFL's official site is www.nfl.com and the NBA's is www.NBA.com

The concept of challenge introduces a whole new aspect to the game, cementing digital technology as an integral part of it. Aware of this, America's National Basketball Association (NBA) allows officials to watch replays only before they rule on whether a shot was released before a buzzer announced the end of a period of play. There are no challenges. European basketball is different again, Italy permitting NFL-style coach challenges.

Milwaukee Bucks guard TJ Ford takes a shot in the 11 February 2006 NBA game v the Charlotte Bobcats. Keen to uphold the integrity of its officials, the NBA has fought shy of introducing a controversial 'video challenge' system.

Pitch and Snick

'When I step across the boundary rope, that is the only time I feel I am in total control.' – Dickie Bird, highly respected test umpire

For all its reputation as a conservative game, cricket has accepted technology as readily as any sport. Indeed, it may be argued that exciting technological gadgetry, from pitch mike and stump camera to Hawkeye (see below), has saved the game as a modern spectator sport. However, in employing technology originally

The old school: umpire Dickie Bird, universally respected throughout the cricketing world, believes that hawk-eyed humans make better umpiring decisions than any piece of technology.

developed to enhance the TV experience, cricket has entered a murky new world for which it has neither map nor compass.

For those new to the game, a good introduction to cricket is offered on: http://uk.cricinfo.com/link_to_database/ABOUT_CRICKET/EXPLANATION

Cricket is a complicated game involving split-second decision-making. Its two umpires on the field of play, at international level quite often ex-players whose faculties are no longer sharp enough for them to continue playing professionally, are asked to rule on the finest of line judgements, the slightest of sounds, the most complex of permutations (non-cricketers look away now!): Did long leg, dozens of metres away and in poor light, catch the ball travelling at high speed 1 mm before it hit the ground? Was that the faintest of tickles to first slip? Did a ball travelling at 90 mph (145 kph) hit the pitch in line with stumps hidden by the batter and, if it did, would it have gone on to hit those stumps if it had not first struck the batter's pads?

Before roaring thousands crammed into the Melbourne Cricket Ground or Wankhede, Mumbai, they can be matters – almost literally – of life and death

Such arcane issues are rarely of life-changing importance in a fixture between Much Binding in the Marsh 2nd XI and Piddletrenthide Over 60s, but before roaring thousands crammed into the Melbourne Cricket Ground or Wankhede, Mumbai they can be matters – almost literally – of life and death, and certainly of millions of rupees in betting money.

Cricket's official flirtation with the technology of judgement began with a quaint system of lights that came on next to the scoreboard as daylight deteriorated: one light = dim, two lights = gloomy and so on. Nowadays umpires are equipped with hand-held light meters which they point in the general direction of the bowler in an attempt to ascertain whether a sharp-eyed young batter can pick out the ball against the background.

More recently, cricket embraced TV replay: in major matches the umpires on the field can ask a 'third umpire' in the pavilion to check with his TV monitor on four issues: catches, run-outs, stumpings and boundaries (whether or not the ball has crossed the boundary for a four or six). This settles some awkward questions but raises many more. On run-outs, for instance, quite often no camera is able to offer a clear view of the incident in question. Where low catches are concerned, there is some doubt about the camera's ability to distinguish the microsecond difference between a ball travelling straight into a player's hand and one that touches the ground fractionally before being caught. Roger Knight, sometime MCC's Secretary and Chief Executive, believes that in such cases umpires should be able to rely on 'the honesty of the players' who could then be cited for acting contrary to the Spirit of the Game if they are subsequently shown by technology to have cheated.[2]

Test yourself: Look at the amazing catches on:
http://www.youtube.com/watch?v=-rla_Rq5FsE
and decide, as an umpire unaided by TV replay, whether or not you would allow them.

[2] http://2knightsviews.blogspot.com, 10 November 2007.

American **football** reckons that, aided **by TV replays,** its officials get 98% of their decisions **right**

Digital Umpires

American football reckons that, aided by TV replays, its officials get 98% of their decisions right. Either other sports are less cocksure or their judges are less competent. Football and cricket are well known for adjudicators who do not always reach the correct decision: 'A study of international cricket suggests a figure of 85% at best.'[3] Awkwardly controversial, therefore, is cricket's decision to limit technological assistance to the four issues mentioned above and not to use it for the two most difficult and often contentious methods of dismissal: (1) LBW (leg-before-wicket) and (2) caught behind (when the ball only brushes the bat or the glove). In pre-technology days, the umpire gave their decision – the batter's pad did or did not prevent the ball from hitting the stumps in the case of LBW or the ball had or had not glanced the batter's pad or glove in the case of caught behind – and all concerned accepted the verdict more or less gracefully.

Early TV coverage did not alter the situation much because cameras were rarely in the right position (i.e. at the umpire's eye line) or sharp enough to determine whether an LBW or caught behind decision was right. In the last 12 or so years, however, the situation has changed dramatically as new technologies – better cameras and replay systems, the Snickometer, Hawkeye and Hot Spot – have allowed commentators, viewers and listeners to sit on virtually incontrovertible judgement on the officials in the middle.

[3] *Guardian Unlimited*, 12 September 2002.

There's more on Hawkeye at:
www.hawkeyeinnovations.co.uk

The latest slow-motion replay system, Hi-Motion, can slow action down by a factor of 12x while retaining genuine high definition. The Snickometer, invented by computer expert Allan Plaskett, picks up sounds from spy-style directional microphones or from those located in the stumps or pitch and reproduces it as an oscillation chart of the ball passing the bat. A peak in the spectrum indicates that the ball has touched something on its way through. This is useful when judging caught behind decisions and also for LBWs – batters cannot be out LBW if the ball has touched their bat, however faintly, before striking their pad.

There's more on the Snickometer at:
http://www.channel4.com/sport/cricket/analyst/technology/ana_15.html

First used by Channel 4 for coverage of a test match in 2001, Hawkeye was developed from missile-tracking technology. Its purpose is to recreate with 99.99% accuracy the trajectory of a moving ball. The ingenious British invention wirelessly links a series of six smart cameras, set in different positions around the playing area, to a computer program that combines the information it receives frame by frame (250 per second) to produce a 3-D image. Hawkeye not only displays the path of a ball or series of balls, useful for analysis of a bowler's performance, but it also predicts where a ball would have gone if its path had not been interrupted. Specifically, in the case of LBW decisions, it can say whether a delivery that struck a batter's pad would have gone on to strike the wicket. Skyscope, a separate system developed for Sky TV, does much the same as Hawkeye.

The result of these developments is that at the end of a session of play, it is possible to say with reasonable accuracy how many decisions an umpire has got right and how many wrong. This inevitably undermines the officials' position as the sole arbiter of fact, especially when they can refer only some decisions, such as run-outs, to a third official. A slight breach of this practice was initiated in the English 2007 Friends Provident Trophy limited overs competition. As an experiment, batters and fielders were allowed to challenge an umpire's decision over a dismissal (both 'out' and 'not out'), referring the matter to a third umpire with

The obvious answer: Hawkeye in action at the 2007 Wimbledon Championships.

access to TV replay, who had the authority to reverse decisions made in the middle. Each team was permitted two referrals per innings.

❝ [The **referral system**] could **undermine** the authority of the umpire on the **field** **❞**

Neither players nor officials appeared over-enamoured with the appeals idea. It did 'not have a place in the game' said Sussex captain Chris Adams, and the experiment was 'doomed to fail' according to English Cricket Board chief Alan Fordham. More specifically, he expressed worries that the referral system 'could undermine the authority of the umpire on the field.'[4]

Overall, then, cricket has got itself into a bit of a mess. Its governing body, the ICC (International Cricket Council) is at the time of writing awaiting a detailed and careful study of how technology may be further used to assist the umpires in their decision-making. Interestingly, the ICC's president-elect, David Morgan, is hoping that this will lead to 'increased use of technology . . . for the good of the game.'[5] He and others like him believe what is increasingly obvious: the modern panoply of cameras, microphones, computer programs, etc., provides more accurate information for complex decision-making than the middle-aged human ear and eye.

Unfortunate officials will be **increasingly challenged**, questioned and confronted to the **point where** their task becomes **impossible**

[4] Both remarks reported by Sarah Holt on BBC Sport website, 1 May 2007.
[5] Speaking on BBC Radio 5 Live, 12 January 2008.

Innovation should be embraced, therefore, and introduced to assist umpires in all relevant judgements. Unless this happens, the unfortunate officials will be increasingly challenged, questioned and confronted to the point where their task becomes impossible. We are not far from such a position already: when media-fed complaints about poor decision-making can force an umpire to be withdrawn from a series, as happened in January 2008 to Steve Bucknor in the Australia v India series, some very disturbing writing is on the wall.

At the same time, perhaps we might hear a word in defence of the cricketing authorities? Most of their problems have arisen because they have been pioneers, going where other sports – most notably football – have feared to tread. As a consequence, cricket has faced many of the teething problems that were bound to occur during the inevitable progress from fallible human officiating to objective, technological umpiring. When others follow, as they certainly will, then a cheery 'thanks mate!' in the direction of cricket would not be out of place.

'You Can't Be Serious'

'I am totally against it. I think it will destroy the game. It will slow it down, lose the momentum and the motion of the game . . . It is bull. This definitely is not the way to help the game.'
– Marat Saffin on instant replay and player challenges, 2006

In tennis, as in cricket, pinpoint accuracy regarding the precise position of a relatively small ball is essential. Over 25 years ago, the Cyclops system was introduced to help judge whether a high-speed serve was in or out. It works by projecting a series of light rays along and just outside the service line, and issuing a loud bleep when it records a ball falling beyond the line. Although fine in the lab, on court the system can be prompted into giving false rulings: uneven surfaces (especially on worn grass courts) and insects are the chief culprits. Because of this, in a Cyclops-equipped court, the final decision of whether a ball is 'in' or 'out' rests with the match referee.

After Cyclops came Trinity, an electronic device that, by measuring vibrations in the net, ruled on net faults during service. As with Cyclops, it was not infallible, especially in high winds, and the final decision remained with the referee.

"Look at the score now!" grumbled the Swiss star. "It's killing me, Hawkeye is killing me!"

The referee's status as the ultimate arbiter of fact remained intact until 2006, when Hawkeye hit the show courts of the US Open. The following year it was at Wimbledon and before long is expected to be a feature of all major tournaments. The machinery is essentially the same as that used in cricket (see above), but with even more cameras. Moreover, tennis officials allow Hawkeye to be used for player challenges. The general rule is two challenges per set, with an extra one if it goes to a tie-break. A correct challenge leaves intact a player's two challenges, while a false one reduces his stock by one. Unused challenges may not be carried over into other sets. When a player calls for a line judgement to be referred to Hawkeye, the incident is replayed on TV and in slow motion on large screens visible to the players, officials and crowd.

The introduction of the challenge brings a fundamental change to the game of tennis. It widens the gap between the top professionals and the rest, it undermines the authority of officials and, most significant of all, it makes the timing of the challenge a key component of match tactics. The challenge can be used not just to check on a line decision but also to break an opponent's concentration. Designed to relegate to history frustrated outbursts such as John McEnroe's famous 'You can't be serious!' (Wimbledon 1981), the appeal system produced a storm of its own in the 2007 Wimbledon Championships, when the device gave a crucial break point to Rafael Nadal over Roger Federer, the world no 1. 'Look at the score now!' grumbled the Swiss star. 'It's killing me, Hawkeye is killing me!'

It didn't, and he went on to win the match and the championship. Nevertheless, Federer, an opponent of the challenge system, had clearly been rattled by the break in play at a key moment in the game.

Even when technology is making all decisions on matters of fact, umpires will still be required to discipline notoriously outspoken players like the fiery John McEnroe.

©ACTION IMAGES/MSI

Press-Button Madness[6]

Once the system of rounds and points had been introduced, boxing matches were decided by the referee or by ringside judges armed with an experienced eye and pencil and paper. The system was always open to controversy, corruption even, and matters came to a head in the final of the gold medal Light-Middleweight bout between American Roy Jones Jr and South Korean Park Si-Hun in the 1988 Seoul Olympics. Jones dominated the fight but lost in a highly controversial decision when the judges split 3-2 in Park's favour. Amid widespread allegations of bribery, those voting against Jones were all suspended and a new high-tech scoring system was put in place for the next Olympics.

The so-called 'computerised scoring' used in amateur boxing from the Barcelona Olympics onwards involves five ringside judges equipped with a panel fitted with two buttons, blue and red. When a judge believes a boxer has landed a punch in the target area, thereby scoring a point, they press the relevant button within a second of the blow landing. When three judges press the same button within a second, the boxer is credited with a point. The points tally is flashed on a score-board visible from the ring.

The arrangement is fraught with difficulties. Indeed, a number of first-class authorities, including former world champion and Hall of Fame star Barry McGuigan, believe that the use of technology has made the situation worse than before, leaving it more unfair and inaccurate, and still open to corruption. Body punches are scarcely recorded and judges are known to be deliberately slow on the button, missing the 1-second time limit and therefore invalidating their scoring.

---

[6] As in the boxing comments in Chapter 1, I am deeply indebted to Barry McGuigan, MBE, for much of the information in this section.

More importantly, as was touched upon in Chapter 1, the very nature of amateur boxing has been altered. Fighters are trained to go for long-range, often light-weight punches, clearly visible to the judges, rather than harder blows delivered at close range. This is because they are scored on the number of punches they land clearly in the target area, irrespective of their quality or power. Indeed, coaches discourage heavy, more draining punches as they simply tire a boxer for no extra reward. Instead we have an endless succession of tall, rangy southpaws, all virtually clones of each other, bouncing round the ring and delivering the same staccato blows that score points but are essentially harmless. In amateur boxing, we almost never now see that thrilling, bout-winning, knockout punch in the last minute of the final round from a fighter down in the points tally.

To compound the problem, with the scoreboard clearly visible above them, boxers know once they are ahead and can adjust their tactic accordingly. This leads to fighters running down the clock by dancing round the ring out of their opponent's reach. This is not what spectators, boxing fans or otherwise, want to see. It was hardly surprising, therefore, that the professional arm of the sport, in the form of the World Boxing Council, flirted only briefly with the new technology before abandoning it.

The Jones v Park fight can be seen on YouTube:
http://www.youtube.com/watch?v=o0cNugcG6zg

What Next?

The Challenge

The issue of the challenge, already available to players at the highest level in American football, tennis, cricket and basketball, raises fundamental questions about the nature of sport. First, because of the price of the required technology, the challenge is available only to the top professionals, thereby deepening the gulf between them and other players. Second, the challenge enshrines a new principle: that those officiating may be wrong. Third, by turning to technology to resolve disputes, the sports concerned are admitting that impersonal science is better at ascertaining fact than the senses of an individual human being.

Bent refs and blind umpires – 'we was robbed' – are as much the stuff of post-match chat as are brilliant goals and stunning centuries

The last two points illustrate the logical foolishness of the challenge: if technology can do a job better than a person can, why not let it make all the decisions? That way the challenge would be redundant and all technology-run sport could concentrate on performance without the distraction of controversial decisions. But perhaps that is precisely what we do not want? Top-level professional sport is ultimately about entertainment – bums on seats in the stands or before the screens – and not about the players' enjoyment. And any form of controversy, including 'bad' decisions, is hugely entertaining. Bent refs and blind umpires – 'we was robbed' – are as much the stuff of post-match chat as are brilliant goals and stunning centuries.

This leaves the bosses of the sporting industry with three possible routes to follow. One, at present taken by football, is to keep things as they are, accepting that mistakes are part of the game and, since that game is the most successful in the world, it would be foolish to tamper with it. The second option, currently adopted by a number of sports, is to admit a limited amount of technology into the process of adjudication: for instance, deciding tries in rugby, whether a catch is held in cricket or whether an athlete has false started. The third option is to embrace the technology of adjudication wholeheartedly.

Super-ref

Given the astounding developments of the last 25 years, there is no reason why, within the next half-century, technology should not handle all matters of objective judgement in professional sport. At a simple level, this happens now in swimming and athletics. Football is going to follow. Hawkeye makers were already experimenting at Reading's training ground when a number of dodgy decisions at the start of the 2007–08 English Premiership season, especially a goal denied to Tottenham at Manchester United, made the call for Hawkeye in the goalmouth irresistible. Once this is the accepted way of deciding whether or not a ball has crossed the line, technology will then be asked to rule on other matters, such as off-side and handball. The tech-ref's verdict will be announced with a unique audio-visual signal. The referee's authority will be enhanced – 'Don't blame me, blame the computer!' – and they will be free to concentrate on more subjective issues such as foul tackles. Similarly in rugby, where a whole range of issues, from forward passes to foot touch, could happily be removed from the referee's charge.

Technology is only doing better what **referees** and umpires were **established to do** in the **first** place

Fencing already employs a high degree of technology, 'hits' being verified by a bleep when a charged sword blade or spring-loaded tip strikes the target area and so completes an electrical circuit. Amateur boxing is said to be exploring something similar, with sensors in vests, gloves and headgear. It should surely be possible, too, in another half-century, to use a network of cameras linked to a suitable program as a replacement for the highly subjective points system that currently decides all matches in which there is no knockout. Meanwhile, on the hockey pitches, tennis courts and cricket pitches of the late 21st century, the human umpires remain to maintain fair play and decorous language. All technical decisions are handled electronically. And why not? Technology is only doing better what referees and umpires were established to do in the first place.

Finally, what's that ridiculous piece of medieval technology hanging round the ref's neck? It is impossible to believe that the mouth-blown whistle, inefficient, slow to be activated and potentially dangerous, will continue for much longer. Within a few years, the referee in the middle and the technological referees on the sidelines will all be connected electronically to the same sound system, and that strange bit of tin with a pea in it will become simply a museum exhibit. Not before time, too.

4 Born of Technology

'The track is my canvas. My car is my pencil.'
– Graham Hill, world motor racing champion

It is now the turn of land sports born of technology – cycling, skiing, skating, sledding and, ultimately, motorcar and motorbike racing. Water and air sports follow in the next chapter. Because they tend to be as much about highly complex and sophisticated machines as about those who operate them, I have decided to deal with two- and four-wheeled motorsports only in overview.

From There . . .

Speed!

Speed is about so much more than just getting from A to B more swiftly than your rival. It's about a quickening of the pulse, wind in the hair, the ground flashing by beneath you, the thrill of danger . . . The first to experience such frisson, around 5,000 years ago, were horse riders and charioteers. Skiers were probably not far behind: the earliest skis, more like slippery snowshoes than the slender modern devices, probably appeared around 2,500 BC – there are rock carvings from that era of a couple of blokes on these primitive slider boards. Some of the heroes of Norse sagas were said to be proficient skiers as well as slaughterers, no doubt using skis made using the same woodworking skills as those developed for longships.

A quickening of the **pulse**, wind in the **hair**, the **ground flashing by beneath you**, the thrill of danger . . .

Although the Norwegian army was holding skiing competitions in the 18th century, it was the Victorians who, as with so many sports, got the activity properly organised. Even so, the technology remained pretty basic until the 20th century. Leather ski boots were virtually the same as normal footwear in everyday use. The most important early developments were in the 'bindings' – the way the boot was fastened to the ski – such as Sondre Norheim's 'birch binding' and Mathias Zdarsky's 'Lilienfeld binding'. These allowed manoeuvres, like the slalom, until then not possible for fear of losing a ski or breaking an ankle, or both. The sinister-sounding Rottafella (rat trap) binding followed in 1920.

> 'Ski' comes from the old Norse word for a piece of wood and the first skis were made from single pieces of timber.

Aluminium skis and laminate construction were introduced in the 1930s. By now skiers could enjoy several runs a day thanks to the development of easy-on-off chairlifts. Technology began to have an even more serious impact after World War II, when rapidly rising prosperity turned the slopes from winter playgrounds for locals and the rich into second holiday venues for the aspiring middle class. TV coverage of the Winter Olympics and other events fed more money into the sport and so encouraged technological innovation. The 1950s brought artificial snow and plastic running surfaces on the bottom of skis. A decade later, fibreglass skis and plastic boots became available and the 1980s witnessed a revolution, still ongoing, in the design of skis and development in their construction.

Some idea of the impact of technology on skiing can be gained from two examples:

- In the 1850s, a skier travelling at 90 mph (145 kph) was just about the fastest creature on the planet; modern speed skiers exceed 150 mph (241 kph).
- During the later 19th century, the world record ski jump stood at 30 m (98 ft); today's ski-flyers travel 200 m (656 ft) further, and Olympic ski jumps range from 110 to 145 m (360–475 ft), depending on the height of the slope.

Blades and Boards

Skates

The most significant development in skate technology was made centuries ago: replacing blades made of animal bone with metal ones. The skate remained a three-piece construction – a blade attached to a wooden base which was then strapped to a boot – until, around 1850, the American E.W. Bushnell came up with an all-steel skate that clamped straight onto the sole of the boot. Technology then gave the sport a massive boost in 1879, when the world's first man-made ice rink was opened in London. Other rinks soon followed, freeing skating from its weather dependency and turning it into a worldwide, all-season activity.

Thereafter, the only significant technological changes were the blades that curled round at the front in a 'closed-toe' design, adding greatly to the skate's strength, and teeth cut into the toe of the blade to aid complex moves, especially jumps.

Snowboards

The modern sport of snowboarding developed in the 1960s out of surfing and skateboarding, and rapidly acquired the youthful cachet associated with these sports. Initially the boards were simple affairs adapted from the parent sports. Within a few years, boards specifically for snow use were being manufactured in thousands, where appropriate incorporating ski technology in areas such as composition, binding and waxing.

Sledding

The main sledding classes are:

Bobsleigh (bob), big sled, team of two- or four-seated crew members
Luge, small sled, one or two crew members travelling feet first
Skeleton, tiny sled, one rider head first

The crew member steering a sled is known variously as the 'driver' or, more commonly, by the French term 'le pilot'.

Until the post-war era, sledding was a largely specialist, amateur pastime that attracted little technological input. This changed when the East Europeans targeted the sled sports in their quest for Olympic gold. All kinds of innovation appeared, including heated, narrow, hard steel composite runners, sophisticated streamlining, complex steering mechanisms for bobs, and even hydraulic suspension to dampen vibration. Worried that the sport was getting out of control, the FIBT (Federation International de Bobsleigh et de Tobogganing) introduced strict regulations on sled weight (a four-man bob and crew, for example, must check in at no more than 630 kg, or 1,389 lb), size and even temperature: the temperature of a sled's runners must differ by no more than 4° C from that of a reference runner left exposed to the air an hour before the slide begins.

Take a bobsled ride down the Olympic track, Lillehammer:
http://www.youtube.com/watch?v=l-U_u8gbS9g

Industrial Sport

The Industrial Revolution, the great technological and commercial upheaval that began in Britain in the later 18th century and thence spread to every corner of the globe, spawned wholly new sports. First came cycling, followed some 75 years later by motor car and motorcycle racing. These three are more dependent upon modern technology than any other sporting activity.

The bicycle is the **most efficient** machine **ever invented** for **transforming human energy** into **mobility**

The bicycle is the most efficient machine ever invented for transforming human energy into mobility. It had its origins in the wooden, freewheeling, foot-driven velocipedes or hobby horses of the early 19th century. By the 1860s, we had pedal-driven, iron-wheeled 'boneshakers', on which the first recorded bicycle races took place. Developments arrived thick and fast: spokes, rubber tyres (solid) and ball bearings by the 1870s, chain drive – a truly revolutionary innovation that transformed the bike into a means of mass transport – and rear-wheel drive in the 1880s, and John Dunlop's coccyx-saving pneumatic tyres at the end of the decade. Reliable gears were added in the 1900s. As a consequence, cycles being ridden at the outbreak of World War I were little different from those we see on the roads and cycle paths today, almost a century later.

We have no idea who first put wheels on a chair to make it easy to push around – early illustration suggests the Chinese – but sporting contests between wheelchair users was not introduced until 1948. The pioneer was Stoke Mandeville neurologist Sir Ludwig Guttmann, who organised inter-hospital games as part of his rehabilitation programme for spinal injury patients. From this small seed sprang the first worldwide meeting for disabled athletes in Tokyo (1960) and the modern Parallel Olympics or Paralympics movement. Specialist wheelchairs made their first appearance at the Toronto Paralympics (1976), since when they have developed almost beyond recognition to suit wheelchair athletics and an expanding range of other sports. Within 50 years, sport technology had brought joy and fulfilment to hundreds of thousands of disabled men and women who in the past could never have been anything but spectators. Many regard this as its most important achievement.

'If I ever did one good thing in my medical career, it was to introduce sport into the treatment and rehabilitation of disabled people.'
– Sir Ludwig Guttmann, 1967

Motorsports

If there is a continuum with 'pure sport' at one end and 'pure technology' at the other, then motor-powered racing and rallying inevitably lie closest to the latter. Indeed, there are many who claim that all forms of motor racing are not sports at all because the most brilliant drivers and riders stand no chance unless given the best machinery. Put another way, motorsport is really about engineering, not human athletic prowess or skill. Or, as Teddy Mayer, one time boss of the McLaren team, put it, 'Drivers are just interchangeable light bulbs – you plug them in and they do the job.'

Defenders of the sport argue that it differs from other sports only in scale not in essence, pointing out that activities such as sailing, cycling and wheelchair racing are also reliant upon technology. They insist that the sport is regulated to the finest degree – no activity more so than Formula One – so that competitions take place on relatively equal terms. Moreover, there are both car and motorcycle races, such as the Renault World Series car races, in which entrants have very similar machinery at their disposal.

Fans argue, too, that the technological competition between teams and individuals is as much part of the sport as the actual racing, in the same way as training is for a track athlete. Finally, it is suggested that a motorised transport machine is simply the modern equivalent of a horse, and no one would dream of claiming that horse racing was not a sport.

As fans will know, there is a mine of F1 information on http://www.formula1.com

The basic technology of motorsport developed early on: the internal combustion engine using pistons, valves, carburetion, cranks, differentials, a gear box and so forth. Technologically speaking, despite Rover's efforts with gas turbine propulsion (Jet 1, 1960) and the Wankel rotary engine (1957 onwards), advances have been largely refinements of the standard design. These included new materials –

When is a sport not a sport? If we exclude motorsport as too dependent upon technology, then do we also rule out horse racing because the outcome is too dependent upon the horse?

❮❮ **Drivers** are just **interchangeable light bulbs** – you plug them in and they do the job ❯❯

Henry Ford was a great plastics enthusiast! – for construction, brakes, tyres, etc., and vastly improved electronics.

> In 1960, F1 Lotus driver Alan Stacey left the track at high speed and was killed after a bird had flown into his face. Full visors did not appear until the end of the decade.

Moving the engine to the rear of the vehicle, a notable advance, was pioneered with the 1959 Cooper. The one-piece monocoque chassis was a major 1960s breakthrough. The same decade saw the first seriously scientific attempts to improve aerodynamics, with the initial result that F1 cars were fitted with wing-like spoilers intended to push the car more firmly onto the road. Not only did the early ones break off and whirl dangerously across the track like huge Frisbees, but when a car spun, as inevitably happened in accidents, the spoilers could lift it clean off the road and send it, literally, flying. Within a decade these technical difficulties had been overcome, producing the modern F1 car whose aerodynamics were so effective that Mario Andretti said it was 'like being painted onto the road.'

For those with a strong stomach: F1 aerofoils, negligible safety precautions and horrific accidents on:
http://www.metacafe.com/watch/47090/formula_1_crash_collection/

... To Where We Are Now

Snowtech

'Skiing consists of wearing three thousand dollars' worth of clothes and equipment and driving 200 miles in order to stand around at a bar and get drunk' – PJ O'Rourke, US writer and satirist, 1984

The most obvious impact of recent technology on skis is their shape. Virtually all modern skis are no longer straight-edged but taper in the middle in a sexy hourglass fashion (a design alternatively known as parabola, deep-cut, side-cut, etc.). The shape was pioneered by Norheim well over a century ago but its efficacy was realised only in the late 1980s. It improves stability and enables skiers to 'carve' turns, a move not possible on straight-edged skis. Knife-like steel edges on the bottom of skis make the carving all the sharper.

All-wood skis are rapidly disappearing from the mountain sides. Although some modern skis have a wooden core, the trend is towards construction of composite materials that include plastics, Kevlar, aluminium, titanium and carbon fibre. Super-light fibre materials using a honeycomb design can bring the weight of a single ski down to a mere 500 g (1.1 lb), several times lighter than traditional wood or even fibreglass models. The grooved base is generally plastic, the more expensive models incorporating 'pre-wax' technology. Waxing – originally rubbing the bottom of the skis with beeswax or a similar water-repellent substance – makes the skis slide faster because, technically speaking, skiing is actually water skiing. That is why snow skis travel faster when coated with a water-repellent.

A skier does not actually slide on the snow itself but on a thin layer of water produced when the pressure and friction of their skis melts the snow directly beneath them.

Whatever the Christmas carol says, no snow-covered surface is ever even and the snow itself is never uniform. The faster skiers travel, the more the skis beneath them twist and vibrate. For years this vibration was one of the biggest problems facing downhill racers. Then came piezoelectric ceramics, the use of which we have already seen in tennis racket technology. Snugly incorporated into the ski's casing near the toe of the boot, these remarkable materials create a small electric charge when stressed. This charge, managed and amplified by chip circuitry, is then returned to the piezoelectric ceramics, causing them to stiffen and thereby dampen the vibration. Clever, eh? But also, at over $1,000 a go, on the pricey side.

The principal development with binding in recent years has been twofold. One is the employment of the 'railroad track', enabling the position of the boot to be adjusted up and down the ski to suit the individual skier and conditions. The second is the launching of integrated binding systems by the big winter sports manufacturers. These take the boot, binding and ski as a single piece of equipment, each specially designed and tailored to work together in perfect harmony. Nevertheless, like the auto-dampening skis, they come at a far from perfect price.

Snowboarding, predicted by US vacation businesses to overtake skiing in popularity within a decade, incorporates much the same technology as its two-legged partner. In some areas, being a younger and less hide-bound sport, boarding has led the way: the concave shape of modern skis, for example, is said to have been copied from the boards. Another board innovation is dividing the base into three parts, each one shaped to suit its purpose – the left part for turning left, for instance. We will have to wait and see whether ski manufacturers are able to incorporate a similar technology in their products.

'I now realize that the small hills you see on ski slopes are formed around the bodies of forty-seven-year-olds who tried to learn snowboarding.' – Dave Barry, American humorist

Icetech

'F1 on ice' – motto of the British Bobsleigh Association. The British Bobsleigh Association's slogan is uncannily apt. Success in the sled sports, like motorsport, depends on a combination of the participant's skill and the technology at their disposal. As we have seen, the FIBT and other governing bodies are only too aware of this and have put in place regulations to ensure that their sports are not technology-dominated. It has even been suggested that the sled sports would be improved if all competitors shared a pool of common equipment, drawing lots to allocate sleds. This would also facilitate participation from the less well off.

In 2006, a top-of-the-range bobsleigh cost in excess of $60,000 to build.

For the moment, however, sleds are individually made and, despite tight regula-tion, there is still scope for technological differentiation. With bobs, for instance, steering reins, seats and external push bars (which retract once the riders are on board) may differ slightly from machine to machine. There has also been quite a lot of work done on sled aerodynamics. While the maximum weight of a sled and crew is fixed, extra weight may be added if it falls below specification. This requires careful calculation since a heavier sled, although faster when travelling downhill, requires more effort to get started.

International sledding regulations currently run to 49 pages of rules and several more of technical drawings.

Stretching the rules: East German bobs with hydraulic suspension on their runners, Sinia, Romania, 1985. The innovation was outlawed shortly after this picture was taken.

Whatever the claims of the intense marketing hype of skate manufacturers, especially those aiming at the ice hockey market, the main impact of modern technology has been on skate boots rather than the blades beneath. That said, metallurgical science has made modern blades lighter, straighter, smoother and better geared to their tasks than older designs.

The blades of all modern skates, some with springing, are generally of lightweight stainless steel, sometimes with added titanium and often chrome plated. The 1990s saw serious speed skaters, who may reach 60 kph (37 mph), universally adopt 'clap skates'. These feature a blade hinged at the front of the boot and detached at the heel, allowing the skater a fuller range of movement. Figure skate blades are wider (0.32 cm, or 0.125 in) but hollowed out at the bottom so that only the outer edges make contact with the ice. The width of hockey blades is somewhere between the two and, like speed skate blades, they are reinforced with hollow tubing.

Metallurgical **science** has made **modern** blades **lighter**, **straighter**, smoother and **better geared to their tasks** than older designs

The straight blade of a speed skate may be as much as 18 in (46 cm) long and is sometimes no more than 0.08 cm (0.03 in) wide.

An ice hockey gatekeeper – technology-clad from tip to toe.

Superbike – Supercheat?

The Men's 4,000 m Individual Pursuit at the 1992 Barcelona Olympics was one of those rare moments in sport considered genuinely revolutionary. The shock came not from the cyclist, Englishman Chris Boardman, but from his machine. Most of those present in the velodrome had never seen anything like it before: no spokes, no two-triangle frame, handlebars – if that was what they were – low down and stuck out in front . . . The superbike's performance was as startling as its looks, allowing Boardman to win in a world record time.

When, 4 years later, it was Atlanta's turn to host the Olympics, all riders had superbikes, some costing a reported $30,000 each. By now the cycling regulatory

The shock of the new: Chris Boardman and his Lotus Superbike took cycling to new levels of efficiency. For reasons of their own, the cycling authorities subsequently banned the innovative design.

©ACTION IMAGES

body, ICU (International Cycle Union/Union Cycliste Internationale), was getting worried lest technological innovation put high achievement in their sport beyond the reach of all but the wealthiest individuals and nations. Regulations, whose relaxation had led to the appearance of Boardman's Lotus-built superbike, were tightened, then tightened again, and are now prefaced by the blunt declaration: 'Bicycles shall comply with the spirit and principle of cycling [and] . . . cyclists will compete . . . on an equal footing. The principle asserts the primacy of man over machine.' – ICU regulations, 2007 (full text available on: http://www.union.ic.ac.uk/resource/governance/constitutionindex.shtml)

To some, only too aware that cycling probably has a worse drug record than any other sport (see Chapter 8), this talk of the 'spirit of cycling' is sheer hypocrisy and simply an attempt by continental Europeans to maintain their dominance in the face of a perceived threat from 'Anglo-Saxon' technophiles. To others the statement is a bold declaration of what sport is about and a model for governing bodies to follow. Nevertheless, laudable though the ICU's stance may be, it does not follow through to its logical conclusion: all competitors riding identical machines.

> **Bicycles** shall comply with the spirit and **principle of cycling** [and] . . . **cyclists** will compete . . . on an **equal footing**. The principle asserts the **primacy of man over machine.**

Young men on old bikes – the 2007 Tour de France. Basic cycle design has changed little over the last 100 years, leading the sport's critics to label it obscurantist.

Trail Blazers

The latest ICU rules are designed to maintain the traditional bicycle. They regulate overall size, shape and dimensions, weight and even the requirement for pedals and a chain drive. Obvious streamlining, in the form of windshields, is banned, as are all other technical innovations that have not received official blessing. Within these strictures, the impact of technology has been largely limited to weight, ride, gearing and braking systems.

All bikes for professional use are computer-designed for optimum aerodynamics, comfort and power transfer. Some of the most exclusive, such as the Trek used by Tour de France legend Lance Armstrong, incorporate slight fairing to direct air around the frame. The frames themselves are of carbon fibre or titanium, or a composite that sometimes includes epoxy. Since no cycle may weigh less than 6.8 kg (14.99 lb), the non-metallic materials are selected not because they are lighter but because of their dampening qualities, giving a smoother ride. This would matter little for someone using their bike to pop down to the shops every now and again, but for the road racer who may spend hours in the saddle every day, it really is important.

'Nothing compares to the simple pleasure of a bike ride' – US President John F. Kennedy. Given his reputation, I wonder whether he really meant 'nothing'?

Although refinement and new materials have improved the efficiency of cables, brakes and derailleur gears, basic design is unchanged. However, one area where innovation has been permitted is in pedal clips. Until the later 1980s, these were

'Death-cleats' were **swiftly** replaced by **versions** that used **ski binding technology** to effect **swift release** by a twist of the foot

just small cages on the top of the pedals into which the riders put the front part of their foot. The first major deviation came when a cleat (a protruding cube of hard plastic), fixed to the bottom of the cyclist's shoe, was slotted into a special fitting on the pedal. Amazingly, the early systems had a near-fatal design fault: apart from taking off their shoe, the rider could release their foot from the pedal only by reaching down and manually operating a special clip! Not surprisingly, these 'death-cleats' were swiftly replaced by versions that used ski binding technology to effect swift release by a twist of the foot.

In contrast to the conservatism of racing bikes, the mountain bike fraternity have taken a much more liberal approach to technological innovation. This probably stems from the sport's later 20th century Californian origins – West Coasters probably appreciate novelty more than any other group in the world, and do not take kindly to being told what to do. The consequence is different wheel and tyre sizes, disc brakes, lockable hydraulic suspension on both front and back wheels, gearboxes and experimentation with different means of transmission.

Want to see what a mountain biker can do? Try:
http://www.youtube.com/watch?v=mYIKfEU8yl8

Chairs for Sport

Sportsmen and women confined to wheelchairs have recently benefited from a vast range of technological developments, beginning with weight. For years the mark of a good wheelchair was its solid construction, i.e. a good wheelchair weighed a lot – perhaps 23 kg (50 lb) or more. Aluminium alloy and titanium frames have altered all that, bringing weights down to 8 kg (18 lb) or less. Modern chairs are also far more stable, with three- or five-wheel versions for sporting events that require maximum manoeuvrability, such as basketball. All moving parts feature hi-tech bearings and seats and rests are fully adjustable.

Many of these advances have been driven by consumer demand, meeting the needs of the expanding range of sports played by wheelchair users. The current list includes most track and field activities, basketball, dance sport, fencing, rugby, tennis, archery, skiing and curling. Most require a specific chair design. For tennis there are three- and four-wheel chairs with raised seats that allow complete freedom to swing the racket, for example, while chairs made for basketball, a contact sport, have a steel foot guard at the front and an extra rear wheel to prevent tipping. Engineers have also markedly improved chair stability with steeply cantilevered main wheels.

We **should first** remember that group of **athletes** whose **sporting lives** would not **even be possible** without it

More innovative is the range of hand-powered tricycles, some with chain drive and others – familiar to most who have watched a large city marathon such as New York's or London's – using the traditional push rims outside the rear wheels. The chair-drive version is generally reckoned to be easier to ride and its multiple gears (over 25 in some cases) are certainly easier on the user's arms, wrists and hands. Even less chair-like are the amazing mono- and bi-skis on which disabled sports-people zoom down the slopes with greater skill, balance and agility than many of their able-bodied colleagues.

On the wilder side of disability sport is a band of daredevils seeking that extra surge of adrenalin. Some go in for Fourcross Downhill Mountain Biking, which involves haring at great speed down the roughest tracks on what is essentially a highly specialised, non-motorised go-cart with bike-type wheels. Then there is jumping, sometimes involving a fourcross machine towed by a motorbike to get up speed. The jumps range from simple ramps to hair-raising leaps over icy lakes or, Evil Knievel-style, over rows of cars. If we are ever tempted to criticise the impact of technology on sport, we should first remember that group of athletes whose sporting lives would not even be possible without it.

While enabling huge numbers of previously excluded athletes to participate in serious sport, the development of high-tech machinery for disabled athletes has widened the already distressing gulf between rich and poor sporting nations.

For more extreme wheelchair sports, with links to amazing video clips, etc., start at: http://www.apparelyzed.com

Motorsport

*'In this business, those who do not constantly implement new ideas are left far behind.'
– Gavin Fisher, chief designer, Williams F1*

It is likely that the technology of motor car and motorbike racing has reached a near-plateau on which significant change is unlikely without there first being a change in the regulations set by the various governing bodies. It may even be argued that the F1 machines of the 1990s, packed with electronic driver aids, were technologically more advanced than their modern equivalents. Computer-aided traction, optimising roadholding and eliminating wheelspin, increased performance to such an extent that it was banned, and recent regulation on matters such as tyres was intended, as with the adoption of single-manufacturer tyres for superbike racing (2004), to produce more closely fought races.

The **chip** is responsible for **almost all aspects of race strategy**, from **pit stops** to weather forecasts

Two other aspects of modern motorsport are worth a mention. One is the impact of computerisation. Although there are now strict limits on the extent to which a car's racing performance may be computer-aided, every aspect of the modern car and motorbike is designed and tested virtually before being put near a track, and the chip is responsible for almost all aspects of race strategy, from pit stops to weather forecasts.

McLaren-Mercedes and Ferrari F1 teams employ as many computer experts as engineers.

There is also the issue of safety. The roll-call of drivers and riders killed in motor-sport before the 1990s reads like a war memorial. Since the double deaths of Ayrton Senna and Roland Ratzenberger at the San Marino circuit in 1994, however, no F1 driver has been killed racing or in official pre-race practice sessions, and serious injuries have been dramatically reduced. Some of the measures to achieve this have been readier use of the safety car, better driver restraint and the incorporation of an extremely strong driver's 'survival cell' around which cars crumple or even disintegrate on heavy impact. A testimony to modern safety technology was offered in the 2007 Canadian Grand Prix, when Robert Kubica lost control of his BMW Sauber at 280 kph (174 mph). The vehicle left the track, hit a concrete wall and went into a series of horrifying rolls. Remarkably, Kubica suffered no serious injury.

Has to be seen to be believed: the Kubica Canadian Grand Prix crash, 2007: http://video.google.com/videoplay?docid=−3119039867907859307

What Next?

Snow Future

Powerful forces militate against a fundamental breakthrough in ski technology in the near future. This is partly because there is a limit to what one can do to make sliding down a frozen hill much more efficient, and partly because the regulators, who already keep a tight grip on the sport, will surely ban an innovation that either markedly alters the sport or gives one group of competitors a distinct advantage. That does not mean there will be no change but merely that it is likely to be incremental rather than revolutionary.

'The future in ski tuning will be two words; nano-technology and electronics.'[1] Skis will become more responsive to both the changing surface and the wearer's

Brains in the boot . . . Are we approaching the era of the 'intelligent ski' that self-adjusts to suit the conditions and the wearer?

[1] From http://www.j2ski.com/ski-chat-forum/posts/list/2298.page

behaviour. Among the ideas under discussion are programmable magnetic bind-ings, assuming power sources can be made small and light enough, and 'intelli-gent' skis that change not only flexibility mid-run but width and length as well. What about electrically heated skis that travel faster because they increase the film of water beneath them? Would the regulators allow such an innovation? Meanwhile, something for the masses on crowded slopes: super goggles incor-porating GPS, radar warning of impending collision with fellow snow hogs, and the condition of the piste ahead.

Powerful **forces militate against** a fundamental breakthrough in **ski technology** in the near future

More important than all of those, however, is the future of the snow itself. As our planet warms, skiers will be driven higher and higher to find the blessed white stuff. Either that, or more and more snow will have to be artificially created. But making snow uses energy, which all too often means electricity produced by burning fossil fuels, so releasing the CO_2 that feeds global warning . . . Then there's the annual problem of millions of people increasing their carbon footprint as they drive or fly to the slopes. What this means is that, a century from now, we may have the most brilliant skis and other equipment imaginable – but no snow on which to use it.

'An OECD report, the first systematic study of the slopes in the Alpine region, . . . warned that climate change posed a "serious risk" to the resorts.' – *Guardian Unlimited*, 14 December 2006

Snow may become a scarce commodity but it is unlikely that ice rinks will close in the foreseeable future. Even so, they are huge consumers of energy and so it is possible that alternatives to conventional ice will be developed which do not require such low temperatures. As for the skates themselves, to go with the new 'hot ice' we may see electrically warmed 'hot skates' that give the skater greater speed. Giro-stabilised skates for beginners would be useful, too.

Uniformity or Innovation?

In the next century or so, cycle technology will follow one of three widely different paths:

1. Maintain the status quo, upholding the present policy of ensuring that all racing cycles are roughly similar so that the victor is, in theory, the best athlete, not the competitor with the best machinery. The problems with this position are that it damages the sport's image and, over time, stifles innovation and technical development. The cycles used in prestige events such as the Tour de France are already looking a bit old fashioned.

   To the uninitiated, the racing bike is a dull bird compared with the banned superbikes, the latest mountain bikes and even, dare one say it, the average super-styled, gismo-laden machine available from your local cycle shop. If, in 50 years' time, racing cycles permitted in major events still look basically the same, the sport will have a serious problem. This could result in falling popularity or, more likely, a breakaway circuit that would benefit from the increased marketing possibilities of its 'sexier' cycles.

Fibre composites will bring down **weight** even further and, coupled with streamlined fairing, **speeds will rise dramatically** towards the 100 **mph** (160 kph) **bike**

2. Select one make and model of machine for a particular event in the upcoming season, and insist that all participants ride it in official competitions. This would encourage cycle development but retain cyclist dominance. The boost for the chosen manufacturer would be enormous, stimulating season-by-season competition for selection and putting a premium on technical innovation within a looser specification than is currently in force. Given certain safeguards (limiting price, for example, and setting up a strict anti-corruption regime to prevent bribery), the system would encourage technological input within the framework of the ICU's current philosophy.

3. Do away with virtually all regulation and allow riders, designers and technocrats to come up with the most efficient machine they can. This might start where the superbike left off. Fibre composites will bring down weight even further and, coupled with streamlined fairing, speeds will rise dramatically towards the 100 mph (160 kph) bike. The trusty derailleur gears will go, replaced by a smoother system, perhaps based on the chain-less, liquid drive that is already being developed. Add disc brakes and suspension, both using hydraulics, some featherweight computerisation, a more streamlined riding position – and there we have it: the super-superbike of the 2080 Megalympics.[2]

[2] See Chapter 9.

There's a fairly primitive Wikipedia article on liquid drives on: http://en.wikipedia.org/wiki/Hydraulic_bicycle

Superchairs

As long as the money can be found, the opportunities for further development of sporting wheelchairs are enormous. Unfortunately, the sort of innovations employed in able-bodied sports, such as fibre compound construction, are extremely costly and would therefore be available only to disabled athletes with major sponsorship or backing from national bodies. The numbers able to achieve this would probably remain small, reinforcing the already distressing gap between disabled athletes from wealthy nations, such as Britain, and those from less developed nations. That said, if the funding were available and regulation kept to a minimum, there would be dramatic improvement in wheelchair and handcycle technology.

As long as the **money** can be found, **the opportunities** for **further** development of **sporting wheelchairs** are **enormous**

Chairs will be more stable, lighter, stronger and more manoeuvrable. For racing events, we may well see aerodynamic and design innovation along the lines of the superbike. Tyre and wheel construction has much to learn from cycle road racing, including narrower, high-pressure tyres. Computer-aided, mouth-operated gearing may well appear, as will chain-less drives for handcycles. It is possible that the basic 'chair' shape may be superseded, too. In fact, the words of Chris Boardman, British Cycling's director of research and development, in relation to bicycle design apply even more readily to that of wheelchairs: 'The most amazing thing is that we are limited only by our imagination' (*Daily Telegraph* website, 15 April 2007).

Future Formula

Even more than with cycling, the future direction of F1 motorsport depends almost entirely on its regulators. It is a fair bet, however, that over the next 50 years a number of changes will be forced upon them. The most obvious one is fuel. By the middle of the century, with oil stocks exhausted and all forms of environmental pollution banned as the world tries desperately to hold down global temperatures, motor racing will have to be driven by a non-polluting fuel like hydrogen or electricity. Safety will be still further enhanced so that injury to drivers, riders, officials and spectators is extremely rare.

Keen to be seen as green, F1 has been behind pioneering work on a mechanical kinetic energy recovery system using a flywheel. For more details, see: http://uk.eurosport.yahoo.com/09112007/23/f1-future-wins-innovation-award.html

Speeds over 650 kph (400 mph) are reached and **each season features** at least **one horrendous** pile-up in which **several drivers die**

It is possible, too, that F1 will adopt the principles behind the innovative A1 Grand Prix. The change would make grand prix racing a truly international contest by providing each team with a car that is mechanically identical. This eliminates possible advantage from better equipment, leaving victory to the most efficient team and skilful driver.

For further speculation on the future of motorsport, see Chapter 9.

There is another, far wilder scenario for the future of motorsport. What if, overcome by the problems caused by temperature rise, the rich-poor divide, overpopulation and global pollution, Western-style liberal democracy collapses and is replaced by different forms of totalitarian regime? And what if, eager to keep its citizens happy by feeding them crude mass entertainment at the expense of individual dignity, these regimes permit unregulated motorsport in which speeds over 650 kph (400 mph) are reached and each season features at least one horrendous pile-up in which several drivers die?

Details of the A1 Grand Prix circuit are on:
http://www.maximummotorsport.co.uk/a1-grand-prix

Formula 2075 may make a modern Grand Prix **look more like a shopping trip** than a car **race**

Fortunately, this technology-unchained scenario remains a Hollywood or video game fantasy. But it is not so very different from what happened in ancient Rome, and one or two unforeseen mega-disasters coupled to a few poor political decisions might easily lead to it becoming a late 21st century reality. Formula 2075 may make a modern Grand Prix look more like a shopping trip than a car race.

5 Afloat and Aloft

'There is nothing – absolutely nothing – half so much worth doing as simply messing about in boats.' – Ratty, in the 'Wind in the Willows' by Kenneth Grahame, 1908

Windsurfing, waterskiing, parachuting, paragliding, hang-gliding, ski gliding, kite surfing, jet ski . . . a quick glance through any activity holiday brochure illustrates the dramatic explosion of technology-inspired water and air sports over the last 50 years. However, given their high dependence upon sophisticated man-made devices of one sort or another, they remain the preserve of the wealthy. This widens still further the techno-divide between sportspeople of the developed and developing world.

A top-of-the-range hang-glider can be acquired for something over £3,000, while the hottest jet skis will set you back a staggering £10,000 or more.

Unfortunately, the haves/have-nots divide is also a feature of traditional water sports like rowing and sailing, where no one can hope to compete at the top level unless in possession of the latest kit. The result is an unfortunate paradox: technology has given us more sports, thereby increasing choice and enabling more individuals to excel in their chosen field, while at the same time limiting those benefits to a small fraction of the world's population.

Challenging, exhilarating . . . dangerous, polluting . . . What are we to make of innovations like the high-powered jet ski?

©ISTOCKPHOTO.COM/VASILYSMIRNOV

From There . . .

Splashing Up the Nile

There was probably not much in it, but rowing – or more likely paddling – came before sailing. Be that as it may, several thousand years ago, boats powered by both oars and sails were splashing up and down the Nile and, humans being as competitive then as now, inevitably there were wagers along the lines of 'Race you to Karnak' or 'Last one to Memphis buys dinner.' The Egyptians appear to have been holding formal rowing races by the second millennium BC, galley races were certainly a spectacular feature of both Greek and Roman festivities, and from the water sports of 13th-century Venetian *regati* (festivals) we get our word 'regatta'.

Competition between sail-powered merchant vessels reached its apogee in the early 1870s, when tea clippers like the *Cutty Sark*, now preserved in Greenwich, London, raced from China to Britain in less than 120 days. By the end of the decade, steamers had taken over the mantle of the swiftest and most reliable ships and sail racing – yachting, from the Dutch word *Jaght* – was left for the enthusiasts. Originating in 17th century Holland, within two centuries the sport was firmly established as a popular pastime with the rich and leisured classes, and entered the Olympics in 1900. The first medal table was dominated by French and British vessels whose design, rigging in natural materials and heavy wooden construction had yet to feel the influence of modern technology.

The year 1851 saw the first race in the competition that has developed into the celebrated America's Cup.

Ply to Plastics

'Rowing: a competitive sport of boats that are narrow.' – Great Soviet Encyclopaedia

After choppy seas had led to the cancellation of the 1896 competition, rowing, too, was first contested at the 1900 Olympics. By this time, boats already incorporated the sport's two most significant technological innovations: metal outriggers that increased an oar's leverage (Oxford University, 1846) and sliding seats (Yale University, 1870) that enabled rowers to use their powerful leg muscles more effectively. Outriggers allowed hulls, known as 'shells', to become significantly narrower in order to reduce drag, leading to the modern pencil design in which the rower's balance is crucial. Outriggers led to longer oars, too.

The first alternative to wood for shell construction was papier-mâché, used experimentally and without much success (for fairly obvious reasons!) in the 1870s. Plywood suffered similar drawbacks until the invention of waterproof glue in the 1930s. By now, thanks to the use of composites and aluminium alloys, boat weights were coming down sharply. In due course this led to the modern rule book, written by FISA (Fédération Internationale des Sociétés d'Aviron/International Federation of Rowing Associations), which set strict parameters for boat weight, design, size and so forth.

The **first alternative** to **wood** for shell construction **was papier-mâché**, used **experimentally** and without much success

Over the course of the 20th century, sailing boats underwent a similar transformation in design and materials. A number of influences were at work, many of the most significant coming via the aircraft industry. Careful analysis, for example, was made of the forces of drag that limit a boat's speed in a similar way to those in play around an aircraft. Scientists identified three types of drag:

(1) friction as the hull pushes against the surrounding water molecules;
(2) pressure building up before the bow; and
(3) wave drag that, at its simplest, is energy expended (and thus wasted) in creating the waves that make up part of a boat's wake.

An understanding of the physics of drag led to changes in the shape of hulls, keels and fins.

From other **branches of science** came stainless steel and **nylon** wire to **replace the traditional ropes** of natural fibres such as hemp

The force that lifts an aircraft is the same as that which drives forward a boat under sail. Thus, the study of aircraft wing design had a major impact on sail shape and construction. Also from the aero industry came the technology for the extruded aluminium masts and spars that are still widely used in most sailing vessels. From other branches of science came stainless steel and nylon wire to replace the traditional ropes of natural fibres like hemp. Such materials were also largely discontinued in sail manufacture, where their weaknesses – lack of strength, water absorbency and liability to rot – put them at a disadvantage beside nylon and polyester, despite the latter's poor UV (ultraviolet light) resistance.

As in other tech-based sports, to prevent victory going to the most technologically advanced – invariably the wealthiest – competitor, sailing's organising bodies arranged classes of sail boat (around 100 classes for keelboats and 130 for dinghies and smaller craft) in which sailors raced each other in craft that were largely identical. Hence the classes of Olympic competition: '470', 'Laser', 'Finn' and so on.

A kayak is an enclosed boat in which the paddler sits. A canoe is open, with the paddler(s) kneeling or sitting.

Drag analysis and the replacement of natural materials, principally wood and canvas, were also a key feature in the way paddle boats – canoes and kayaks – developed over the last 100 years. The result was lighter, more manoeuvrable and yet stronger boats. With the exception of surfing, whose Hawaiian origins go back

The surfboard, sporting technology at its best – simple, cheap, accessible and tremendous fun.

many centuries, the huge variety of other board-based water sports came into being well after the 20th-century materials revolution had begun. Surfers, however, had to dig in to their pockets to replace their original plain planks of wood with man-made versions in plastic and other light, bright materials.

Take-off

The technology behind parachute jumpers, hang-gliding, paragliding and all the other forms of gliding stems from the development of reliable parachutes for aircraft pilots and crew in the early part of the 20th century. The story mirrors that of most other tech-sports. Natural products, canvas then silk, were eventually replaced by man-made nylon as the preferred material for the canopy and cords. Hang-gliding became possible with the light yet immensely strong aluminium alloys, again a by-product of the aero industry. On the design side, advancing knowledge of aerodynamics enabled the conventional hemispherical parachute to be remodelled into the 'flying wing' shape of the rectangular parafoil or ram-air canopy employed in sports, such as paragliding, that require jumpers or pilots to direct their flight with precision.

Fancy paragliding? Try:
http://www.youtube.com/watch?v=oFl9qyiRHvY&watch_response

. . . To Where We Are Now

Sculls and Shells

The modern sporting rowing boat is about as high-tech as FISA will allow. At the top level, wood has all but disappeared from rowing, replaced by plastics, carbon

The modern **sporting rowing boat** is about **as high-tech as** FISA will **allow**

fibre, fibreglass and lightweight metals. While the weight, width and length of a shell (hull) are strictly regulated, oars can be of any length and design, giving sports technologists some scope for creativity. At this stage, to help those not acquainted with the esoteric world of rowing, it may be useful to point out that an oar is not just an oar: rowers distinguish between 'sweeps' and 'sculls'.

Sweeps are used in boats with an equal number of rowers pulling on either side – one, two or four, making a pair, a four and an eight.

Sculls are used when each rower has a pair of oars, one in each hand – one, two or four, making a single scull, double scull and quadruple scull.

Modern oars, both sweeps and sculls, feature two significant innovations:

1. Composition, with hollow fibreglass or carbon fibre replacing the old solid wood
2. The shape of the blade (the flat bit that goes into the water)

In the early 1990s, the traditional bottle-profile was replaced by asymmetrical hatched-shaped blades whose powerful shape has been further refined by computer design to make the catch (entry into the water) and finish (leaving the water) as smooth as possible.

Add better grip, adjustable lengths for sculls and other small refinements, and the result is an oar significantly lighter and more effective than the age-old instruments used by Ratty and Mole.

The women of Hollandia Roieclub, Holland, battling it out with the South Australian Institute, Henley 2007. Like cycling, rowing has eschewed major technological innovation in order to keep down costs.

Between the oar and the shell comes the (out)rigger with a rowlock, known in the USA as an 'oarlock', on the end furthest from the boat. Boats designed for international competition boast adjustable, streamlined riggers of lightweight titanium alloy crowned with rowlocks that hold the oar with a minimum of friction. The shell to which it is attached is constructed as a honeycomb sandwich of epoxy resin, Kevlar and meticulously laid carbon fibre. Its design, including the fin, which may double as the rudder in coxed boats, incorporates sophisticated input from fluid dynamics experts to reduce drag. The moulded seats zip backwards and forwards with a minimum of friction as composite wheels spin along anodised metal runners. Perfection, claim the boat builders.

Rowing is still a sport in which talent and determination triumph over technology

There are, however, dissenting voices. For example, nearly all leading manufacturers, such as the world-renowned Filippi of Italy, emphasise the stiffness of their shells – but boat manufacturer Burgashell record this unspecific but interesting anecdote. A certain manufacturer, while sticking to the FISA Minimum Weight, used exotic composites to produce a shell with the maximum possible level of stiffness. To most people's surprise, 'The boat was judged to be unrowable as a certain amount of give was determined to be desirable.'[1] Burgashell also query the value of being too concerned with weight, suggesting that, in certain conditions, the greater momentum of a heavier boat is an advantage.

World records are not officially recognised in rowing because variable conditions, such as wind and water speed, are so crucial to race times.

Such challenges to received rowing orthodoxy are to some extent born out by world best times for certain events. In 2007, the best time over a straight 2,000 m for a men's heavyweight coxed four (5:58.96) was still that set way back in 1991 by a German crew rowing in Vienna. Of the 24 men's and women's world best times, no less than nine (37%) dated from the 1990s, suggesting either that rowing boat technology has reached some sort of plateau or that it does not necessarily bring the sort of advantages that manufacturers crow about. Either way, it probably means that FISA's control of technology (including drug taking) is both well aimed and well policed. As a result, rowing is still a sport in which talent and determination triumph over technology.

[1] http://www.burgashell.co.uk/page.php?id=87

Plain Sailing

'Those who fall in love with practice without science are like a sailor who . . . can never be certain whither he is going.' – Leonardo Da Vinci

Over the past 30 years, technology has revolutionised leisure sail cruising so that in normal circumstances, a large – around 60 ft (18 m) – modern vessel with all the latest equipment can be handled from within the cockpit by a single person. Electric winches hoist and reef (reduce the size of) the sails, and a computerised autopilot using GPS takes care of the navigation. The only tasks left to the captain are to pour the drinks and keep an eye out for other vessels sneaking in beneath the radar. As an old hand growled recently, 'It's not bloody sailing in one of those things – more like driving a car!' Not quite, but one knows what he meant.

Technology may have made cruising under sail simpler and, arguably, safer, but it has also made it a hobby only for the opulent. A new Discovery 55 with all the extras, for instance, will not leave the purchaser with much change from £1 million.

Interestingly, at the other end of the scale, aluminium masts and fibreglass or plastic foam sandwich hulls are quicker and cheaper to make than wooden ones, and require a great deal less time- and money-consuming maintenance. Simple boat trailers and car roof racks capable of holding a small dinghy have also made the sport more accessible: in the 1950s, it was common to take time off before a regatta to sail one's boat round the coast to wherever the races were being held. That automatically ruled out most men and women engaged in regular 9 to 5 jobs.

The range of small sailing boats is so vast that perhaps the impact of technology on dinghy performance is best covered by looking at a single class, Lasers. The world's most popular single-hander, the 4.23-m (13.8-ft) Laser is raced at all levels, from local yacht clubs to the Olympics. Features are standard and must be made by an accredited manufacturer. The glass fibre hull makes the boat light enough to be car-topped, and the overlap between the hull and deck mouldings gives a convenient grip, as well as spray protection. An aluminium mast and boom (spar along the bottom of the sail) allow a single Dacron sail of 75 sq ft (7 sq m) to be carried without shrouds (supporting ropes at the side of the mast) or forestay (supporting rope at the front of the mast). The rudder and dag-gerboard (a small, retractable keel) are made from tough, lightweight reinforced polyurethane foam, and all other parts from corrosion-resistant metals and other materials.

Technology for all – the immensely popular and exciting Laser class of sail boat, here seen racing in Northern Ireland, is a classic example of how technology can enhance a sport.

Such a **craft** would have been **inconceivable without** the post–World War II **materials** revolution

The result is a simple, flexible, relatively cheap and utterly serviceable boat, capable of being sailed enjoyably by almost anyone. Such a craft would have been inconceivable without the post–World War II materials revolution.

The F1 of the Seas

'Everybody seems to want a new boat that is bigger, more exciting, difficult to sail, and faster.' – Brad Butterworth, skipper of Alinghi, winner of the 2007 America's Cup

The last 20 or so years have witnessed dramatic developments in the design of the super yachts, single- and multi-hulled, that participate in ocean racing and the blue ribbon event, the highly prestigious America's Cup. A whole host of highly complex technologies have been brought into play, especially materials science and aero- and hydrodynamics. Over time, some of the cheaper developments trickle down to other classes of boat (as happened with aluminium masts, for instance), but the process is slow and in general the techno-gap between the average weekend racing dinghy and the winner of an event like the America's Cup continues to grow.

The **techno-gap** between the **average weekend racing dinghy** and the winner of an event like the **America's Cup continues** to grow

In simplest terms, the racing yacht may be divided into two parts: the hull and the rig, the latter including mast, sails, spars and attendant ropes that drive the boat along. Since the 1980s, top-end hull design has been increasingly influenced by computational fluid dynamics (CFD) and what the jargon-juggling nerds of the sport call 'real-time, model-based performance analysis'. Initially at least, ideas grew from programmes developed by NASA for space flight analysis.

At the time of writing, the 2009 America's Cup has been cancelled due to lack of sponsorship – has high-priced yacht technology finally reached its limit?

These developments and tighter regulations have led to a convergence of performance which places greater emphasis on rigging and the actions of the crew. The precise nature of materials and construction used for the composite hulls of top-of-the-range racing yachts remains an in-house secret, but they are all based around the carbon fibre honeycomb sandwich principle, with many precise details of construction, such as temperature, laid down by the organisers.

The keel's **fin shape** has been replaced by something that **looks more like a banana** suspended **beneath** the hull

To the layperson, the most obvious change in hull design has been in the keel, whose fin shape has been replaced by something that looks more like a banana suspended beneath the hull. It is in fact the 19-tonne, torpedo-shaped lead weight (known as a 'bulb') used to keep the boat from being lain flat on the water when a strong wind blows on the beam (from the side). Embarrassingly, when the ACC (America's Cup Class) regulations were redrawn for the 32nd Cup (2007), the use of lead weighting was not written in, making all competitors technically illegal. Faced with a bill of $8 million per boat to replace the lead with legal silver, even the super-rich backers of the world's costliest race blanched a bit – and mutually agreed to a swift rewriting of the rules to allow the humble lead to remain.

There's a fascinating amount of detailed technical information on an America's Cup yacht on:
http://www.americas-cup-2007.com/bmw.html

The high-tech rig of the super-yachts is even more impressive than that of their hulls. It is based upon the understanding (from a phenomenon known as Bernoulli's principle – see Chapter 1) that sailing is not simply a matter of the wind blowing a boat along, but of the forces created by the aerofoil shape of the sail that allows air to pass more quickly over one side than the other. This results in a pull and push on the sail, conveyed to the hull via the mast. The two forces combine in what is called the 'apparent wind': the velocity of the wind relative to the boat's motion. One consequence is that a sailing boat may actually travel faster than the wind that is powering it.

There's an apparent wind calculator on:
http://www.sailingusa.info/true_wind_calculator.htm

How the aerofoil shape of a sail enables a vessel to sail close to the wind.

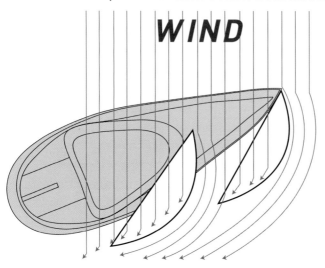

Only fairly recently has computer technology enabled designers to treat the whole yacht – hull, sails, stays, mast, spars – as a single racing machine with each item conceived as part of an integrated whole. With shaped composite masts stripped of most of the drag-inducing stays of olden days, square-headed and asymmetrical sails with inflatable carbon fibre battens, different sails for upwind (Mylar or Kevlar laminate) and downwind (nylon) . . . such vessels are truly the F1 machines of the ocean. Finally, dozens of electronic sensors strategically placed over the boat collect hundreds of items of information per second which are then used to improve performance the next time out, albeit by perhaps only fractions of a knot. But that's enough: the Swiss Alinghi team won the 2007 America's Cup by a single second.

It takes about 20,000 man-hours to build a yacht capable of competing in the America's Cup.

Up and Away

'Aeronautics was neither an industry nor a science. It was a miracle.' – Igor Sikorsky, helicopter pioneer

Paragliding – flying along on a material aerofoil weighing scarcely more than 12 kg (26.5 lb) – is possible only because of modern materials technology. The two-layered wings, with an open leading edge that allows incoming air to inflate the wing into its aerofoil shape, are made of special materials, such as Porcher's polyamide-based 'Skytex'. The lines that support the pilot and hold the whole structure together are made from an artificial fibre such as aramid, an 'aromatic polyamide' from the same family as Kevlar, and sophisticated controls include 'brakes' and a 'speed bar'. The modern paragliding experts in a good thermal might be excused for believing themselves to be Superman incarnate.

Suspended from a more rigid wing, the hang-glider pilot can soar thousands of feet into the air, stay aloft for hours and travel hundreds of miles. The most skilled can perform aerobatics. As with paragliders, they owe it all to technology. The details of the super-strong, lightweight materials from which hang-gliders are made do not differ widely from those employed in many other branches of sport, such as sailing and paragliding, although it is perhaps worth mentioning one. PET film is a strong and stable material from the polyester stable, widely sold under the trade name Mylar. It was developed in the 1950s and came to prominence in the engineering world when used in the manufacture of NASA's first communications satellites. Hang-gliders may not reach such altitudes, but they are a fine example of how spin-offs from the space race have impacted on sporting activity.

They **owe it all** to technology

Birdman – hang-gliding technology makes an age-old dream come true (almost).

What Next?

The Row Goes On

No one can be sure where rowing will go from here. Although boat builders assure us that every year's model is better than the last, offering less drag, smoother seating and friction-free mounting for the oars, there is little evidence from either the timings of races or their outcomes that there is much difference at the highest level between individual boats. This is, of course, just what FISA intends. As with cycling, every effort is made to maintain rowing as a sport dominated by talent rather than technology.

It is unlikely, however, that technology can be put on hold indefinitely without the sport's governing body being made to look irritatingly reactionary. If a means to

Every effort is made to maintain rowing as a sport dominated by talent rather than technology

make a boat go noticeably faster is available, then the chances are that in the end it will be adopted. Rowers currently 'feather' their oars – turn the blades 90° at the end of a stroke so that they are parallel with the surface of the water as the oar is returned for the next stroke, thereby reducing drag through the air. Oars fitted with a lightweight electronic or mechanical self-feathering device would make this operation easier and more efficient, and free the rower to concentrate on the power and rhythm of the stroke. Another benefit would be oars whose length would adjust automatically during a race: short for super-quick strokes at the start, lengthening for mid-race power and perhaps shortening again for a sprint at the end.

Sliding riggers can be seen on:
http://www.youtube.com/watch?v=Yq5jlHYxkME

More exciting than these is the idea of sliding riggers, which were experimented with around the same time as the introduction of sliding seats but not developed seriously until the early 1980s. By 1983, boats with sliding riggers dominated the World Rowing Championships. With heavy rowers no longer heaving up and down the boat, 'pitching forces and rapid momentum reversals were dramatically reduced and, for a given effort, the boats went faster.'[2] As rowing was already

[2]Christopher Laughton in conversation with the author. I am most grateful to Messrs Laughton and Hooper for giving so freely of their expertise on this subject.

under attack from the IOC for being an expensive, Western and élitist sport, FISA took fright at the cost implications of rendering every conventional single sculling boat redundant and outlawed sliding riggers forthwith. In time, lest rowing be perceived as a fossilised, anti-technology sport, they will surely return?

Still more radical is the concept pioneered by the small ROCAT company of Cornwall of a catamaran rowing boat in which the rower remains on an unmoving seat, driving the oars directly with their powerful leg muscles, through a 'swingarm rigger', before finishing the stroke with their arms. This eliminates pitch and employs the rower's power extremely effectively, while the twin-hull structure gives the boat remarkable stability in conditions that would swiftly sink a conventional monohull.

The ROCAT principle is demonstrated in an animation found on http://www. rocat.co.uk

The shape of things to come? The highly innovative ROCAT may revolutionise the way we row.

©FREYA LAUGHTON

While we are probably decades away from the sight of ROCATs zipping along the Thames during the Oxford v Cambridge Boat Race, there must be a chance that before too long the rowing world will introduce a twin-hull class featuring sliding or swingarm riggers, perhaps even in open sea racing? After that, we might be treated to the sight of catamaran eights powering along at speeds way beyond anything achievable by conventional shells. Such a stirring sight would prove a major TV draw and also attract young, techno-aware athletes to the sport of rowing. FISA take note: the boaters and blazers on the banks of the Thames might not like it, but in the end technology invariably triumphs.

Techno-sailing

The use of new materials for hulls, sails, spars and ropes will continue to improve the overall performance of sailing boats, especially at the yachting end of the spectrum. Here we are likely to see sails made of a pliable-rigid fabric. While easily foldable under normal conditions, when stressed this will become rigid in order to better maintain the sail's aerofoil properties. Another major change within the next half-century will be the further use of electronics in boat management. This will have little impact at the dinghy level, where cost control is paramount, and its incorporation in competitive yacht racing will depend on the officiating bodies.

It will **be possible** to travel in a completely automated **yacht**

Beyond this, it is likely that within 50–75 years it will be possible to travel in a completely automated yacht. The captain sets the course, unties the moorings and sits back. The ship's computer starts the engine, uses precise radar and satnav to take the vessel out to sea, cuts the engine, hoists, sets and trims the sails after noting the direction and strength of tides and winds – and continues to pilot the boat precisely and safely to its destination. Round the world yachting? A piece of cake for those who can afford the millions such a vessel would cost.

As with dinghies, the world of kayaks, canoes and sailboards is also restricted by what enthusiasts are willing or able to pay. That means technological improvement will be limited to the gradual introduction of lighter, stronger, more practicable materials. In the kayak world, for example, there is currently excitement over 'Mouldable Fabric Technology' (MFT) moving in from the world of body armour. Self-feathering paddles may arrive via the rowing world and top-of-the-range sailboards will benefit from the new pliable-rigid fabrics developed for the sails of conventional boats.

Want to see what the fuss is about? Try:
http://www.youtube.com/watch?v=24L8fk4DgKs

Away with the Birds

The technologies of paragliding and hang-gliding are in their infancy. Lighter and stronger materials will make the sports safer and more exciting, enabling pilots, like birds, to stay aloft for almost as long as they wish. In this they will be assisted by two pieces of lightweight electronic gadgetry. One will be used to direct the aerofoil above them, the other to produce an accurate map of the surrounding air within, say, a 1 mile radius.

Electronic piloting will be possible by means of a tiny control panel, hand-held or even one day directly wired via sensors to the pilot's own thought processes, which will adjust the shape of the aerofoil to produce whatever changes the pilot wishes

– with the obvious provision of a safety cut-out in case a command is unrealistic or impractical. At the same time, the radar- and microwave-operated 'surrounding air reader' (SAR) will produce an invaluable read-out on a small screen or even feed directly into the electronic pilot. It will provide information about the local wind speed and direction, as well as air currents and temperatures. Even the eagles will be jealous.

The **technologies of paragliding** and hang-gliding are in their **infancy**

6 Theatres of Dreams

On 17 October 2007, England's football team faced Russia at Moscow's Luzhniki Stadium in a vital group game for a place in the upcoming Euro 2008 finals. If England won, they would qualify; if they lost, their chance to progress would be out of their own hands, dependent upon the results of other group matches. It was a crucial confrontation.

As always, for days before the match the media offered frenzied analysis of every possible selection, tactic, outcome, etc. Should Chelsea's Frank Lampard start? Would captain John Terry be fit? Was the manager, Steve McClaren, really the man to lead England to the heights? All these were the usual sorts of questions that flew around before every big game. This time, though, there was a new element in the mix: what effect would the pitch have on England's chances?

The Luzhniki Stadium sported what the English press disparagingly referred to as a 'plastic' pitch. In fact, the FieldTurf synthetic surface was highly sophisticated, third-generation artificial turf virtually identical to that on which many of England's players trained every week back home. But doubts persisted over the ball's bounce, its speed over the surface and the possibility of 'carpet burns' on the limbs of sliding players. The replacement of good old grass with this ersatz stuff, grumbled the pub pundits, was a sneaky Russian trick to help their team get through.

There is video of this match on:
http://www.broadcastyoutube.com/watch?v=8xQ_QdZweJy&feature=related

As it turned out, the Russians did get through, 2-1. But not because of the pitch or any other skulduggery – they just played better. Afterwards, disappointed English fans blamed the players' lack of pride, the manager's ineptitude, the referee's myopia and the groundsman's heavy watering of the ground before the game and at half-time. But hardly a word was said about the impact of the synthetic turf itself.

Was this the turning point, the moment when Blake's 'green and pleasant land' finally accepted that technology, as well as nature, could provide a playing surface for its national game?

From There . . .

Grassy Banks

For those who want to take the stadium issue further, there's useful information on:
http://www.worldstadiums.com/stadium_menu/architecture/historic_stadiums.shtml

The Greeks, needless to say, had a word for it: 'stade'. Originally a unit of measurement equivalent to around 180 m (200 yd) – no one is quite sure – it was adopted as the name of the original Olympics' highly prestigious sprint race. This gave rise to the name 'stadion' for the place where the event was held, which in turn became 'stadium' in Latin. And that, more or less, is where we are today. Not that the first Olympians would have recognised our vast concrete and steel temples of sport: their track was little more than a dusty strip marked out with poles and furnished with stone toe grips at one end. The spectators milled about along the sides or packed the nearby hill to get a better view of what was going on.

Not far from Olympia's stadium stood a much more impressive construction, the hippodrome or horse-racing arena. It was a huge oval, some 1,500 m around with a wooden partition down the middle and banked seats on either side. Some reckon it held up to 40,000 spectators. Pretty impressive for something built well over 2,000 years ago miles from anywhere, but nothing compared with Rome's

Outdated technology: toe grips on the starting line of the track used for the original Olympics.

150,000-seat Circus Maximus, which is still one of the largest sports arenas ever. The unforgettable chariot race in William Wyler's memorable *Ben Hur* offers some idea of what these vast stadia may have been like: not too hot on health and safety but unsurpassed for atmosphere.

Emperor Constantine's enlarged circus, a Roman version of the hippodrome, perhaps held a staggering 250,000 spectators.

It was almost two millennia before modern stadiums approached the grandeur and sophistication of the ancient world. Athens built a horseshoe with an impossibly tight bend for the inaugural modern Olympics (1896) but London's part-covered 68,000-capacity White City Stadium at Shepherd's Bush (1908) was the true pioneer. All subsequent stadiums, from Pasadena's Rose Bowl to London's new Wembley, have been essentially variations on the Shepherd's Bush theme.

Slings and Arrows

At the dawn of the modern era, the natural and near-universal sporting surface was grass. Everyone played on it: footballers and wrestlers, rugby, hockey, badminton, golf and tennis players; bowlers bowled on it, boxers boxed on it, athletes ran and jumped on it. The exceptions were winter and motorsports, of course, and hard-wall games such as squash and fives which emerged in strangely contrasting built environments. Fives grew out of a ball game played up against the buttressed wall of an English public school, while squash began with the inmates of the Fleet debtors' prison, London, taking exercise by batting a ball around the gaol walls.

The outcome of a match might well be decided by a downpour rather than skill

As sports became formalised in the 19th and early 20th centuries and professionalism emerged, so more attention was paid to the places where they were played. Even then, it was remarkable how long the old amateur attitudes and ethos lingered on into the professional era. Take the cricket pitch, for example. All cricket lovers know that rain livens up a pitch alarmingly, allowing the ball to fly about unpredictably after it has landed on a drying wicket. Pitch covers were introduced in the 1970s but did not become genuinely effective until the 1980s – or, in many regions, beyond. Before then, despite the batters' best efforts, the outcome of a match might well be decided by a downpour rather than skill.

A classic and oft-quoted example is the 1974 Lord's test match between England and Pakistan, played in the middle of a rain-swept August. Pakistan were twice caught on a sticky, drying pitch – conditions ideally suited to the bowling of Kent's left-arm 'Deadly Derek' Underwood. Although they managed to draw the game, Pakistan's much-vaunted batting line-up was twice ripped apart by Underwood who ended up with the remarkable match figures of 13 wickets for 71 runs. Faced with an understandably furious Pakistani management, the English responded with shamefaced apologies for the poor pitch covers (which had leaked) and mutterings about 'sportsmanship', 'the spirit of the game', 'taking the rough with the smooth' and other platitudes.

It is curious that million-pound industries permitted, even welcomed the Dance of Chance in areas where simple technology could easily have eliminated it

Similar remarks were still being heard 30 years later to justify the retention of grass playing surfaces at the Wimbledon tennis tournament, as well as excusing the occasional poor playing surfaces in other sports such as golf, football and rugby. Although it may be argued that 'the slings and arrows of outrageous fortune' will always play a key role in sport – as in life itself – it is curious that million-pound industries permitted, even welcomed the Dance of Chance in areas where simple technology could easily have eliminated it.

Perfect Pitch

Grass – muddy, threadbare or lush – remained the principal sporting surface until after World War II. Thereafter, it retained its pre-eminence with football (including, until recently, American football), rugby, cricket and most other pitch-based sports thanks to two important developments. One was undersoil heating that kept a pitch frost-free, the other was gradually improved drainage to limit deterioration in winter weather. Finance was both an incentive and a problem. The under-pitch electric blanket at Scotland's Murrayfield stadium, for example, was installed only when a generous benefactor came up with £10,000. This in turn enabled the Scottish Rugby Football Union to raise greater revenue by not cancelling matches because of frozen pitches.

On the other hand, the American NFL, which never cancelled a match whatever the weather, encouraged the installation of undersoil heating for safety reasons after the 1967 game between the Green Bay Packers and Dallas Cowboys (nicknamed the 'Ice Bowl') was played on what was virtually an ice rink in temperatures of −25°C.

The 'Ice Bowl' can be seen on:
http://www.youtube.com/watch?v=DVXFS6nzJrU

An alternative solution, the wholly artificial playing surface, appeared at London's QPR (Queens Park Rangers) football ground in 1981. The so-called 'plastic pitch' or astroturf was widely condemned for its high and uneven bounce and for the 'carpet burns' that players suffered when sliding on it.

In other sports, though, artificial surfaces were rapidly taking over. *En-tout-cas* constructed the first hard, all-weather tennis court in 1909. After that, all the leading tournaments except Wimbledon switched to artificial surfaces of one sort or another. The US and Australian Opens opted for hard courts comprising an acrylic, rubber and silicon surface on a concrete or asphalt base. Red clay, used in the French Open, was in fact crushed and compacted brick with a loose surface, while green clay, also widespread in parts of the USA, really was clay.

Hockey moved to artificial surfaces in the 1970s, making the game faster and helping the wealthier nations, such as Australia and the Netherlands, which could afford the expensive pitches. Almost all golf courses retained grass for the fairways and greens but introduced various types of matting to the tees to reduce wear and tear. Experiments with all-weather, polyurethane-based horse racing tracks began in the 1960s and were gradually introduced over the next 40 years. As with artificial football pitches, though, there were plenty of snags to overcome. Perhaps the most controversial was the effect the new surface had on the form book: the percentage of favourites winning on all-weather surfaces was significantly lower than on grass.

❚❚ It **feels like** running on **air** out **there** ❚❚

Athletics tracks and jump take-offs were surfaced with crushed cinders, or some similar substitute, until polyurethane surfaces (the famous Tartan) appeared in the 1960s. The 1968 Mexico Games was the first summer Olympics in which races were run on the new surface. It immediately caused controversy as records tumbled. The hardness of a rubberised track – the latest version of which was created by Mondo for the 2008 Beijing Olympics – clearly allowed athletes to perform better than on the old cinder tracks.

There's plenty of interesting track information on www.mondousa.com and http://www.tennissurfaces.com/rekortan.htm

This led to suggestions that a new category of records should be instigated for the surface, and there were even suggestions in some circles that, to make the Games more exciting, the Rekortan track laid for the 1984 Los Angeles Olympics had been specially prepared to increase the chance of record-breaking perfor- mances. US superstar Michael Johnson praised the Mondo track of the 1996 Atlanta Olympics as a 'magic carpet', while the 100 m winner Justin Gatlin drooled, 'It feels like running on air out there.'[1]

Light and Shade

'If . . . natural light is deteriorating to an unfit level, the [umpires] shall authorize the ground authorities to use the available artificial lighting.' – ICC test match regulations

[1] http://www.slate.com/id/2105744/

Although floodlit sport is generally associated with the spread of TV after the Second World War, speedway racing was taking place under floodlights by 1923 and the first night-time NFL game took place 6 years later. It was another 20 years before British football embraced artificial lighting. Cricket and rugby followed even later, lured by the extra revenue to be gained by offering evening entertainment that could be beamed live around the world at a time when the maximum audience was available.

Sports that had traditionally been outdoor, such as swimming, badminton, boxing and other martial arts, went indoors as lighting and building design improved. The same improvements permitted other open-air sports – cycling, athletics and tennis, for example – to develop indoor competition. Thus did technology defy the seasons by giving sportsmen and women an opportunity to compete year-round.

Finally, there was the impact of technology on travel. It is often forgotten that all of the major modern sport competitions – national and continental cups, Olympic Games, world cups, etc. – are possible only because of the development of mechanised mass travel. This began with the train and the steam ship, expanded into the car and omnibus, and culminated in the age of cheap air travel that not only enabled teams (and even horses) to travel halfway round the world for a single event, but also enabled spectators from every nation to come together for major competitions. By the 1990s, the whole fabric of international sport was supported on a vast network of high-tech travel.

. . . To Where We Are Now

Green Credentials

Technology provides most of the sports that have traditionally played on grass pitches – essentially football, American football, rugby, Aussie rules and Gaelic football, hockey, cricket and baseball – with a range of options: traditional grass, fully synthetic and hybrid. As synthetic surfaces improve and become more sport-specific, the number of major games played on them increases year on year.

Artificial surfaces are today truer than **grass** ones, **reducing the element of chance,** speeding games up and rewarding **skill**

FA guidelines on artificial pitches can be found at: http://www.thefa.com/GrassrootsNew/Facilities/GroundsAndPitches/ Postings/2004/05/ArtificalGrassPitches_Guidelines

The reasons for the spread of synthetic playing surfaces are threefold. Although the cost of installing an artificial playing surface may be high, its maintenance costs are slight compared with the £250,000 or so needed annually for the upkeep of a top-class grass pitch that is heavily used. Secondly, modern, steeply banked stadiums, fully or partially roofed, allow insufficient sunlight and air to reach the pitch for natural grass to flourish. Finally, whatever the purists may say, artificial surfaces are today truer than grass ones, reducing the element of chance, speed-ing games up and rewarding skill. Nowhere is this more apparent than top-class field hockey.

Someone **sticking a fork deep** enough into the **playing surface** might receive a **fatal electric shock!**

Even where grass is retained, the impact of technology is considerable. A lawn-like look can be achieved by piping warm air beneath the surface to keep it frost-free and encourage root growth. The smartest and most costly systems combine this with a drainage capability. Far cheaper and more common are undersoil electric blankets, although they may cause problems as Falkirk FC, Scotland, discovered when they were told that someone sticking a fork deep enough into the playing surface might receive a fatal electric shock!

In the warmer south, at Twickenham, the Rugby Football Union's prestigious HQ, under-pitch heating is eschewed in favour of covering the pitch with a giant inflatable tent in freezing weather and pumping it full of warm air. On all first-class grounds, a gravel, sand and pipe drainage system swiftly takes excess water from the carefully aerated and spiked surface soil. And if there are still problems, notes BBC Rugby Correspondent Ian Robertson with only a little hyperbole, 'You can just roll out a new pitch in 24 hours, bringing the grass from China.'[2]

English Premiership rugby union pitches are a classic example of what can be done. Before the sport went professional in 1995, by mid-February most first-class pitches, especially the low-lying ones such as Bath's Recreation Ground, resembled First World War battlefields rather than sporting arenas. Ten years later, thanks in no small part to technology borrowed from the farming industry and other sports, most of the top clubs were playing on pitches that more or less retained their level, grassy surface throughout the year.

Twickenham has even borrowed the technology of Dutch bulb growers to keep its grass green and healthy. Six giant rigs beam artificial light onto the pitch, stimulating root growth in all weathers. Similar systems have been installed at Arsenal's Emirates Stadium and, most recently, at Cardiff's Millennium Stadium,

[2] In conversation with the author, 15 January 2008.

where the pitch is divided into 7,400 square modules that can be lifted out and replaced individually or en masse.

Wise Crack

Commentator Mark Taylor, responding to comments on cracks in the WACA pitch: 'Boy! Now we know what happened to all the Aussie cricketers we have seen come and go over the years – they fell into the cracks!'

More innovative is the portable grass cricket pitch (25 m × 3 m × 200 mm) that can be transported to a field and dropped into a pre-prepared slot as a single piece, thereby transforming a football stadium to cricket ground literally overnight. The system has been used at such prestigious venues as Lords (London), Eden Park (Auckland, New Zealand) and Melbourne's Telstra Dome (Australia).

Greener Grass

Despite all the technology available to groundsmen, it is still extremely difficult to maintain a grass pitch through a long and dark winter when it is played on once or twice a week. In recent years, the grounds of certain English Premiership football clubs, notably Chelsea and Newcastle, deteriorated badly. Dave Roberts, responsible for the football pitch at Southampton's St Mary's Stadium, observed, 'As soon as you put a stadium around a pitch you deprive it of sunlight and air movement and the grass struggles to grow . . . You can't cheat nature.'[3]

[3] Cited on http://news.bbc.co.uk/sport1/hi/football/eng (13 January 2003)

But technology can. One answer is to bathe the pitch in artificial light (see above). Another, used at Liverpool's Anfield, Arsenal's new Emirates Stadium and Real Madrid's Estadio Santiago Bernabeu, is to reinforce natural grass with artificial fibres. Originating in Holland, the system involves planting a newly dug pitch with fresh grass, and then, using a purpose-built, computer-controlled machine, injecting 20 million polypropylene artificial strands between the grass roots. Projecting 15–20 mm above the surface of the soil, they give added strength to the natural grass, markedly reduce wear, and aid drainage.

The hybrid arrangement, pioneered by Desso with its DD GrassMaster system, claims to combine the feel and playing characteristics of natural grass with dura-bility enhanced by a factor of at least three. Moreover, there are no reports of 'carpet burn'. As well as at football grounds, the surface has gained wide accep-tance in the American NFL and has also been laid down on rugby pitches.

▌▌ You can't cheat nature ▐▐

The advantages of the new grass over the old were vividly shown when the former was chosen as the playing surface for London's new Wembley stadium. After

Liverpool FC's Anfield stadium, where technology maintains a near-perfect playing surface throughout the year.

hours of torrential rain, it was mercilessly chewed up by the elephantine players of the Miami Dolphins and New York Giants in NFL's inaugural European match, 2007. When the English football team came to play on it shortly afterwards, it was deemed a national disgrace. Even Slaven Bilic, the manager of England's Croatian opponents, remarked tactfully, 'The pitch here is not good, it is not the condition which Wembley . . . is known for.' Not surprisingly, there were immediate discussions about relaying the surface with a hybrid turf.

One step further is to employ 100% artificial fibre, as at the Luzhniki Stadium, Moscow (see above). The current product leader, FieldTurf, mixes flat, 50 to 65 mm blades of polyethylene with others that have spines, like natural grass. This ensures the 'blades' spring back into position after they have been depressed, giving the surface much the same characteristics as natural grass. Unlike the original artificial pitches, with their high, unpredictable bounce and low resistance on a speeding ball, the new ones are tested by FIFA to ensure that bounce, rebound and roll are within the parameters expected of a normal pitch.

The benefits of the new high-tech surface are many, some even surprising. Synthetic pitches drain easily, water permeating swiftly through the porous woven backing to which the fibres are attached, seeping through the shockpad to graded stone and into drainage pipes. Muddy goalmouths are a thing of the past, as are divots and unlucky bounces. On a 'plastic' pitch, no one can blame the groundskeeper for their poor performance. Gone, too, are the abrasions that arose from sliding on the old 'carpet' pitches.

Statistics show that there are **certainly no more knee and ankle injuries** when playing on a 'plastic' pitch, and perhaps **even fewer**

Third-generation synthetic pitches are not only fairer but, remarkably, easier on the players. The silicone-lubricated fibres of the 'grass' rest on an impact-absorbing 'shockpad' (see below). This comprises smooth-sided cryogenic (produced at very low temperature) rubber pellets made from old lorry tyres in a polymeric binder. On average, such a surface is less cloying and more resilient than grass, statistics showing that there are certainly no more knee and ankle injuries when playing on a 'plastic' pitch, and perhaps even fewer.

In 2005, *New Scientist* magazine reported UEFA figures that there were only 3.2 muscular and ligament injuries for every 1,000 hours of play on artificial surfaces compared with 7.6 on grass.

Given their clear advantages, it comes as little surprise to find synthetic pitches gradually creeping across the sporting world, from European football grounds to NFL stadia and rugby practice pitches. International field hockey has been played on artificial surfaces for decades. These were originally sand-based astroturf. Nowadays, water-based synthetic surfaces are almost universal at the highest level as they are less abrasive and favour players with greater ball control. Essentially, they are a short-pile (around 12 mm) woven carpet of artificial fibre, such as nylon or polypropylene, which is continually wetted, even at half-time, to keep the surface lubricated.

The development of such pitches has had unforeseen consequences. The faster surface helped more skilful players and led to a change in stick design to facilitate techniques such as reverse stick trapping. But a swifter game, with the ball whizzing about at high speed as in a pinball machine, made it less likely that hockey would get widespread TV coverage – it was just too fast for the uninitiated to follow.

Even more important, high-tech, water-based pitches made top-flight hockey an expensive sport and, in poorer countries and those blighted by water shortages, an élitist one too. India and Pakistan, once masters of world hockey, have suffered greatly. This is yet another unfortunate example of technology widening the gap between the haves and the have-nots.

Cracks, Keys and Alternatives

No sports surface is subject to as much punditry as the humble cricket pitch. More than in any other game, the crucial strip (only 22.64 m long and 2.64 m wide) determines the duration, nature and, frequently, the outcome of a match. Before the start, it is examined by experts, prodded, leered at by TV cameras and even has keys shoved into its cracks. During play it is stared at, glared at, kicked, covered, swept, rolled and repainted. And when the game is over, if it has not behaved itself, it may be reported to the bosses.

Although matting wickets, plastic or natural fibre, are used for practice and in junior and lower league games, the grass pitch remains the only acceptable surface at the game's top level. Even then, 'grass' is often something of a misnomer for the brown, barren and almost bald length of compacted soil which is frequently offered as an international cricket pitch. Portable pitches (see above) offer one, albeit expensive, solution.

No **sports** surface is subject to as much **punditry** as the **humble cricket pitch**

Another, longer-term one comes from expert analysis and advice, such as that offered by Cranfield University's Centre for Sports Surfaces, which has money from the England and Wales Cricket Board (ECB) to examine pitch technology in such esoteric areas as rolling intensity, 'soil water status' and mowing. Even so, for all the technological input, a pitch usually manages to come up with a few surprises.

Fancy a postgraduate degree in Sports Surfaces? Try:
http://www.cranfield.ac.uk/students/courses/page1823.jsp

High Court

Once the basic tennis court division – grass, clay (green and red) and hard – had emerged by the last quarter of the 20th century, the divisions were further complicated by the multiplicity of variations upon them. 'Clay' was always a misleading term –most 'clay' courts having little or no clay in them – and it became more so as two types of soft or 'synthetic clay' court emerged. Both start with a concrete or asphalt base on which is laid either a carpet or a layer of rubberised material. They are dressed with rubber granules to allow players to slide as on a natural clay court.

Most 'clay' courts have little or no clay in them

Hard courts also use a solid base topped with acrylic and a range of other materials such as silica. In truth, the range of hard, soft and clay courts has expanded to the extent that it is now almost impossible to generalise about manufacture.

The US and Australian Open tournaments, for instance, both nominally played on hard courts, offer significantly different surfaces provided by different firms: the multilayered acrylic-silica-rubber of DecoTurf (US) and the rubber resin of Plexi-cushion (Australian, replacing the cushioned acrylic of Rebound Ace for the 2008 tournament). Add to the mix the interlocking polypropylene tiles of suspended courts and the variety of carpeted (and even super fast wood) surfaces of indoor courts, and the mind – and the poor player – boggles.

There's some US Open Tennis on:
http://www.youtube.com/watch?v=WgUrOQQXspk

So what's the effect of all this court technology on the game of tennis? At the lower levels, probably not a lot. Players like my willing but unfit brother, who slap a ball about for fun and recreation at weekends, pleased just to see the ball clear the net and stay within the court, are not overly concerned about the court's characteristics. But for the many players who perform at a higher level, court differences really do matter. Here we find individuals specialising in certain surfaces. The doubles expert Jonas Bjorkman likes a suspended court, Britain's Tim Henman operated best on the hallowed turf of Wimbledon, while Justine Henin-Hardenne and Rafael Nadal are happiest on the slow clay courts of the French Open. It takes an especially fine player like Henin-Hardenne also to thrive on the much faster surfaces offered by the US Open, where she triumphed in 2007, and Wimbledon. As she noted during her 2007 Wimbledon campaign, the ability to switch surfaces is as much mental as physical: 'Grass is a funny surface – you can suddenly lose a few games so quickly that you have to remain calm when it happens.'

Finally, there is the ongoing controversy about whether Wimbledon should persevere with its grass courts. Purists and traditionalists and those who thrive on the 'fast' surface – 'fast' because although grass reduces a ball's velocity more than other surfaces, it skids through quicker and lower, coming on to the racket earlier – want no change. Modernisers disagree. Grass courts militate against rallies, they argue, making the game more boring (but see the section on balls in Chapter 1). They also suggest that grass is more dangerous as it becomes very slippery when wet. Besides, no matter how well it is prepared, after 2 weeks of continual play, a grass court wears unevenly, producing quirky bounce.

Is it really right, the reformers plead, that a fortune-earning final, played when the court is at its worst, is able to be decided not by a player's skill but by a fault in the surface?

Happy Landings

In other sports, the impact of technology on playing surfaces has been rather less controversial. After initial worries about synthetic running tracks giving athletes unnaturally enhanced performances, the IAAF has tightened up its specifications considerably and is in the process of going even further by producing lists of officially certified track products.

The current cost of getting your track IAAF certified is a cool $25,000.

All track and field event surfaces with a synthetic covering have to meet standards of thickness, force reduction and vertical deformation. The latter two are tested using the android-sounding Berlin Artificial Athlete and Stuttgart Artificial Athlete.

For information on the Berlin and Stuttgart Artificial Athletes see: http://www.isss.de/publications/ArtificialAthlete/CalibAA.pdf

Test positions and temperature range are also specified. By 2007, there were only 50 track and field installations with IAAF Class I certification.

Technically, the challenge of track manufacturers has been to produce a surface that provides the right balance of grip, spring and durability while still remaining porous to allow swift drainage in a downpour. Various manufacturers have taken different approaches, although they all begin with a solid base overlain with some kind of rubberised mat, then maybe a corrugated carpet-type layer topped with minute granules (perhaps of ethylene-propylene-diene monomer – sounds complex but it's simply a form of industrial grade rubber) in a polyurethane binder that is coloured to give the track its specific hue.

Technological advance has made the modern athletics track safer, too. Athletes accidentally falling are far less likely to injure themselves on the surface and also less prone to stress-related injuries that arose from pounding old-fashioned hard tracks.

The safety aspect extends to a wide range of other sports, from gym to judo, with the replacement of canvas and horsehair by plastic foam and other materials that are far more effective as shock absorbers. The result is fewer accidents and athletes, especially younger ones, with greater confidence to try more complex manoeuvres. This is particularly evident in gymnastics, where sprung floors and effective matting have considerably increased the sport's appeal. Elsewhere, while technology has enabled pole-vaulters and high jumpers to soar to heights previously unimaginable, it also ensures that they land safely – not that long ago, high jumpers were coming down in a sandpit!

Crowing glory – the National Stadium, Beijing, which houses a track tested, like all such surfaces, by an artificial athlete.

Walls, Waves and Winter

Indoor athletics tracks, such as those at the Britain's Commonwealth Indoor Stadium in Manchester and Birmingham's National Indoor Arena, are technologically very similar to outdoor tracks except that they are often demountable and the surface is glued to a plywood base. Perhaps surprisingly, wooden construction remains the standard for indoor velodromes, with concrete the preferred surface

Want to know more about velodromes? You could do worse than start with: http://www.velodromes.com

outdoors. Indoors, technological innovation is usually to be found in the enclosing building rather than in the track itself. Traditional wood construction is also preferred for top-level courts used by the NBL, although a whole range of synthetic surfaces are found in other indoor and outdoor courts. The technology of the better ones is similar to those employed in tennis courts.

An eco-friendly ice rink? Not exactly. But in 2007 the state-of-the-art ice hockey facility at Phillips Academy, Andover, Massachusetts, installed equipment that saved 6,700 therms a month simply by recycling the heat generated by its compressor to power its dehumidification process.

The most exciting innovation in the world of squash court construction has been walls of safety glass. Beginning with just the rear wall, the modern all-glass-walled court greatly enhances TV presentation and opens the arcane and sweaty world of the squash court to public gaze, making it a genuine spectator sport for the first time. Another innovation comes with the option of replacing traditional sprung wooden floors with hard-wearing man-made materials with much the same characteristics. Finally, with the introduction of glass walls comes the fully portable squash court ready for erection wherever a tournament is to be held.

The influence of technology on swimming pool construction has concentrated less on materials than on attempts to reduce wave disturbance. These began in earnest at the 1996 Atlanta Olympics. A number of measures were pioneered: recycling water from the bottom to the top of the pool, using variable speed pumps to maintain a 'crown' of smooth water on the surface; motion-absorbing lane markers to reduce the wake of the leading swimmers; designing the edge of the pool to deflect waves downwards rather than back across the pool; installing a moveable floor that allowed the pool depth to be increased, thereby further reducing waves;

and increasing the depth of the side gutters in order to reduce 'splashback'. The way swimming records continue to tumble at almost every major competition is no doubt due largely to improved training methods, but better pool technology must also play its part in a sport where differences are measured in fractions of a second.

Minimal splashback – the latest pool technology seeks to allow each competitor to swim in still water.

In no sport is human intervention with the playing surface more controversial than in skiing. The bête noire is the snow cannon, also known by the more consumer-friendly name of a 'snow-making machine'. Accounting for perhaps a quarter of all ski centres' investment and using more power than the entire ski-lift network, giant snow cannon are now a key but costly feature of many ski resorts and competition slopes.

A snow cannon gobbles 1 cubic metre of water to produce 2 metres of snow and roars at up to 80 decibels.

Forcing a mix of compressed air and water into the atmosphere through nozzles, the snow cannon is about as environmentally unfriendly as the patio heater: global warming brought about by the emission of greenhouse gasses means there is less snow on ski slopes, so we produce more snow with machines that use electricity produced by burning fossil fuels, thereby adding to global warming . . .

A water- and power-guzzling snow cannon – the future of skiing or its death knell?

The same charge can be levelled against refrigerated bobsleigh runs. Further-more, Europe's snow cannon are said to consume as much water per annum as a city of 1.5 million inhabitants. And if environmentalists are not upset enough by the snow cannon, there's always the American idea of adding ice-nucleating bacteria to the cannon water, allowing snow to be produced at higher tempera-tures than possible with a conventional cannon.

Roofs and Screens

After reinforced concrete had become the norm for stadium construction by the middle of the 20th century and all-seating was introduced in most large arenas for safety reasons, the two most significant stadium innovations have been roofing and media facilities. The two are not disassociated. Although purists might dis-agree, a torrential downpour or, worse still, a blizzard can make a sporting event a miserable lottery or even lead to cancellation. Neither eventuality is really acceptable in an age when so much of a sport's income comes from broadcast fees. Perhaps more regrettable is the loss of the wind factor in a fully enclosed modern stadium, although Ireland rugby star Tony Ward, a kicker, would not agree. Speaking in 2003, before the old Lansdowne Road stadium had been demol-ished, he said, 'The biggest problem . . . is the unpredictability of the wind. Because of the way the east and west stands are built up, and because there is nothing at either the Lansdowne Road or Havelock Square ends, the wind tends to come in around the back and causes real problems.'[4]

The air-conditioned Houston (Texas) Astrodome, with a capacity of 62,000, was the first fully roofed large stadium. Retractable roofs, appearing in the 1980s, reached something of an apogee with London's new Wembley Stadium (2007), which has a partly closing roof. Here the clash between aesthetics and practicality,

[4] On http://www.ercrugby.com/eng/5018_2742.php

All new **stadiums** are designed to negate **the 'wally factor'**

so apparent in earlier stadiums with retractable roofs, such as Wales' Millennium Stadium, Cardiff, was overcome with steel cables and an enormous arch spanning the entire building.

Modern stadiums are designed to act as TV studios, as well as sports venues. London's Emirates Stadium (2006), home to Arsenal Football Club, claimed to be the world's first HD (high-definition) streaming stadium. Others soon followed. Making a stadium digital-friendly is about much more than linking up a few wires. It involves building camera positions into the design (remarkably, the original Emirates design did not feature a TV camera gantry!), remembering that different

The Houston Astrodome, Texas, the world's first fully roofed large stadium.

sports require different viewpoints. The best example of this is probably the separate needs of football and athletics, one of the more usual sport-sharing combinations.

It is not just the presentation of games that is dictated by the extra-stadium audience. Timings have to be internationally dovetailed, too. Thus, a boxing match between European fighters in a European city will start in the small hours of the morning to meet the needs of the event's prime funders: the US pay-to-view audience.

Sound systems have to be capable of acting as public address systems and a tie-in for concerts or public meetings. And what about siting the TV studio? In many old grounds, where these have been added as an afterthought, broadcasters are sometimes thrown by the 'wally' effect – members of the public performing antics in front of the windows in an effort to get on TV. All new stadiums are designed to negate the 'wally factor'.

I found myself looking up at the screen rather than reaching for my binoculars to see what was happening at the other end of the pitch

Lighting is another key issue. Broadcasters require better lighting than is necessary just to view the game. Yet the lights must not diminish the picture on the large screens that are a feature of all modern stadia. These screens are a powerful symbol of the dramatic impact of technology on sport. In the 2007 Rugby World Cup, for instance, they were on long before kick-off, showing clips from previous cups and matches, featuring players, and displaying advertisements. During the nail-biting final few minutes of England's form-book-shattering quarter-final win over Australia in Marseille, for instance, on several occasions I found myself looking up at the screen rather than reaching for my binoculars to see what was happening at the other end of the pitch.

Rugby is happy to relay the TV pictures onto the stadium screens. Other sports are less keen to do so. Programme directors do not want to become cricket umpires, for example, and so controversial decisions are not broadcast within the stadium. Rugby has no such qualms, so not only are live pictures shown but the crowd can also see the same images as the video referee when they are asked to adjudicate on questionable scores. In the 2007 Rugby World Cup final between England and South Africa, after watching replays for two whole minutes the bulk of the crowd was sure that England's Mark Cueto had scored a try in the right-hand corner. Studying the same pictures, the video ref disagreed and the try was disallowed – to a cacophony of howls and boos from disappointed spectators. Techno-justice or techno-incitement?

In sports where crowds are traditionally less well behaved than those at rugby matches, officials are less willing to risk riots by exposing the decision-making process so openly.

Sound and Safety

Design technology has its quirky side. To help build up a frenzied atmosphere, the roof of Stadium Australia, built for the 2000 Olympics, was shaped to reflect crowd noise back on itself. Dutch technicians, on the other hand, have devised a way of recording offensive crowd chants and playing them back at a 0.2 to 1-second interval. The echo effect makes it almost impossible for the chanters to hear their own words and keep time with each other, so they stop.

Computer design at the early stages impacts upon a host of stadium features, from sight lines to toilets. Safety is another area that has benefited enormously. It became a top priority when 39 supporters were killed after the collapse of a retaining wall at Brussels' Heysel Stadium an hour before the start of the 1985 European Cup final, and 4 years later nearly 100 died at Sheffield's Hillsborough Stadium. Not only are major grounds now all-seater and the crowd kept under CCTV surveillance, but computer programs work out the number and positioning of exits for stadium evacuation in an emergency. In an era of increased terrorist threat, this has become an even higher priority.

Such apparently simple matters as tickets have also been swept up in the techno revolution. It is now common for tickets to be bar-coded for reasons of security and safety. More recently, it has become possible to have tickets relayed to a purchaser's mobile phone, where they appear as an image that can be scanned for access to the ground. Tight security (unless you have your phone nicked) and also eco-friendly.

The same applies to 'pregrammes' – electronic programmes accessed through the web. These contain a host of add-ons not found in their printed paper equivalents: video clips, opinion polls, tactical graphics, endless statistics, and even odds with links to online bookmakers. And, of course, to those with web-friendly phones all this is available inside the stadium. A far cry from standing crammed onto a terrace with a tepid pie in one hand and the other stuffed firmly into your pocket to prevent the bloke behind you from emptying his bladder into it.

What Next?

Carpet Ball

Within 50 years at the most, synthetic surfaces will be universally better than natural grass or wood. Global warming will make it increasingly difficult and expensive to maintain natural surfaces, too. It is inevitable, therefore, that the route pioneered by field hockey will be followed by other sports. True, over the last few decades major league baseball has shifted from grass to synthetic and back to grass again. Some 90% of 2005 games were on natural grass. But American football is making the synthetic shift as is the version of the game (aka soccer) so popular in the rest of the world. Baseball will come back. With the development of soft landing materials, rugby will follow, as will Aussie Rules and Gaelic football, and virtually all other field sports played professionally. New synthetic horse racing tracks are being built all the time. Lawn tennis will soon be reserved for vicarage gardens only.

Within **50** years at the most, **synthetic** surfaces will be **universally better** than **natural** grass or wood

The point about lawn tennis brings home a painful truth. With playing surfaces as with so many other aspects of sport, technological development will benefit only the opulent. Top professionals will practice and play on superb surfaces. Those without access to such facilities will fall farther and farther behind. We have already seen this with hockey, where the controversial decision to move over to water-based synthetic pitches has put the game beyond the reach of millions in parts of the world where the sport was traditionally strong.

Finally, there's the 'TV Turf'. Just emerging in 2007, the idea is to place fibre optics between the blades of polyethylene grass. These fibres carry light upwards from the trays in which they are planted, turning the field into a gigantic TV monitor of some 128 million pixels. Fed images from a central computer, the TV turf can carry adverts, scores, statistics or just simple messages: Happy birthday coach, from all your fans and admirers!

The senses reel.

Pitch and Putt

What of sports in which the playing surface is essentially part of the game, notably cricket and golf? Let's begin with the latter. Golfers are traditionalists, unwilling to change any aspect of their precious game. But in the end it is not tradition that talks but money. Teeing off from an artificial surface is no problem – indeed, it is what many golfers are used to nowadays anyway.

When three-quarters of the world is **short of water**, **who** will feel happy seeing **millions** of gallons of it **squirted over the playgrounds** of the **wealthy**?

The difficulty is at the other end, with the greens. It is here that a synthetic surface would be most useful but most strongly resisted. Maintaining a carpet-like swathe of grass is extremely expensive, not only in labour but also in water. And since that surface is still less reliable than a synthetic one, persevering with it will come to be seen as just wrong-headed and environmentally selfish. When three-quarters of the world is short of water, who will feel happy seeing millions of gallons of it squirted over the playgrounds of the wealthy?

The joins between natural fairways and synthetic greens may prove a difficulty at first, but not an insurmountable one. No doubt one day the fairways themselves will also be synthetic.

The 10th at the Master's Course, Augusta, Georgia . . . For how much longer will it remain acceptable to use precious water to maintain such unnatural perfection?

And so to cricket . . . There is no reason whatsoever why one-day and Twenty20 games should not be played on synthetic pitches, and before long they certainly will be. This will make them cheaper to stage and remove much of the grossly unfair effect of a mid-match change in the weather.

Five-day test matches are a different proposition. Because synthetic pitches would make bounce and turn (spin) more consistent, they would probably enable batsmen who became accustomed to them to notch up huge scores. Currently many tests are decided because the pitch gradually wears and deteriorates, making victory difficult for the side batting last in a four-innings game. Synthetic pitches would remove this handicap, making the game fairer but, in conjunction with easier batting, produce more drawn games.

In all likelihood, however, this position will never be reached. The reason is not that officials will refuse to adopt synthetic pitches for tests but that test matches themselves will disappear before the decision has to be made. For years now the trend has been towards shorter, more exciting cricket – Twenty20 being the obvious example. In many countries, notably South Africa and New Zealand, test

Techno-sport for the 21st century: the tele-friendly slog of Twenty20 cricket is not for the purists.

matches attract pitifully small crowds and there is no reason to envisage this trend reversing. Sad, perhaps, but inevitable in an age when in entertainment speed is of the essence. As a consequence, top-class cricket, like all other sports that were once played entirely on grass, will be using exclusively synthetic pitches.

The Virtual Stadium

Over 2 years ago, the Italian politician-cum-media magnate Silvio Berlusconi suggested crowds should be allowed to watch Seria A games for free. By the 2020s, the idea may become a reality to avoid empty stadiums.

What sort of emporium will we be sitting in to watch top-class sport in 50 years' time? Well, there is a very real possibility that fewer and fewer of us will bother to go to the stadiums themselves as the online digital alternative will be so attractive. Moreover, the concept of 100,000 people traipsing across the country just for fun, leaving an enormous green footprint, may well be unacceptable. That said, what will the stadium be like for the privileged, wealthy or fanatical who still attend?

Every spectator is **invited** to don a '**binomask**' that **zooms in as close as one wishes** to the **action** taking place below

To make the cost of the entertainment package viable, stadiums will have to be bigger than ever and as multi-sport as possible. Architects have even suggested that it may be possible to roof over not just the arena itself but the whole complex – perhaps even a whole town. Crazy though this may sound, it would create the possibility of reducing harmful emissions within the structure to nil. So the place where the game happens, serviced by swift, pollution-free public transport, is entirely sheltered from the elements. Its power needs are provided by highly efficient solar panels spread around the upper surfaces. The seats are padded and access to them by electric escalator.

On all four sides of the synthetic pitch, which doubles as screen, there are more huge synthetic one-way screens: the crowd behind them can see the pitch per-fectly while those opposite see only the images which they carry. Each seat has its own monitor – or you plug in or tune in your own hand-held version – which has replaced the old paper programme long ago. The menu offers replays of past games and of individual players, every statistic one wants, betting and voting opportunities and, of course, advertising. During the match it will replay any chosen moment of the match from any angle.

> There will soon be the facility, at home and in the stadium, for you to become a virtual player, and in that capacity to have a go at the missed penalty, the dropped catch, the failed tackle that you have just witnessed live.

The match package begins with a meal, followed or accompanied by live entertainment related to the coming event. The on-screen build-up comes next, leading to the emergence of the players. Sound systems enhance desired noise and dampen the undesirable. At this stage, every spectator is invited to don a 'binomask' that zooms in as close as one wishes to the action taking place below. All decisions and officials' comments are relayed through speakers or the binomask. After the game, spectators are invited to stay for post-match entertainment and analysis before making their way to the transport home. Far fetched? Compare the experience of going to a large-scale match before the First World War and today, then imagine the pace of technological development over the next century . . .

Surfing in London? Yes, from 2011 onwards when the world's first outdoor wave machine starts sending down 2-metre rollers in Tower Hamlets' new 'chlorine surfing' facility. Environmentalists are torn between delight at helping overused beaches and horror at the energy consumption of the new pool.

There is also the stay-at-home option before the wall-sized 3-D screen. Again, one puts on a headset, although this version has a number of pads that connect directly with your brain. Down the line come not only the sounds of the stadium as heard from a specific seat, the voices of the commentator and the match officials, but also electronic stimuli that persuade you that you are actually there. You can feel the atmosphere, smell the beer, hear the person next to you yelling in your ear, and taste the nervous expectation in your mouth before the game begins. Sitting 'in the comfort of your own home' – as the commercial cliché goes – you are virtually pitch side.

7 Gear, Gadgets and Gismos

Date: 20 July 1984.
Place: Friedrich Ludwig Jahn Sportpark, East Berlin.
Event: Javelin.

A tall muscular figure wearing striped tracksuit bottoms and a matching singlet over a white T-shirt gathers speed down the approach. About four strides from the line he draws back his arm, leans back and, with a strangled cry of determination, launches the javelin into the air.

From a technical point of view, the throw is just about perfect. The athlete, East Germany's Uwe Hohn, stops before the line and lifts his head to watch. A second or two later, his face breaks into a grin and he raises his arms in delighted triumph.

This is incredible! The javelin is soaring across the stadium on an ideal trajectory. It's a world record, certainly. But just how far will it go? Officials and spectators hold their breath and watch in a nerve-tingling mix of amazement and disbelief as the deadly missile finally hits the grass just a few feet from the edge of the running track.

It was a truly extraordinary performance and Hohn's throw of 104.80 m, beating the previous world record by an astounding 5 m, has never been bettered. It is most unlikely to be, too. Shortly afterwards, the IAAF changed the javelin regulations to remove the possibility of a competitor hurling the instrument right out off the field and piercing an unfortunate official or fellow competitor.

Few other events or athletic activities display more clearly the complex relationship between sport and technology in modern sport. After scientific training and javelin design had made Hohn's throw possible, science was called on again to ensure that it could not be repeated. It was almost as if the officials were saying to the scientists, 'You got us into this mess: now get us out of it!' By 1984 (ominous date), the link between sport and applied science – and by definition technology – had become unbreakable.

Hohn's throw can be seen on:
http://www.youtube.com/watch?v = QGuVV7UYe7g

From There . . .

Spin and Stall

We saw at the beginning of this section how apparatus technology, in the form of swinging weights for the standing long jump, was used to enhance sporting performance in the original Olympics. The long jump was not an exception, either. Early javelin throwers used a leather thong wound round the implement's centre of gravity to spin it as it was released. This helped nullify the vibrations and waving that might otherwise have arisen because of minor imperfections in the javelin's construction. Another early innovation was a crude form of starting stall, now employed just for horse racing but apparently once also used for human sprints.

Early **javelin** throwers used a **leather thong** **wound round** the implement's centre of gravity to **spin it** as it was **released**

In contrast, other than being standardised, the apparatus used in a number of field events – particularly the shot (or 'weight'), the discus and the hammer – has changed hardly at all. 'Technology' glamorises a fairly basic development in hammer throwing: the original implement, some form of weight on the end of a wooden shaft, was superseded by the modern ball and chain design towards the end of the 19th century. In 1895, the solid wooden obstacles that had hitherto been used in hurdle races were replaced by lighter ones that fell over when hit. At least, that was the theory. In practice they remained heavy enough to cause heavy bruising if struck. The modern L-shaped hurdles made their debut in 1935.

Spears and Poles

Throwing a metal-tipped spear or javelin was revived in the 1896 Olympics, although without the leather throwing thong. By this time, the original olive wood of the shaft had been replaced by hickory or Scandinavian birch, the weight was fixed at 800 g and the length 2.6 m.

The year 1950 saw the start of a javelin revolution when the American Richard Held introduced the hollow javelin of steel and aluminium. Its tube composition enabled Held to increase the surface area by 27%, while maintaining the same weight. This allowed his javelin to 'fly' and the world record was soon shooting up towards Uwe Hohn's life-threatening launch. The response was interesting: instead of increasing the instrument's weight, as non-scientists proposed, IAAF officials moved the centre of gravity forward 4 cm. Women's javelins underwent a similar change 15 years later.

Bringing forward the javelin's centre of gravity had a double effect: (1) it flew shorter distances and (2) it fell nose first, making distances easier to mark.

The impact of technology on the pole vault was even more dramatic than that in javelin throwing. In a sort of early bullfight, the Greeks and Cretans vaulted over bulls; further north, the Celts levered themselves forward to see how far they could go; finally, it was left to the Germans to instigate the modern era with vertical vaulting in the late 18th century. Until the turn of the next century, poles were of a strong, solid wood such as ash. These were replaced by bendy bamboo, then aluminium (1957), by when planting the pole in a box at the foot of the jump had come into general use. The next few years saw the key developments that are with us today: the highly flexible fibreglass pole, which inspired a revolution in vaulting technique, and deep foam cushioning for the landing.

The Dutch claim that pole-vaulting grew out of an ancient tradition of using long sticks to lever themselves over water-filled dykes.

Pumping Iron

'Tennis is . . . a spontaneous sport that . . . depends upon . . . the keenness of the player . . . Real training will do tennis far more harm than good.'
– Helen Wills, 20th century tennis champion (in Tennis, *1929)*

From time immemorial, athletes have been preparing themselves for upcoming challenges. Systematic training was a regular and widespread feature of the lead up to the original Greek Olympic Games and included care over diet, as well as work to improve skill levels and increase physical prowess. Competitors were known to improve their strength with what we now call 'progress resistance training', using early forms of weights – and anything else that came to hand. The wrestler Milo apparently lugged a newborn calf about on his shoulders, a form of training echoed in the 20th century by the All Black legend Colin 'Pinetree' Meads, who was said to train by running up hill and down dale on his New Zealand farm with a ram tucked under each arm.

Athletes planning to compete in the ancient Olympics trained intensively for 10 months, often employing professional coaches who might refer to manuals, such as Philostratus' *Handbook for a Sports Coach*.

❝ The **eye is a muscle** which needs **to be exercised** like any other ❞

By the 19th century, 'bodybuilding' with weights was a regular practice, and the hollow dumb-bell filled with some sort of heavy material was gradually replaced by the barbell – an early technological innovation that is still with us. Partly thanks to the widely advertised work of Charles Atlas, the archetypal mid-century 'he-man', strength training and isometric exercise – muscle contraction without joint movement – expanded considerably between the world wars. Then, starting slowly in the 1960s, sport was swept along in the gym avalanche, each training centre filled with an expanding and bewilderingly sophisticated array of exercise machines.

Meanwhile, growing out of an initiative from the University of Leeds in the 1950s, most serious athletes incorporated an element of circuit training into their routines. At the same time, sports analysts were beginning to break down sporting activities into separate qualities and skills, each of which could be worked on individually. This replaced the practice of preparation by playing the sport itself or running through certain elements of it. One of the clearest examples of this was the development of sports vision training to increase ball-game players' spatial awareness, vision reaction time and the like. Many traditionalists pooh-poohed Clive Woodward when he introduced such coaching to the English rugby team and explained, 'The eye is a muscle which needs to be exercised like any other.' His detractors were obliged to partake of humble pie after his team's victory in the 2003 World Cup.

Head and Heart

Out of the 1928 St Moritz Olympics emerged the First International Congress of Sports Medicine, the organisation that actually coined the phrase 'sports medicine'. Sports psychology dates from a book published by a German psychologist the previous year, although it was not for close on four decades before the International Society of Sport Psychology emerged. For some time thereafter the principle focus of sports psychologists was in motivation, helping sportsmen and women build self-confidence and an aggressive 'will to win'.

▌▌ If **they'd told me about bananas** I might still be playing ▐▐

Our obsession with sporting diet – hyped by manufacturers cashing in on the fad for 'sport' drinks and so forth – is a more recent development. Herb Elliot, the great Australian middle-distance runner and a supposed pioneer of modern-style diet – admits that apart from a bit of muesli he ate nothing special. British professional footballers were regularly tucking into red meat, sugary drinks, chips and dairy fats well into the 1990s. On a lighter note, BBC Rugby Correspondent Ian Robertson recalls how '60s and '70s rugby legend Willie John McBride, on learning that modern players were told eating bananas would lengthen their playing careers, observed ruefully, 'Bananas? If they'd told me about bananas I might still be playing.'[1]

---

[1] Ian Robertson in conversation with the author, 15 January 2008.

. . . To Where We Are Now

Sport as a Science

On a typical sports blog, US baseball 'Coach Bob' wrote recently, 'Over the years, incremental advances in technology have accumulated to proportions which clearly affect the games today.' Clearly unsettled at what was happening, he urged: 'It is time for those who not only watch our favourite sport, but LOVE it, to decide how we want to handle these problems – most of which relate to technology development.'[2]

Bob is clearly not alone in feeling that sport is losing something as it becomes more and more scientific-technological. So just what is he so worried about?

> ❝ It is time for **those who not only watch** our favourite sport, but **LOVE** it, to decide how we want to **handle** these **problems – most** of which relate to **technology** development ❞

As at Loughborough and Exeter Universities, most of Britain's earliest university departments of sports science grew out of the PE side of teacher training. During the 1970s, as the profile of sport grew nationally and internationally and it created more and more specialist jobs for administrators and trainers as well as athletes,

[2] From http://www.infosports.com/baseball/arch/1031.htm, 22 November 2007 – just one of many discussions on the topic.

sport became a subject in its own right. Today there is hardly a self-respecting university anywhere in the world without its own school or department of sport, with courses increasingly linked to 'exercise' in general.

This expansion has been so dramatic and the consequential research output so far-reaching that the last 20 or so years have witnessed little less than a techno-logical revolution in the way athletes in virtually every sport prepare, perform and recover. Sadly, though, as with so many of the other aspects of sport we have examined thus far, this process of 'technologisation' has meant that the wealthy, or those with access to wealth, now have an almost unassailable advantage over the poor and amateur.

Of course, every now and again the media feature uplifting stories of the boy or girl from nowhere who has burst upon the international sports scene. The Cam-eroon footballer Roger Milla is a good example. But he did not become an inter-

The Ryder way: the Sports Technology Institute at Loughborough University used this motion analysis system to fine-tune the swings of the victorious 2006 European Ryder Cup team.

national figure, helping his country reach the quarter-finals of the 1990 World Cup, until he moved to Europe and began playing for French clubs.

'If I can join hands with FIFA . . . to promote football globally, then I can do more than that to raise African football to new heights.' – Roger Milla

Traditionally, sports science, defined as the employment of scientific principles to improve sporting performance, divides into three principal areas – biomechanics, physiology and psychology – with other supporting disciplines such as statistics and sociology. Like all academic subjects, biomechanics, physiology and psychology are essentially umbrella terms covering a host of subdivisions that range from diet to performance analysis. For the purposes of this brief survey, we will view

All is revealed: high-speed imaging developed by Loughborough University allows batters and other sportspeople to analyse their technique in great detail.

the present situation from the purely practical perspectives of (i) preparation and training, (ii) performance, and (iii) recovery, recuperation and the treatment of injury.

Preparation and Training

Technique

'Not every person . . . knows everything about the game, and teaches every stroke perfectly. Why not go to a specialist if you have a little problem?'
– Tracy Austin, US tennis star and TV analyst

Want to see a top athlete in training, using all the latest sports science gadgetry? Go to:
http://www.ganges.com/High_Jump_Promo_Tora_Harris_2_30m_7_6_50_ v2654313

As good a starting point as any is 'motion analysis', the must-have tool for technique improvement. Information is acquired by video cameras and/or a 'force plate' that measures the forces exerted on it by an athlete. The evidence is fed into a computer and analysed by a number of sophisticated programs, such as 'Motion Composer' and 'Skeleton Builder'.[3] The wide range of very detailed

---

[3] Examples from http://www.motionanalysis.com/applications/movement/sports/products. html (12 December 2007)

information provided pinpoints specifics such as inefficiencies in technique, which in turn can be rectified by careful coaching. In the case of the shot put, motion analysis spearheaded the change from the glide to rotational delivery.

For more on motion analysis, try:
http://www.sportsmotion.com

In pole-vaulting, it is impossible to separate technique from apparatus. Unusually, the IAAF has imposed minimal regulation on pole specification: its length and material are unrestricted, for instance. This has given the scientists a field day as they seek the best way to catapult an athlete over a bar 6 m above the ground. Physicists realise that hollow poles are better than solid ones, that tapering poles operate better than parallel ones (a contribution from Cambridge University), and that the vault is achieved by releasing the stored strain energy in a bent pole. All this has resulted in the extraordinary technique – basically turning themselves upside down in order to 'pour' over the bar – of today's vaulters. In other words, technology dictates technique.

The javelin story is simpler. It is more tightly regulated (2.60 m to 2.70 m in length with a minimum mass of 800 g), with a carefully delineated centre of mass. This is no longer at the mid point of the implement's length, theoretically making throws like Hohn's impossible. Technique is honed by computer modelling so that athletes know the ideal trajectory for their launch, the right moment at which to pull their throwing arm back, etc.

In pole-vaulting, it is impossible to separate technique from apparatus. This came from the science of **biomechanics**, the study of the interplay between forces and an animal body (normally human). It overlaps with **anthropometry** (body measuring), and its more recent and sophisticated cousin **kinanthropometry** (using measured data to predict the condition of a body and thence its performance potential).

Nobles had **calculated the precise body angle**, timing and all other movements needed for a **perfect jump** – and Edwards **obliged**

If all this seems a bit anoraky, then let's go back to Jonathan Edwards, the finest triple jumper the world has ever seen. It was only after working with Florida State University biomechanics expert Dennis Nobles that in 1995 he was able to realise his full potential and establish the world record of 18.29 m that, amazingly, still stands. Nobles had calculated the precise body angle, timing and all other movements needed for a perfect jump – and Edwards obliged.

Jonathan Edwards' world record jump can be seen on:
http://www.youtube.com/watch?v = la0aslRvbAM

The same skills-analysis techniques are used for high jump, hurdling, ski jumping, kicking a football, and a variety of other sporting activities, including bowling in cricket. Where the latter is concerned, precise analysis of skeletal position produces not only greater accuracy and consistency but also reduces the risk of injury.

Honest spin: Loughborough University has developed the world's first device to capture the 3-D spin on a ball in flight.

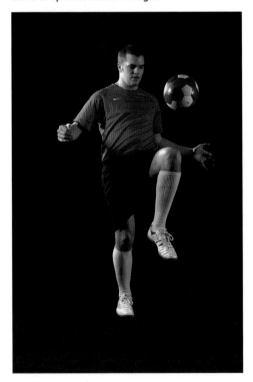

For some insight into biomechanical analysis, try:
http://www.sporthorizon.com/sports_page.htm

Another interesting piece of research from the University of Western Ontario, Canada, confirms what many have believed for several years: that simply watching a skill being performed helps the uninitiated, when given the opportunity, to perform it themselves. By watching a video or TV programme, for example, observers learn complex movements, forces and timings of such refined activities as wielding a cricket bat. Extraordinary – but don't tell the kids or you'll never get them off the sofa!

Ball analysis apparatus at Loughborough, part of the University's specialist facilities for the design, simulation, testing and manufacture of sports equipment, footwear and apparel.

Apparatus

Modern technology provides a bewildering – and often unnecessary – array of machinery to assist sportsmen and women in their training. There is scarcely a muscle group in the body that is not targeted by some gadget or other. Brute strength is built up with bars, dumb-bells and weight machines designed to develop muscles, ligaments, tendons and bone density. Coupled with the right diet, they can have dramatic effects. 'Bulking up' is the current phrase, often applied to players of contact sports such as rugby and American football. In preparation for the 2007 RWC, for example, the entire Scottish team was put through an intensive course of weights and diet that produced surprising trans-formations in shape and size in a matter of a few months.

During pre-season training, a first-class rugby player of around 90 kg (198 lb) will often require 4,000–5,000 calories per day – a costly business.

The impact of technology on its apparatus is clearly visible in every sport

Nor is machinery just there to add strength. Instead of plodding for hours along wet winter roads and tracks, the modern athlete can stay snug in the gym and work on aerobic fitness with cycling, running and rowing machines. Then there are machines to replicate human opposition: for rugby players rolling scrummage machines that do just about everything an opposing pack would do, except bite your ears; and for cricketers, hockey and baseball players bowling (or, more accurately, ball-launching) machines capable of sending down 95-mph snorters.

These go alongside all the other pieces of equipment, such as nets, sprung stumps and moveable goals, which enable outdoor sports to be practised indoors.

'Preparing to play on the sub-continent . . . can be replicated very successfully with a bowling machine.' – John Abrahams, 2 i/c England's National Cricket Academy

At a more general level, there is hardly a sport in which the impact of technology on its apparatus is not clearly visible. It is seen, for example, in the safety padding

Not quite human: the latest Bola bowling machine does just about everything – except unpredictability.

Some sports have an **extraordinary aversion** to the benefits afforded by the **simplest of technologies**

wrapped around rugby posts, in the elasticised 'ropes' around boxing and wrestling rings, and in rot-free nets in football, tennis, hockey and handball.

Starting stalls, pioneered in Australia in the 19th century but introduced into Britain for flat racing only in 1965, have eliminated much of the hit and miss associated with other methods of getting a horse race under way. Although technology has made the alternative system – starting tapes – a bit more efficient, its weaknesses were plainly and embarrassingly visible to a worldwide audience of 300 million when the 1993 Aintree Grand National had to be declared void after horses became tangled in the tapes and 30 of the 39 riders set off on what was belatedly called a false start. Some sports have an extraordinary aversion to the benefits afforded by the simplest of technologies.

The 1993 Aintree fiasco is on:
http://news.bbc.co.uk/onthisday/hi/dates/stories/april/3/newsid_
4216000/4216143.stm

Training

At the top level, sports training is now a precise science that is beyond the ken of most ordinary fans. Even journalists get left behind. In 1998, one unsuspecting

At the top level, **sports training** is now **a precise science** that is beyond the **ken** of **most ordinary fans**

hack asked Sir Clive Woodward – or plain Clive as he was then – whether he wanted his England rugby team to be physically stronger. Given its recent hammering on the 'Tour to Hell' against larger New Zealand and Australian sides, the questioner was clearly expecting the answer to be 'yes'. It was not. Strength, Woodward explained, was not the issue: what his players really needed was power. Knowing nods failed to hide the confusion felt by many in the audience.

At its simplest, in sport, power = strength × speed.

The difference between strength and power, one involving a muscle's ability to operate against resistance and the second incorporating speed with that ability, is just one of the concepts arising from precise analysis of how a sporting body operates. It is this analysis that is now brought to bear on all aspects of training. According to Jean-François Toussaint, head of the Irmes (France's Institut de Recherche Biomédicale et d'Epidémiologie), the result is that today's top athletes perform at 99% of their physiological capacity compared with 75% a century or so ago.

Integrated Training

In 2007, Manchester United's assistant manager, Carlos Queiroz, described the 'integration concept' of his training regime: 'All things are related to the preparation of the players. The technical, tactical and fitness aspects, everything together is an integrated system.'[4]

Amid the jargon and all too prevalent mumbo-jumbo of the training ground, certain concepts are universally accepted. As well as **power**, these include:

Aerobic and Anaerobic Exercise and Fitness

The former is exercise that increases the amount of oxygen being delivered to the muscles; the latter is explosive exercise over a short period of time that uses energy stored in the form of glycogen because oxygen is being used faster than the body can replenish it.

The Wikipedia article is useful here:
http://en.wikipedia.org/wiki/Aerobic_exercise

VO2

The rate at which the body can absorb oxygen and use it. Described as the 'gold standard' measurement of aerobic fitness, it is based on the efficiency of the

[4] *Guardian*, 1 December 2007.

cardiorespiratory (heart-lung) system. VO2 max (measured with a 'max test'), the maximum amount of oxygen a given body is capable of transporting and utilising, can be improved with training. However, it is possible to test budding athletes to see whether their cardiorespiratory systems will ever allow them to compete at the highest level.

So you think you're fit? Lab testing an athlete's VO2.

More on:
http://www.runningforfitness.org/faq/vo2.php

Lactic Threshold

The point during exercise when the amount of lactate (lactic acid) in an athlete's muscles builds quicker than it can be removed, leading to eventual standstill.

Detailed scientific stuff on:
http://home.hia.no/~stephens/lacthres.htm

Fast and Slow Twitch Muscle Fibres

In a given bundle of muscle fibres, about 50% are fast twitch, good for sprinting and anaerobic exercise, and 50% are slow twitch, good for aerobic exercise. It seems that some athletes may be born with more of one kind than the other, that muscles can be trained to act as fast or slow twitch, and that some people's twitches are quicker than others!

For more on fast and slow twitch fibres, see:
http://sportsmedicine.about.com/od/anatomyandphysiology/a/MuscleFiberType.htm

Plyometrics

An 'in' word (coined in the USA using incorrect etymology, 1981) for an age-old training technique: increasing power by the repeated stretching and contracting of muscles.

The Wikipedia article on Plyometrics is pretty good:
http://en.wikipedia.org/wiki/Plyometrics

Obviously not a lot of this stuff impinges on the average amateur who plays sport for the fun of it and to keep fit; but at the professional level it's vital. In fact, so time-consuming and expensive is top-level training today that expert back-up, an array of equipment and full-time professionalism are virtually a prerequisite for international success in all major sports. Hence the 2006 provision by Britain's Chancellor Brown of a £600 million war chest for athlete training, including a national School Olympics, in preparation for Britain's 2012 Olympics.

Those who boggle at such figures are in good company. No less a body than the National Audit Office ran an eye over British athlete funding in 2005 and came to some pretty startling conclusions. In what was dubbed the 'Glory Index' – the ratio of funding to Olympic medal winning – swimming came out worst with £3.3 million, while archery proved the best bargain at £0.3 million. The overall index was £2.4 million per medal.

For more on this subject, try:
http://www.guardian.co.uk/Columnists/Column/0,,1711864,00.html

Of course forking out cash is no guarantee of success, but it does help. How else can one explain the relative sporting success over the last 15 years of a country like Saudi Arabia, which, camel racing apart, has no sporting heritage or traditions whatsoever? And the relative underachievement of talented sportsmen and women from poorer nations?

It **thickened the blood** to the point where it caused **heart failure**

High-tech training invariably involves input from a sports physiologist, perfor-mance-measuring equipment (such as the force plate – see above) and computer power to analyse the data, a gym, a coach or two, and suitable facilities. Training programmes, marketed under catchy names like 'Lactate Doser', the 'Herb Elliott' and 'Oxygen Special', are tailored to the needs of individuals. For those travelling to compete in a different environment, acclimatisation is considered essential, teams taking up residence abroad for days, even weeks before their competition. It's all a far cry from the time when Don Thompson, Britain's sole track gold medal winner in the 1960 Rome Olympics, trained in his parents' bathroom after recreat-ing what he hoped would be Italian heat and humidity by placing a boiling kettle on a lit paraffin stove in the corner.

Accurate measurement of VO2 has led to interest in ways of improving it other than by simple aerobic exercise, such as interval or 'Fartlek' training. Oxygen is carried to the muscles by the red blood cells. The more of these cells an athlete has, therefore, the more oxygen can reach their muscles and the better they can perform. In the 1970s, it was discovered that the body's red blood cell production is regulated by the hormone erythropoietin, better known as EPO: more EPO = more red blood cells. Providing athletes with large doses of an artificial form of the hormone was tried as a way of boosting the red blood cell count. It was swiftly declared illegal, however, not least because it thickened the blood to the point where it caused heart failure. Next came altitude training.

Athletes **who sleep in a hypoxic tent** perform **better** when emerging to compete in a **normal atmosphere**

At altitude, because of the lower atmospheric pressure, the body takes less oxygen from the air. To compensate, stimulated by increased secretions of EPO, it produces more red blood cells. So over a 2-week period, athletes training at over 2,500 m (8,000 ft) will naturally increase their red blood cell count. If they then compete nearer sea level, they should be at an advantage over adversaries who have trained at lower altitudes. But the toing and froing is expensive and tiring, and the results of altitude training are short-lived.

The BBC is good on EPO:
http://news.bbc.co.uk/sport1/hi/in_depth/2001/world_athletics/1481126.stm

As an alternative, therefore, the Finnish scientist Heikki Rusko came up with a special 'house' in which the oxygen concentration mirrored that at high altitude. The body, tricked by the atmosphere within the 'oxygen' or 'hypoxic' tent, compensates by increasing red blood cell production. It is claimed, although it has yet to be proved definitively, that athletes who sleep in a hypoxic tent perform better when emerging to compete in a normal atmosphere.

Before the 2002 World Cup, England football captain David Beckham slept in one of these wonder tents after breaking a bone in his foot. He hoped it would help maintain his fitness during the period of enforced inactivity needed for the break to heal. When fellow England star Wayne Rooney suffered a similar injury before the next World Cup, the tent was made big enough to accommodate both the injured footballer and his fiancée, Coleen McLoughlin. Judging by what followed, neither player seemed to have benefited much from their camping experience.

Diet

'How, what and when we eat is now a real issue. Vital.' – Barry McGuigan, former world flyweight boxing champion (conversation with the author, 14 January 2008)

When double Olympic gold decathlete Daley Thompson was at the height of his powers in the early 1980s, he declared innocently that because of the amount of exercise he took his diet didn't matter: he could and did eat whatever he wanted. Ten years on, British Division One (now the Premiership) footballers were still sitting down on match days to large fried breakfasts and celebrating victory or drowning their sorrows afterwards with plentiful pints and shorts. Not any longer. At least, not when the training team is around.

Some reckon that **potatoes boiled** for 20 minutes and **eaten 3 hours before** kick off are the **ideal** pre-match fuel

The myth of 'anything goes' on a sportsperson's plate was officially debunked almost two decades ago, when a diet providing 60–70% of calories from carbohydrates, 12% from protein and 18–28% from fat was recommended by an international conference meeting in Lausanne. The ruling was based on firm scientific evidence.

We now know that carbohydrate is the key food for exercise because it converts readily to glycogen. This is stored in the liver and muscles. The body's other energy store, fat, delivers energy much less readily. As glycogen storage is limited, athletes in endurance events, such as cycling, top up en route by eating. This is not an option available to runners who have to make do with the more digestible but nutritionally less effective carbo-drinks. All sportspeople participating in events requiring aerobic activity indulge in 'carbohydrate loading' in the days before they compete. Some reckon that potatoes boiled for 20 minutes and eaten 3 hours before kick off are the ideal pre-match fuel.

Olympic decathlete Daley Thompson thrived in an age when 'diet' meant simply eating whatever he fancied.

It was not so long ago that rugby players, boxers, weightlifters and other power athletes were encouraged to gobble down slabs of red meat in order to build up their muscles. Another sporting myth. Although power players need a bit more protein in their diets than ordinary citizens, this is better taken in the form of eggs, white meat and fish, although lean red meat is rich in iron. This mineral is now recognised as a key ingredient of an athlete's diet and especially important for runners, whose iron levels often become worryingly low, and for menstruating women.

Then there's fluid intake. Backed by extensive research, this has become almost an obsession with modern sportsmen and women. Not a second's break in play goes by without a swig at the water bottle. Water? No longer. Although plain old H_2O is adequate for most people in most circumstances, modern athletes go for isotonic and hypotonic drinks rich in glucose and salts. Sadly, these are also marketed for everyday consumption as somehow 'healthy' or 'sporty', when in fact their high sugar content merely manifests itself as a few more centimetres round the waist. So does booze, which also leads to dehydration (a principal factor in hangovers) and slower recovery from vigorous exercise. So much for the post-match pint! Not surprisingly, many of today's finest athletes, from Jonny Wilkinson to David Beckham and Andy Murray, are non-drinkers. (Although Wilkinson broke his rule – apparently with painful consequences – after the 2007 Rugby World Cup final.)

Performance

Engage Brain . . .

'90% of cricket is played in the mind' – Sir Richard Hadlee, great New Zealand bowler, 1991

Winners, as always, are tough in mind as well as body

It has long been understood that in all stressful activities, from athletics to 'A' levels, attitude is as important as raw ability. Enter sports psychology, a discipline that claims roots back to the late 19th century and the era of Sigmund Freud. Its impact has grown ever since, from the first sports psychology laboratory in 1920 (Berlin) to the position we are in today where its teachings are evident in every stadium, on every pitch, on every course and court around the world: the 100 m runners staring fixedly ahead, going through their routine with meticulous care . . . the goal kicker or penalty taker blotting out the noise of the crowd . . . the golfers prowling round the 18th green to calm themselves, as well as to assess the lie of the ball before taking the final putt.

Winners, as always, are tough in mind as well as body. In essence, sports psychology is about understanding the mental or psychological factors that influence sporting performance and finding ways of controlling them to improve team and individual performance. Inevitably these vary from person to person, which is why top teams and individuals employ the services of a coach with sport psychology qualifications or even an out-and-out sports psychologist on a full- or part-time basis.

In recent years, the practitioner with the highest profile has been Dave Aldred, MBE, formerly kicking coach to the England Rugby team – most notably to record points scorer Jonny Wilkinson – and sometime advisor to football teams such as Newcastle United, rugby league teams, golfers and other leading sportsmen and women. Partly through studying the behaviour of dolphins, creatures that are not hampered by fear of failure or other anxieties when displaying their supreme aquabatic skills, Aldred's premise is that 'skills and behaviours are often in fact the same thing. When you treat a skill as a behaviour, then there is a greater likelihood that the individual will consistently perform at a high level.'[5]

Techniques developed by sports psychologists include Dissociation, Reframing and Visualisation. The first is learning to switch off your brain's 'I'm-at-my-limit' mechanism; the second means mentally breaking a protracted task, such as running a marathon, into manageable chunks. Visualisation, the most obvious to the spectator, involves what is termed 'mental practice of action' or 'imagery' in which athletes create in their mind an image of what they are about to do. One of the clearest examples of this is a high jumper visualising the approach and leap before making the attempt. This involves tremendous concentration, or 'attention focus' in sports psychology jargon, which overlaps with control and may involve rituals. All of these are no good without challenging yet realistic goal-setting, another area on which sports psychology has had an impact. Then there's the whole field of motivation, which experts divide into intrinsic (achieving something for internal, private satisfaction) and extrinsic (seeking public acclaim or reward). And all of the above needs to be underpinned with effective anxiety control.

Happily, despite all the analysis, neurological and psychological input, the bizarre rituals, brow-furrowing focusing and imaginative visualising, footballers still miss penalties, golfers still go to pieces on the 18th green and teams still find it easier to win at home than away. In other words, the only predictable element in sport remains its glorious unpredictability.

'Golf is a game that is played on a five-inch course – the distance between your ears' – Bobby Jones

[5] http://www.abingdonmanagement.co.uk/index.cfm?page=showspeaker&sp=da (4 November 2007)

Match Day

Training over, body carb- and liquid-loaded (if necessary), mind focused, match day is when the coaches and their tactics come into their own. The day's routine will already have been carefully planned, including meal times and content, event-related meetings, urine tests (to check hydration) and other last-minute medical checks and treatments. At the 2007 World Athletics Championships in Osaka, Japan, 400-m runner Tim Benjamin was amazed at the precise support given to the British team by a back-up staff of 31 (including 10 medics) for a team of 56 athletes: 'It is the little things . . . If you are back at the hotel, and you need someone there is always somebody there . . . '[6]

In extended-time events and matches, especially team games, computing power is increasingly important. Coaches at rugby, American football, baseball, motor racing and cricket sit before their screens, pouring over statistics, technical infor-mation and replays. Football and other sports have back-room staff performing the same function, feeding information to those pitch side.

The result is that those watching can understand what is going on better than those on the pitch. This led to the late Bob Woolmer, coach to the Pakistan cricket team, establishing a radio link between himself and his captain in the middle. The ICC swiftly stepped in to ban the practice.

Nevertheless, there remain plenty of other ways of relaying information to the players, from simple hand signals to verbal messages brought out by carriers of new equipment and the ubiquitous water bottles. And in American football, of course, the regular swapping of offence and defence teams gives ample opportu-nity for mid-game coach input based not just on the state of the game but also on the condition of individual players: some teams, for instance, have experimented

[6] *Guardian*, 20 August 2007.

with heat sensors inside players' helmets in order to alert the coach staff, via a transmitter, when a player's temperature is rising dangerously.

Recovery

Physical Recovery

In the old days, we simply 'warmed down' with a desultory jog, took a quick bath or shower and repaired to the bar to mull over the game. No longer. Nowadays at the top level, it's massage, ice baths, recuperative and restorative drinks and carefully balanced meals. Even serious amateurs have massages and try to emulate the professionals in the recovery process.

A swimmer's damaged ankle, needing to return to the **great flexibility needed in kicking**, will be treated differently from that of a runner

The physiology of the ice bath, widely used in rugby, is an interesting example of the application of science to sport. Reacting to the cold bath water, the body goes into a self-defence mechanism to prevent a drop in overall temperature: blood vessels shrink and blood drains from the limbs. With it goes the unwanted lactic acid, too. When after around 10 minutes the athlete leaves the bath, 'new' blood pulses into the limbs, reinvigorating them with a tingling fresh feeling!

Enormous strides have been made on the medical aspects of recovery, particularly in the analysis and treatment of injuries and in the rehabilitation process.

Athletes, as well as medical staff, are all too aware of how important early diagnosis and treatment are: the icepack and scan are now almost as prevalent as lineament and bandage were in the old days. Diagnosis is more precise, too. A fracture is no longer just a fracture but one of a range of breaks that occur for different reasons and take different forms. Each sport has separate ways of treating similar injuries. For example, a swimmer's damaged ankle, needing to return to the great flexibility needed in kicking, will be treated differently from that of a runner whose movement may be more intense but limited in range.

New maladies and syndromes are identified all the time. Some 10% of endurance athletes, for instance, are said to suffer from UUPS (Unexplained Underperformance Syndrome) during their careers and sports physicians have begun to unpick the complex web of physical, mental and dietary factors that lie behind the debilitation.

If technology is **killing sport** in some ways, in others its effects are **almost Lazarus-like**

More dramatic are the surgical procedures used to treat sports injuries. England football star Michael Owen had a double hernia operation at the hands of German surgeon Dr Ulrike Muschaweck and was back playing again in 2 weeks. Anterior cruciate ligament repair, although still a lengthy process, is increasingly successful.

Not so long ago any operation on the spine was considered a risky business and certainly sufficient to put a stop to any sporting career – when I had a lumbar 4–5 disc problem back in the '70s, I was wrapped in a plaster cast, doped with Valium, tied to a bed for 3 months and told never to play rugby again. And now we have

Patched-up England prop Phil Vickery (the tackler) plays on after spinal surgery. Twenty years ago, his injuries would have brought his playing career to a premature close.

'Raging Bull' prop forward Phil Vickery captaining England's rugby team to the World Cup final in 2007 after no fewer than three major back operations! If technology is killing sport in some ways, in others its effects are almost Lazarus-like.

Performance Analysis

Ever wondered how amazingly detailed statistics are flashed up on your TV screen – for example: 'Distance covered by Stephen Gerard during the match = 8,426 m'? The answer is that the TV company, along with coaches and managers, is using a sport tracking system such as the well-known ProZone. A bank of digital cameras tracks the movement of each player and the ball, feeding the information into a computer system that gives positional breakdown every 0.01 second. At any point

Lots of interesting material on:
http://www.pzfootball.co.uk
http://www.eis2win.co.uk/gen/news_performanceanalysis020205.aspx

in the game, therefore, it is possible to tell how many passes, runs or tackles a player has made.

More on performance analysis on:
http://www.pponline.co.uk/encyc/performance-analysis.html

This also means that at the end of a game there is no hiding. Experts reckon that players and coaches correctly recall only 30% of overall performance, while the digital tracking system doesn't miss a thing. The English rugby team were surprised when one of the first bits of kit handed to them by Clive Woodward when he took over as manager was a laptop; they were even more surprised when, after each match, they were given a CD of their individual performance, warts and all.

Video playback and technological performance analysis is now used by virtually all top athletes in all sports. It allows them not just to review past performances but to improve their game, sometimes by displaying their play beside that of world leaders, and sometimes by breaking it down, move by move, to identify tiny errors or inefficiencies. The technology is a vital tool for analysing the style and tactics of future opponents. Of course, all this makes it even more extraordinary that the officials responsible for the development of some sports still refuse to allow technology to assist refereeing decisions. It exists, it's being used by players, coaches, managers and the media – so why not the officials?

The latest, fascinating, bit of high-tech performance analysis and skills improvement kit is the sportswizard developed by Dartfish. Top performers are filmed demonstrating a skill, which is then broken down so a coach or athlete can compare their own videoed performance with that of the expert. See: http://www.rugbysportswizards.com/default.aspx

Enabling the Disabled

It is impossible to overestimate the impact technology has had in enabling physically disabled people to play sport. From artificial limbs for runners to electronic devices that enable the blind and partially sighted to play cricket, the story is one of a technologically aided series of personal triumphs over adversity. The subject, like so many we have touched upon, merits a book of its own. What follows, therefore, is just a quick look at some of the technology that has benefited sportsmen and women with disabilities.

'Count Me IN' – motto of the British Federation of Disability Sport.

Visually impaired archers use a simple system of feet markers and a spring-loaded pin on a tripod that meets with the back of their bow hand. By adjusting

It is impossible to **overestimate** the impact **technology** has had in enabling **physically disabled people to play sport**

the pin, they can record precisely the direction and angle of each arrow release. The technology behind 'Blind Cricket' is even simpler, consisting of a soccer-sized ball filled with small objects – often ball bearings – that rattle as it moves, larger wickets and less rigorous laws. A similar ball is used in blind football.

The Blind Cricket Association can be found on:
http://www.blindcricket.org.uk

Disabled swimmers benefit from a wide range of buoyancy aids. For amputee runners, engineers have produced a striking range of lightweight carbon fibre prostheses. The best known are those worn by the South African athlete Oscar Pistorius, who was born without fibula bones and had both legs amputated below the knee at the age of 11 months. Developing superb balance, the man dubbed 'Blade Runner' has played a wide variety of sports, including rugby, and has clocked under 11 seconds for the 100 m, 21.58 for the 200-m and 46.56 for the 400 m. 'The fastest man on no legs' achieved worldwide fame when his request to compete with able-bodied athletes was turned down on the grounds that his J-shaped sprung prostheses (called 'Cheetahs') gave him an unfair advantage. The decision was later reversed, then reviewed again before being finally upheld in January 2008. Still, the legend runs on.

An athletic leg **prosthesis** may cost up to **£14,000** and a **foot** another **£4,500**

Cheetah Cheater?

Investigating the case of disabled athlete Oscar Pistorius who wished to take part in able-bodied competitions, Prof. Peter Bruggemann reckoned that his subject's 'Cheetah' prosthetic blades gave him an unfair advantage because they 'return 90 per cent of the impact energy, compared to the 60 per cent of the human foot.'[7]

Another superb prosthetic-wearing sportsman is US sprinter Marlon Shirley, who had his left foot sliced off by a lawnmower at the age of 5. Bounding along on one good leg and a carbon fibre J, he has recorded an amazing world record 10.7 seconds for the 100 m. There is, needless to say, a snag. It is one that must have struck everyone who has taken even just a passing interest in disabled sports – money. An athletic leg prosthesis may cost up to £14,000 and a foot another £4,500. Small wonder, then, that the bulk of medals in the Paralympics are carried off by the teams from developed nations. It is, sadly, yet another example of how technology is developing sport in ways that benefit the haves rather than the have-nots.

Oscar Pistorius can be seen on:
http://www.youtube.com/watch?v = 1so1ZMgpg2w

And Marlon Shirley on:
http://www.youtube.com/watch?v = gnKd-94a3Pw

[7] *The Times*, 20 December 2007.

What Next?

Superpole?

If regulations were relaxed, technologists could produce javelins capable of flying 150 m, even 200 m. At that stage the event would become literally lethal in any ordinary stadium. Danger might also attend the vaulter's pole, where it would be possible to manufacture one with sufficient spring to send a jumper soaring over 25 m – what about a mini parachute to help them come down safely?

There is little chance of this happening – unless, of course, some bright spark of an entrepreneur, a Kerry Packer of athletics, decided to launch a series of alternative track and field events geared to extraordinary performances and record-breaking. A certain category of viewer – those who currently watch Extreme Fighting Sports, for example – might find it compelling TV. However, to get the most spectacular results in events where apparatus was irrelevant, such as running, the organisers would also probably have to do away with drug testing. The consequences, a sort of Megalympics, are examined in Section II.

If regulations were **relaxed**, technologists could **produce javelins capable of flying** 150 meters, even **200 meters**

Other sporting machinery and apparatus is likely to improve along lines already clear. 'Intelligent' scrummaging machines could be produced to mirror an opposition pack, pulling down, screwing round – and perhaps throwing the odd punch when the coach wasn't looking? Similarly, it is only a matter of time before a cricket bowling machine can be programmed to send down deliveries in the exact manner and pattern of a real bowler who has been digitally analysed and the information fed into the machine's hard disc. It won't be long before all serious horse racing abandons the haphazard tapes as a means of starting a race and adopts instead a more equable, reliable form of stall.

In the gym, too, the trend will be towards more sophisticated – and more expensive – equipment linked to electronic monitoring that provides instantaneous printouts of what is going on: calories burned, moisture expelled, power employed, and so on. All this is not far away: GPS is already used to monitor running performance and, at the time of writing, Exeter University's School of Sport and Health Sciences has just received funding to develop a SMART shoe to monitor running style, stride length, etc., for coaching feedback.[8]

Another emphasis will be on doing as little bodily damage as possible during training, perhaps installing equipment under water. And what about a space gym, where muscles can be exercised and developed without the extra loading on the joints brought about by gravity?

The question of finding ways of increasing the red blood cell count, and therefore the amount of haemoglobin available to convert to oxyhaemoglobin, is likely to remain controversial. Current techniques, such as the oxygen tent (see above), come perilously close to doping, so it is likely that significant developments in this field will be reserved, officially at least, to our fantasy Megalympics.

---

[8] For this information and for several other valuable comments, I am deeply indebted to Dr Sharon Dixon of Exeter University.

Designerthlete

Whatever developments there are with springy poles, starting stalls and the like, they are nothing compared with what is likely to happen in the medical field. The buzz phrase here is 'stem cell', so before we go any further it is perhaps useful to define terms.

Stem cells are taken from **embryos** and **directed to replace** damaged heart muscles, **spinal** columns, and tendons

Wikipedia is useful here:
http://en.wikipedia.org/wiki/Stem_cell

The human body is made up of some 300 different types of cell. Stem cells are the basic cell forms that develop into each of the specific cell types found in the body's different tissues, such as muscles, bone and nerve cells. They come in two types, embryonic and adult. Adult stem cells are found in bone marrow, for instance, and produce the continuous supply of different cells needed in the blood. Current research focuses largely on embryonic stem cells because they appear to be more flexible, although the very latest Japanese research may obviate the need to use embryos.

Would it be right for humans to **play God** in this way, perhaps even employing material from **their own eggs**?

Many who work in the medical field believe that stem cell research can lead to a revolution in medical treatment even greater than that brought about by antiseptic surgery and antibiotics. The first steps have already been taken with research on animals and with human bone marrow transplants. What follows could be far more dramatic: stem cells taken from embryos and directed to replace damaged heart muscles, spinal columns, muscles and tendons.

For athletes, the potential ramifications of this technology are staggering. A bone-crunching tackle damages Wayne Rooney's anterior cruciate ligament beyond repair . . . End of career? No way, just grow a replacement from stem cells. Instead of England's rugby hooker Steve Thompson having a broken disc in his neck replaced by an artificial one, doctors grow a new one. Playing careers are extended by years. Perhaps even more amazing, the Paralympics is phased out for lack of competitors: all those with severe physical disabilities have been made whole again by the new miracle treatment.

The 'fastest man on no legs', Oscar Pistorius, becomes the fastest man on two legs . . . Huge practical and ethical barriers remain before such a dream can become reality. Would it be right, for example, for humans to play God in this way, perhaps even employing material from their own eggs? And if it were, would it be acceptable to grow spare parts for athletes or should stem cell development be limited to the cure of illnesses such as diabetes and Parkinson's? The choice is ours.

Oscar Pistorius, the highly sprung South African athlete whose career raised important questions about the boundary between disabled and able-bodied sport.

There is, too, an even more sci-fi step in which stem cell research might take us. Cloning entire people. This takes us into the world of designer babies and *The Boys From Brazil*: a football team of 10 Maradonas and a Gordon Banks, a cricket team of five Bradmans, a Sobers, a Truman, a Godfrey Evans and two Wes Halls . . . Fanciful? Maybe today, but in 100 years' time the technology will almost certainly be available to make it a reality. Then we really will have our Megalympics.[9]

[9] See Chapter 9.

8 | Diet Plus . . .

The marathon at the 1904 St Louis Olympics was as gruelling as the event can be. The weather was hot and dry, and the race was held along rough cinder tracks. Clouds of choking dust, thrown up by motors, added to the athletes' discomfort. Indeed, the going was so tough that, after just 9 miles, the experienced New York runner Fred Lorz gave up and hitched a lift in a passing car.

British-born Tom Hicks, a resident of Cambridge, Massachusetts, was made of sterner stuff. He ran, exhausted and dehydrated, until his supporters, horrified at the way he was lurching from side to side, feared he'd collapse before he reached the finishing line.

Eager to help, a friend rushed up to Hicks with a small glass of brandy laced with strychnine. Downing it in one gulp and gesturing his thanks, the grateful runner recovered immediately and bounded off into the dust. A few miles further on, flagging again, he gulped down a second draft and once more sprang forward with chemically induced – and perfectly legal – dynamism.

Eager to help, a friend rushed up to Hicks with a small **glass of brandy laced** with **strychnine**

In Hicks' day, it was not uncommon to use strychnine as a stimulant (and as a laxative!). The normal maximum dose was just over 3 mg and patients were known to die after taking 5 mg. Hicks' fix – 2 mg plus alcohol coupled with enormous physical exertion – was extremely dangerous. Strychnine use is now banned in the UK, even for mole poisoning.

No one overtook Hicks and he finished the race in what he believed was first place. But no! Lorz, having travelled most of the course by car, had got out at the 21-mile point and then dashed to the tape ahead of his rival. Fortunately, the cheat was soon uncovered and promptly disqualified.

Hicks had won the gold. In doing so, though, he came perilously close to paying the ultimate price. Having absorbed two near-lethal doses, he passed out immediately after completing the course and remained unconscious for several hours. Nothing new about drugs in sport, it seems.

From There . . .

More Ram

Quite how those extraordinary Greeks came up with the idea is a bit of a mystery. Presumably it started when they held feasts in the period leading up to some great trial of male physical prowess – a battle, a sporting championship or even a wedding – and the guest who had previously consumed most of the delicacy performed best when the time came to act. This must have happened a few times before anyone cottoned on, connecting cause and effect, but eventually the link was made: eating ram's testicles enhanced physical prowess.

As we now know, it was all a matter of testosterone. And any athlete today who dined off testicles on toast would almost certainly test positive for an illegal performance-enhancing substance. The sportsmen of the ancient world were known to use alcohol, mushrooms and various herbs to give themselves a boost, although the results were not always efficacious. The Romans also doped their horses for chariot races.

Eating **ram's testicles** enhanced physical prowess

Not until 19th century developments in chemistry did the partnership between drugs and sport become serious. Too serious for some: as noted, small doses of strychnine may offer a temporary boost, but as little as 1 mg too much can be fatal. The Victorians also experimented with cocaine, which stimulates the central nervous system, and with ether as a way of deadening the pain attendant on extreme sporting competition. Pain-killing drugs are said to explain how bare-fisted prizefighters managed to fight on despite having suffered fractured bones. Drug-taking – famously practised by Sherlock Holmes – was not illegal and there are no statistics for the fatalities it caused. Nevertheless, it is safe to assume that the lives of a good many of our sporting ancestors were brought to abrupt and untimely ends through the use of dubious and noxious substances.

Welsh Cyclist Arthur Linton was the first athlete whose death (1886) was directly attributed to the misuse of drugs. He had overdosed on 'tri-methyl', a stimulant said to have comprised a mind-blowing (literally) combination of alcohol, strychnine, heroin, caffeine and cocaine.

Cat and Mouse

In modern times, the sport-drugs drama has mirrored the painfully predictable plot of a Tom and Jerry cartoon. The drug developers and users play the role of the sharp-witted mouse, while the keep-it-clean brigade are the well-meaning but hapless cat. As in the films, just when it looks as if Tom will triumph, Jerry comes up with a new trick to stay one step ahead.

In the years on either side of World War I, cocaine, strychnine, heroin and caffeine were the favoured poisons. However, because their employment in sport was not against the rules, it is impossible to know just how widespread use was. It was sufficiently common and worrying, however, for the IAAF to proclaim a ban on performance enhancing substances as early as 1928. In the absence of precise definitions and any testing regime, the move was no more than a well-meaning gesture.

The International Amateur Athletics Association allowed athletes to be paid for performing in 1982 but did not change its name to the International Association of Athletics Federations until 2001.

The 1930s saw the development of powerfully stimulating amphetamine tablets and, more serious, the creation of synthetic hormones, or steroids, based on testosterone. There are unsubstantiated stories of Nazi scientists experimenting with testosterone on German athletes competing in the 1936 Berlin Olympics. To begin with, experimentation with hormones, real and synthetic, was carried out for genuine medical purposes, either as a matter of pure research or as a way of combating muscle-wastage brought on by diseases such as muscular dystrophy or polio. Nevertheless, it did not take sportsmen and women long to realise the significance of what was going on and turn it to their own dubious ends.

> Synthetic derivatives of testosterone, the natural male hormone, divide into two classes: 'anabolic', meaning 'building up', and 'androgenic', meaning 'making masculine'.

An unfortunate side effect of the East v West Cold War was increased competition between the two camps in the sporting field. Success on the pitch or track was illogically heralded as demonstrating the greater worth of the politico-economic system that it represented. The drug-backed drive for medals and prestige, which ruined the health of countless athletes, began in earnest with weightlifters and spread to almost all sports where greater power brought advantage. Nowhere was the sacrifice of the individual for the benefit of the state more prevalent than in communist East Germany. Masterminded from the 1960s onwards by Manfred Ewald and Manfred Hoeppner, the systematic administration of anabolic steroids, often passed off as 'vitamin pills', enabled the athletes from a state of only 16.9 million (1973) inhabitants to become a major force in world sport. The effect of male hormones on female competitors from Eastern Europe, especially in power events, made their androgynous appearance a standing joke in the West.

In the 1976 and 1980 Olympics, East Germany's female swimmers won 11 of a possible 13 gold medals.

Finally, in 1966, football and swimming took a stand against the growing scandal and introduced compulsory testing. Following the death of amphetamine-using cyclist Tom Simpson on the slopes of Mont Ventoux, in 1968 drug testing was instigated at both the winter and summer Olympics. Other sports followed suit, some very slowly: the NFL did not have random testing for steroids until 1987. By then the cat and mouse game was well established.

The Tom Simpson monument, Mont Ventoux, France, is also a monument to irresponsible technology.

Film of the tragic death of Tom Simpson is available on YouTube (not for the fainthearted):
http://www.youtube.com/watch?v=e4viqf-qL9I

From this time onwards, the drugs in sport story developed into a sorry catalogue of accusations, denials, charges and counter-charges, of careers made and careers broken, of criminals, cheats and barefaced liars. It would be wrong to portray it as a simple fairy tale, good v evil. Victory brought those concerned honour and the celebrity of sporting stardom. But for many athletes from developing nations and poorer segments of Western societies, top-level sport was about much more than this: it was a lifeline, a precious way out of poverty, disease and depredation for their families as well as themselves. If the price was popping a few pills – hardly a great crime compared with those they saw perpetrated all around them during their childhood – so be it. If it endangered their health, then so did the poverty and alcoholism amid which so many of them had grown up. Before we rush to an oversimplified judgement, it is worth bearing such circumstances in mind.

Useful history of the efforts to get drugs out of sport on:
http://www.uksport.gov.uk/pages/history_of_drug_free_sport

Great Names, Great Disappointments

The great sport and drugs scandals of the last 30 years are too numerous to list. As one takes the roll-call, it is difficult to avoid a sense of disappointment, even of despair, that so many fine athletes had for years been lying to their colleagues and to the public at large. We feel cheated.

Ben Johnson's infamous 100 m is on YouTube:
http://www.youtube.com/watch?v=cCh5QswxQ6k&search=%26quot%3Bben%20johnson%26quot%3B

Perhaps the greatest scandal – although it hardly came as a surprise to those who had gazed in disbelief at his extraordinary musculature – was Ben Johnson's 1988 Olympic Gold and 9.79 world 100 m record. Shortly afterwards, traces of the steroid Stanozolol were found in his urine and 3 days later he was retroactively disqualified, his medal taken away and his record discounted. In his defence, he said that he had taken drugs simply to keep up with other world-class sprinters, many of whom were doing the same. At the height of his fame the previous year, he was said to have been earning almost $500,000 pm in endorsements.

 The **Tour of Shame**

Johnson shown to be right? Four of the first five runners in the Seoul 100 m subsequently tested positive for banned drugs. At the end of 2007, three of the five men who had run the 100 m in under 9.8 seconds had also tested positive for anabolic steroids.

Four years after the Ben Johnson affair, Maradona, considered by many at the time to be the world's greatest playing footballer, tested positive for the stimulant ephedrine and was sent home from the World Cup in disgrace. In another 4 years – strange how major drug scandals were following the Olympics in a 4-year cycle – it was the turn of the Tour de France. Following the arrest of a masseur found to have over 400 doping products in his car, searches, tests and protest withdrawals meant that 'the Tour of Shame' was left with only 14 teams of the original 21. The number of riders had been almost halved, down from 189 to 100.

The tragic death 2 months later of world record holder Florence Griffiths-Joyner at the age of 38 only added to suspicion that the world of sport was awash with illegal and dangerous substances. In 1988, 'Flo-Jo', as she was popularly known, had set remarkable new world records for the 100 m and 200 m. Both still stand and are unlikely ever to be broken. She always denied taking drugs and put down

More than a wee problem – urine samples taken at the 2000 Sydney Olympics.

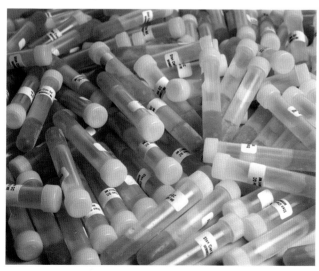

the notable change in her physique to special training. Not everyone believed her and those who worked with her have subsequently confessed to giving her performance-enhancing substances. Nor were all Britons wholly convinced when sprinter Linford Christie and tennis player Greg Rusedski explained their positive tests for the steroid nandrolone as the result, respectively, of the body's natural overproduction and officially sanctioned supplements.

▌▌ One of the reasons why **doping** can be so **corrosive of sport** is that it leaves audiences not knowing **what** to **believe** ▌▌[1]

Lying and Forgetting

Our brief map of the troubled road to the present ends with two singular and contrasting cases. The first is that of Marion Jones, the outstanding woman sprinter who added three golds and two bronzes from the Sydney Olympics to the three golds and a bronze she had gained at earlier World Championships. In her book *Marion Jones, Life in the Fast Lane*, she stated categorically, 'I am against performance-enhancing drugs. I have never taken them and I never will.'

Able to come up with such a staggeringly blatant terminological inexactitude, Jones should consider going into politics – when she is free to do so. In October 2007, she confessed before a shocked US court that she had taken the designer steroid known as 'Clear' before the 2000 Olympics, adding pathetically, 'I have let my country down, and I have let myself down.' Sadly, it was the confession rather than the fact that she had taken drugs that caused the greatest surprise and she was given a 6-month prison sentence for lying to investigators.

[1] David Owen, *FT Magazine*, 3/4 February 2007.

> ** I am **against** performance-enhancing **drugs**. I have **never taken them** and I never will. **

Equally unsettling was the case of the British 400 m runner Christine Ohuruogu. After missing three consecutive drug tests, she was banned from competitive running for a year. Then, after she had returned to win her event in the 2007 World Championships, the British Olympics Association (BOA) overturned the lifetime ban on Olympic participation it had given her, freeing her to run for Britain in the 2008 Beijing Games.

Fair enough, probably. Ohuruogu appeared an intelligent (if absent-minded), articulate and honest citizen, and her excuses for missing the tests seemed plausible enough. But what if . . . ? I cannot have been the only person feeling a little uneasy about the BOA's leniency only weeks after Marion Jones' confession.

. . . To Where We Are Now

Eliminating Doping?

'Athletes today must either give up their dream . . . or use performance-enhancing substances.'
– Victor Conte, former drugs supplier (BBC Radio 5 Live, 2007)

The independent World Anti-Doping Agency (WADA), established in 1999 after the previous year's Tour de France fiasco, has the stated aim of 'eliminating all doping from sport'. So where has it got to?

In optimistic mood, one might point to the statement from the International Rugby Board (IRB) after the 2007 Rugby World Cup that during the 7-week tournament, 212 drug tests were conducted and not one of them provided a positive result. Pretty hefty blokes those rugby players, but if they've got like that with weights and milkshakes, then well done them.

The mood might darken a little if one turned to the IRB's small print. This stated that the samples collected were being stored in WADA's Paris laboratory until an effective test for human growth hormone (HGH) became available. In other words, the World Cup sportsmen had not been tested for one of the most powerful muscle-builders.

During Operation Raw Deal, the US DEA made 124 arrests, shut down 56 illegal laboratories in 27 states and seized 240 kg (530 lbs) of raw steroid powder.

Gloomier still was the fact that, even while the World Cup was being played, on the other side of the Atlantic, the US Drug Enforcement Agency (DEA) was announcing the first results of its Operation Raw Deal against the illegal industry that manufactured and traded in steroids, HGH and other performance-enhancing drugs. Apart from frightening statistics revealing the prevalence of drug manufacture and use, other depressing pieces of information became common currency:

- Huge quantities of steroids were being imported into the USA from China.
- There were at least four steroids undetectable by WADA tests.
- Pessimists reckoned that by the time of the Beijing Olympics, there would be around 100 undetectable performance-enhancing drugs available to athletes.

If you are reading this with one eye on the pictures beaming in from a major sporting event, I hope it doesn't spoil the show too much. A victory is a victory, after all. And the athlete's joy will still be genuine, even if the performance has not quite been.

The steroid testosterone – use or lose? Illicit drug use, often rendered undetectable by the use of masking agents, has seriously damaged the image of athletics worldwide.

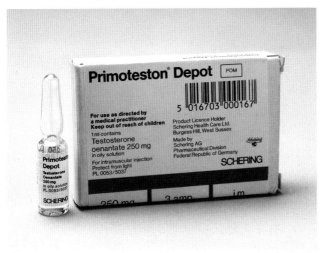

What They Take – and Its Effects

What follows is a brief summary of some of the main performance-enhancing substance groups and practices currently found in sport. The list is by no means exhaustive and is growing all the time.

Acronyms used: POM = prescription-only medicine (but often available over the internet); OTC = available over the counter; CD = controlled drug listed according to the British Misuse of Drugs Act (other countries have similar legislation).

The full WADA 2008 prohibited list can be found on:
http://www.wada-ama.org/rtecontent/document/2008_List_En.pdf

Supplements

The range of so-called sports supplements being marketed is stupendously wide – and equally worrying. The advertising blurb, coming under ridiculous trade names and deliberately complex pseudo-scientific jargon – offers unbelievable advantages. One powder, such claims run, will build muscle, power, strength, endurance and resistance to fatigue, while also improving blood flow and enhancing focus, mood, energy levels, alertness and even motivation . . . and all for a few quid!

An excellent guide to the supplement scandal can be found on
http://www.quackwatch.org/index.html

251

diet plus . . .

Eat me! Like Alice's cake in Wonderland, inviting supplements offer magical growth.

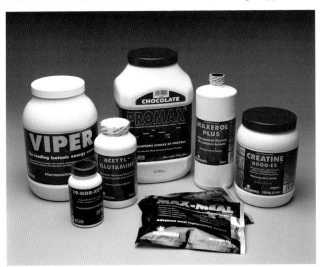

The contents of such quack-boxes range from creatine ('nature's muscle-builder') to steroids, herbal products (such as the potentially fatal ephedra), vitamins, minerals, amino acids, caffeine, whey protein, amino acids, appetite suppressants, aphrodisiacs (e.g. 'Yohimbe HCL' – said to be collected, no doubt with great difficulty and at huge expense, from the dried bark of Corynanthe Johimbe trees found only in the southern Cameroons and the Congo!) . . . and so on and so forth.

Many supplements are misleadingly and irresponsibly advertised. A few may benefit athletes, but only at prices many times higher than everyday products with similar characteristics. Some are virtually useless, while many verge on the downright dangerous. Across the industry quality control, especially with regard to cross-contamination, is poor. A number of athletes testing positive for the banned steroid nandrolone, for example, had ingested it in supplements that did not list it among the ingredients.

'UK athletes are advised to be extremely cautious about the use of any supplements.' – UK Sport

Turn-on or turn-off? Drug-induced musculature is marketed as attractive, as well as performance-enhancing.

©ISTOCKPHOTO.COM/CHANG

Stimulants

What: Amphetamines, cocaine, ephedrine (in heavy concentrations), strychnine, modafinil and dozens of others, but not caffeine.
Status: Definitely CD, therefore most POMs – but ephedrine can be a constituent of nasal sprays, so OTC.
How administered: Tablet and other forms.
Effect on athletes: Increased heartbeat, alertness and energy levels; amphetamines can help build muscle mass.
Side effects include: Hyperactivity, nausea, headaches, tremor, heart and sexual problems and paranoia. Users may even die.
Testing: Most can be successfully tested for, explaining their declining use in recent years.

Narcotic Analgesics

What: Heroin, methadone, morphine, pethidine and others.
Status: Not all are CD. Some lower-strength morphine solutions are POMs.
How administered: Usually injected but there are oral preparations.
Effect on athletes: Small doses allow training and performance though the 'pain barrier'.
Side effects include: Addiction, nausea, drowsiness and possible death.
Testing: Reliable tests are widely available.

Diuretics

What: Acetazolamide, amiloride, bumetanide, chlorthalidone, etacrynic acid, indapamide, metolazone, thiazides and others.

Status: Most POMs. Some diuretics OTC and a wide range available online.

How administered: Tablet, injection.

Effect on athletes: Increases urine production so used by those (e.g. boxers, jockeys) who need to lose weight quickly. By flushing out the body, they may also be used to get rid of the residual effects of other drugs, thus acting as masking agents.

Side effects include: Dehydration producing headaches, heart and kidney disease, collapse.

Testing: Usually picked up.

Anabolic Agents (Steroids)

What: The vast WADA list of naturally occurring and laboratory-made compounds ranges from androstane to zilpaterol, taking in clenbuterol, DHEA, nandrolone, stanozolol, testosterone and THG on the way. More appear every month.

Status: Some POMs, others not. Many produced in illegal laboratories. Widely available online.

Side **effects** include: (male) **kidney damage**, breast **enlargement**, baldness, **shrinking of testicles** and sexual problems, **acne**; (female) **facial hair**, **deepening of voice**, irregular periods, **acne**

How administered: Injections, tablets, creams, drops, capsules, chewing gum – you name it. Sometimes used in conjunction with insulin injections (see below).

Effect on athletes: Can increase aggression as well as muscle size, strength and power.

Side effects include: (male) kidney damage, breast enlargement, baldness, shrinking of testicles and sexual problems, acne; (female) facial hair, deepening of voice, irregular periods, acne.

Testing: New drugs appear as quickly as tests are developed for the old ones. Many athletes are caught but there are strong suspicions that even more escape unpunished.

Note: The WADA ban also covers asthma-treatment drugs known as 'Beta-2 agonists' which may have anabolic (organ- and tissue-building) properties.

> DHEA and THG are the common acronyms for dehydroepiandrosterone and tetrahydrogestrinone.

Blood Doping

What: Removing a litre or so of blood from an athlete's body and freezing it. It is then reintroduced just before the event when the body has made good the deficiency.

Status: Illegal in many countries.

How administered: The blood is injected back into the athlete's body, not necessarily in sterile conditions.

Effect on athletes: Boosts red blood cell count, allowing more oxygen to be carried around the body. This increases aerobic capacity and muscle endurance.

Side effects include: Rise in blood pressure and risk of infection.

Testing: An abnormally high red blood cell count can be detected with a blood test.

Note: The WADA ban also covers any other means of 'artificially enhancing the uptake, transport or delivery of oxygen' by the use of chemicals or blood substitutes.

Certain substances are banned in specific sports only: alcohol in archery (!), for example, and beta-blockers in billiards.

Hormones and Related Substances

Hormones are complex chemical compounds that carry messages around the body to tissue and organs. For some time, doctors have realised that hormone imbalance is the cause of many diseases (such as diabetes) and that stimulating hormone production can also help treat the symptoms of other conditions (such as anaemia). Sadly, the same technology is also used to stimulate the body to behave in unusual ways; it can also be employed to deaden normal reactions. This, of course, is where doping comes in.

The manipulation of hormones is a perilous business but in sport, as we have seen, the rewards are such that many athletes and scientists are prepared to take the risk. Using the WADA classification as a guide, the subject may be considered under three headings:

Erythropoietin (EPO)

What: A synthetically produced version of the kidney hormone that stimulates red blood cell production.

Status: POM (for kidney failure). Expensive.

How administered: Injection.

Effect on athletes: Boosts red blood cell count, allowing more oxygen to be carried around the body. This improves aerobic capacity and muscle endurance.

Side effects include: Thickening of the blood, increasing the risk of heart attack.

Testing: Tests now pick up EPO use.

Human Growth Hormone (HGH)

What: The pituitary gland hormone, sometimes harvested from cadavers, that stimulates growth of muscle, cartilage, bone and tendons. There are also (often safer) synthetic versions.

Status: Specialist POM.

How administered: Injection.

> **❚❚** The test for HGH we have is **imperfect** and it's probable that **an awful lot of people** who appear to be negative are in fact **doping ❚❚**

Effect on athletes: Increases muscles, builds up cartilage and tendons, reduces fat, and speeds up recovery from strenuous exercise and injury.

Side effects include: Swelling of soft tissue, sweating, raised blood pressure, abnormal bone growth, enlarged internal organs that can lead to their failure; linked to diabetes. Injecting HGH may even explain cases of CJD (Mad Cow Disease) which is passed on via infected material. In 2007, the University of Queensland, Australia, announced a possible link between HGH and certain cancers.

Testing: No reliable test yet (January 2008). 'The test [for HGH] we have is imperfect and it's probable that an awful lot of people who appear to be negative are in fact doping.'[2]

Also in the WADA ban are (a) insulins, (b) corticotrophins that stimulate adrenalin production and (c) anabolic gonadotrophins (banned for men only).

Hormone Antagonists and Modulators

What: Products such as anastrozole that counteract the behaviour of naturally produced hormones, like oestrogen and myostatin, which can inhibit the development of a sporting body.

Status: POMs.

How administered: Injection.

Effect on athletes: Greater muscle bulk.

Side effects include: Uncertain but certainly include tiredness, nausea, hair thinning and rashes.

Testing: Unsure.

[2] Prof. Peter Sonksen, world drugs expert from St Thomas' Hospital, London, on BBC Radio in November 2007.

Masking Agents

What: Drugs like epitestosterone and dextran used to disguise the presence of performance-enhancing substances in the body. Diuretics (see above) are the best-known.

Status: POMs (widely used in operating departments).

How administered: Normally tablet.

Effect on athletes: Reduces chance of doping being detected.

Side effects include: Dehydration, headaches, nausea, pain in joints and stomach.

Testing: By definition extremely difficult.

Gene Doping

'The non-therapeutic use of cells, genes, genetic elements, or of the modulation of gene expression, having the capacity to enhance athletic performance, is prohibited.' – WADA, 2008

What: Already touched upon in the previous chapter, this is the process of transplanting a hormone- or protein-producing gene rather than the substance itself. Legally experimented upon successfully with mice, we cannot be sure that it has been tried on humans yet. Circumstantial evidence gained in Germany, however, suggests that it has.

Status: Illegal.

How administered: Injection.

Effect on athletes: Whatever Frankenstein wishes.

Side effects include: The technology is wholly experimental – anything might happen.

Testing: Nothing yet developed.

> UCL Professor Geoffrey Goldspink's experiments with Mechano Growth Factor (MGF) have led to injected mice gaining an extra 25% of muscle bulk in just 3 weeks.

Testing

In the end, the efficacy of an anti-doping programme stands or falls on the quality of its testing. Each nation adopts its own rules and practices, as we saw with the state-sponsored doping practised by the East Germans in the decades before the collapse of communism. Even today, of the 200 states that compete in the summer Olympics, only around 25 have independent anti-doping organisations. Each sport has its own regulations, too, some clearly more rigorous than others.[3] Moreover, athletes are prepared to go to extraordinary lengths to avoid detection. Stories abound. Missing tests are the most common. Others are far more spicy, telling of athletes having their coaches' 'clean' urine injected into their bladders, of women athletes hiding whisky-filled condoms in their vaginas in order to provide urine samples so high in alcohol that they are invalid, and even of 'enemy' agents doping a competitor's toothpaste so they test positive.

---

[3] Those wishing to take this further might like to compare the NFL's list of banned substances, found on http://www.nflpa.org/pdfs/RulesAndRegs/ProhibitedSubstances.pdf, with the WADA equivalent on http://www.wada-ama.org/rtecontent/document/2008_List_En.pdf

Over half of all **athletes** would be **prepared to take a pill** that guaranteed Olympic gold even though it **would kill them** within a year

Apart from the occasional positive test or a confession by a conscience-stricken individual, there is no way of telling the extent of drug abuse. The worldwide trade in HGH is rumoured to be around $600 million, that in steroids probably twice as great.[4] Top sportsmen and women themselves believe doping to be rife. Several surveys have shown that they reckon at least 50% of their competitors take performance-enhancing substances. In support of this, one poll revealed that over half of all athletes would be prepared to take a pill that guaranteed Olympic gold even though it would kill them within a year.[5]

WADA, the one worldwide testing body, prohibits all 'chemical and physical manipulation' of samples taken, explaining further that '*Tampering*, or attempting to tamper, in order to alter the integrity and validity of *Samples* collected during *Doping Controls* is prohibited' (WADA regulations, 2008). Nevertheless, each test is only as good as the tester. Doping officials are as susceptible to human error as the rest of us. Moreover, taking home a fraction of the wealth earned by the athletes they are asked to test, they are obvious targets for bribery or even intimidation.

'*Tampering, or attempting to tamper, in order to alter the integrity and validity of Samples collected*

[4] http://scienceofsport.blogspot.com, 29 October 2007.
[5] *FT Magazine*, 3/4 February 2007.

during Doping Controls is prohibited.'
– WADA, 2008

Then there's the question of overall budgets. Sport is very, very big business. The 2012 Olympics is expected to cost Britain at least £9 billion (over $17 billion). Manchester United is valued at $1.2 billion. Tiger Woods may earn as much as $100 million in a single year. In 2006, F1 racing driver Fernando Alonso pocketed $35 million and David Beckham around $30 million. The big names in the mega sports – NFL, NBL, MLB and European football – are all comfortably millionaires. Even in less opulent sports such as track and field, rugby and cricket, it is possible for those at the top to earn millions.

The paymasters – audiences, spectators and sponsors – prefer success over honesty

Compare those figures with these: In 2006, the last year for which the figures were available at the time of writing, the total budget of WADA, the world's leading anti-doping authority, was around $26 million – yes, that's one quarter of the earnings of a single sportsman, Tiger Woods. Admittedly the WADA figure is only a fraction of the worldwide total spent on anti-doping measurers, but it is a fair indication of why modern sport is in such a pickle over doping. What's more, WADA conducts no more than few hundred tests per annum.

Led by the widely respected former US Senator George Mitchell, a 2007 investigation into drug use in the MLB revealed widespread use of steroids and HGH by the sport's 'All-Stars'.

It's simple: when it comes to drugs in sport, the forces of law and order are hopelessly outgunned by the bandits; or, to put it more bluntly, the paymasters – audiences, spectators and sponsors – prefer success over honesty. Never was this more apparent than in interviews conducted with members of the American public following the 2007 MLB drug scandal: a fair proportion of those questioned said they could not care less whether the players took drugs or not as long as they performed well. Until such attitudes change, drug-taking will remain an embedded feature of modern sport.

> For reasons that are not entirely clear, in 2008 alcohol was removed from the list of substances banned for boules players. Merci WADA!

What Next?

The Choices

The future of drugs in sport is in our own hands. The choices are simple:

(1) Continue as we are, muddling along one step behind the dopers, wringing our hands in virtuous despair.
(2) Find the necessary resources to guarantee that all professional sport is drug-free.
(3) Accept that the battle against drugs cannot be won and make every effort to ensure that doping is above-board and safe.

'Saying we should ban drugs in sport because they improve performance is like saying we should ban alcohol at parties.' – Oxford Professor Julian Savulescu (Observer Sport Magazine, *February 2007)*

Taking each option in turn, let's see where it might leave us in around 50 years' time.

Continue as We Are

This is probably the worst option. Sadly, it is also the most likely. What would it mean for sport in the second half of the present century? If present trends continue, it looks as if testing will eventually be able to eliminate most of the booster substances added to the human body by injection or ingestion. That would end the use of HGH, steroids, EPO and so forth. Problem solved? No way.

The real challenge in the years ahead lies not in what chemicals we add to our bodies but what chemicals we enable them to make for themselves. This is gene doping. Two questions come to mind. One: Surely it will be obvious what's going on when a shot-putter, say, turns up at the Olympics with post-spinach Popeye arms the same size as their legs? Of course. But what if the doper is more subtle, increasing the muscle bulk by just 8%, enough to bring victory but not quite enough to make the intervention obvious? Two: Won't testers be able to find the genetically modified cells that are causing all the rumpus? Not necessarily. They don't have to be placed where such material would occur naturally – testosterone-producing material in the testes, for example – but hidden elsewhere in the body.

The real **challenge in the years ahead** lies not in what chemicals **we add to our bodies** but what chemicals we enable them **to make for themselves**

There is a possibility that failure to detect gene doping will bring the whole testing process into disrepute, leading to the collapse of the WADA. Each sport would then regulate and police itself. Standards would vary between sports and perhaps even between different venues within the same sport. Such doping anarchy might so disillusion the consumers – the paying crowds and TV audiences – that they begin to switch off. In this case, the second of our future scenarios might develop.

Do Everything Necessary to Eliminate Doping

WADA evolved from the 1998 Tour de France drugs scandal. It was born not out of moral outrage but of commercial necessity. Consumers were simply losing interest in the package – live and in the media – that cycling was offering. There was talk of cancelling the Tour, a move that would have cost millions.

What if there were a drug scandal of similar proportions at the Beijing, London or a later Olympic Games? With world records falling like confetti, crowds grow restless, TV viewers switch off, sponsors withdraw their cash . . . The whole system is in danger of collapse.

Then, when things are at their worst, into the dismal black hole rides a white knight media consortium guaranteeing a 'clean Olympics'. At first there is scepticism – haven't we heard all this before? But when the competition is razor sharp and performances realistic, confidence returns and with it the money. The sport is saved.

'You want to beat people who are dirty to prove it's not worth cheating.' – Kelly Sotherton, World Athletics Championships heptathlon bronze medal winner, 2007. Will such honourable attitudes soon be outmoded?

This is not an unrealistic scenario. But for the Clean Sport initiative to materialise, systems would have to be in place to make sure that what was on offer really was whiter than white.[6]

(A) The first requirement would be money. To get the best in a commercial world you must pay the most, so the anti-doping regime needs to employ the best scientists, the best officials, and operate the tightest, most carefully scrutinised systems. These are funded by a levy on all money changing hands in the sport industry – on salaries, transfer fees, ticket sales, media contracts, sponsorship payments, etc. No payment, no entry into a validated competition.

The rate of anti-doping levy would be determined and levied like a sort of international VAT, perhaps called the Anti-Doping Tax or ADT.

[6] Ideas along the lines of what follows have also been put forward by Victor Conte, the one-time boss of a San Francisco company (Balco) that manufactured and sold undetectable steroids.

(B) The second requirement for guaranteed sporting cleanliness is comprehensive and thoroughly credible testing. All athletes must agree to whatever testing regime is required and the tests must be based on the very best scientific research and advice. Following the same principal as that which puts judges among the top earners, thereby attracting the finest brains and reducing the temptation of corruption, so it is essential that all those working in the anti-doping sector are generously rewarded.

Random tests are useless. As long as there is a chance of getting away with it, there will always be athletes prepared to risk their luck and cheat. To counteract this, testing must be regular and universal. For example, all players wishing to play in a football world cup need to be registered by their national association and tested fortnightly, or even weekly, for 6 months before the competition. As a precaution, doped athletes – well rewarded, of course – will be slipped unannounced into the system to make sure that their particular drug or practice is being picked up in the testing.

(C) Finally, it will be obligatory in the weeks prior to a major competition for all competitors to be installed in safe environments where they can be monitored and shielded from outside influences. Something similar happened in ancient Greece, where all athletes assembled near Olympia several weeks before the games began. As many of today's teams go into pre-tournament training camps anyway, involving the anti-doping authorities in such camps will not involve too much upheaval. All of this may appear too draconian and athletes themselves might rebel against it. Do we really want a 1984-style sporting world?

There is also the possibility that a rival, untested sports circuit might be launched, either carrying on from the bad old days before the Clean Sport initiative or starting up as a rival. This harks back to the Megalympics idea floated in the last chapter, championships of superhuman sportsmen and women performing at levels way beyond those currently achieved . . . 100 m in 8.9 seconds, gigantic rugby players powering into each other with thunderous crashes that shake the stands, bowlers pinging down deliveries at 130 mph, strikers dribbling like supercharged George Bests before sending shots sizzling into the net from the centre circle. Wow! The appeal of this computer game stuff, featured in Chapter 9, would be very hard to resist.

Legalise Doping

'I think Ben Johnson's 'victory' in the men's 100 meters at the 1988 Seoul Olympics is just about the most exciting 10 seconds of sport I have ever witnessed.' – David Owen (FT.com, 10 February 2006)

This is where the passions get really stirred. As with recreational drugs, if we can't prevent the use of performance-enhancing substances and practices in sport, why not take the radical but rational step of legalising them?

The arguments against are well known:

The Corinthian Position

'Play up, play and play the game!' In other words, sport is more about taking part than winning. Legalising drugs distorts the true picture by putting an exaggerated emphasis on victory. This deters those who might otherwise play for fun and to improve their general well-being. Eventually, the health of an entire nation deteriorates.

The Sporting Spirit

Sporting success is about rewarding unique combinations of talent and hard work. Drug-taking, therefore, distorts the true 'spirit of sport'.

Danger

Doping puts the human body under strains it is not designed for, leading to mental and physical breakdown. Professional athletes might have access to a reasonable level of advice and care, but most amateurs do not. The consequences of legalising doping, therefore, could be catastrophic. Moreover, the long-term effects of many practices, such as gene doping, are unknown. Limiting drug-taking to known, safe substances is no answer: it merely reintroduces the question of cheating and testing by another door. Besides, who would determine which substances were safe and which harmful? Testing for health not drugs, as some suggest, is a non-starter.

Lawlessness

Allowing drugs in sport promotes drug-taking in general, bringing into disrepute both the law and government-sponsored health programmes. Also, could a ban on the advertising of drugs like tobacco and alcohol at sporting venues be upheld if the athletes themselves were taking drugs?

The arguments on the other side are equally impressive:

Play up, **play and play** the **game**!

The Best

All sport lovers want to see the best possible performances. That is why Premiership matches attract larger crowds than Division Three games, and why a race in which there is a chance of a new world record will always attract more viewers than one that does not. As performance-enhancing substances produce better sport – enhanced strength, speed and skill – then dish them out!

**As good as it gets . . . Top-class women's football, Arsenal v Charlton Athletic.
Would the sport really be more entertaining if players' performances were artificially enhanced?**

©ACTION IMAGES/ANDREW COULDRIDGE

Blurred Boundaries

When should something that enhances performance be outlawed? Do we ban altitude training and hypoxic tents because they're available only to the well off? Do we make personalised clothing and equipment illegal? When does a supplement or a food become unfairly performance-enhancing? A while ago caffeine was an illegal substance and athletes were penalised for taking it. Now it is back on the permitted list, should the confiscated awards of coffee addicts be returned?

Safer

The present regime, which drives drug manufacture and drug-taking underground, only encourages the backyard production of shoddily made, impure and potentially dangerous substances. If the process were legal, it could be regulated and therefore made safe. Besides, many substances currently banned, some

Grey areas . . . Where's the boundary between a normal diet and a performance-enhancing substance when an innocent latte may be listed as both?

steroids for instance, are known to be harmless. It is widely reported that the present regime favours not the best sportsmen and women but those with the best chemists and lawyers.

Fairer

For example, the use of EPO (see above) would enable all athletes to compete on equal terms with those who lived or trained at altitude.

Old-Fashioned

Railing against drug-taking is a hangover from the old amateur days when athletes were (in theory) jolly good chaps who played games for fun and blackballed cheats for being 'not quite decent'. That sort of thinking should have died out with the officer class that walked to its death on the Somme on 1 July 1916.

Pragmatism

We have neither the technology, the money nor the inclination to test effectively for illicit drugs, so why bother? The current regime puts a ridiculously unfair burden on athletes, too. Consequently, as we normally catch only the stupid or the unlucky, it would be much better to stop the sanctimonious whining and let people get on with it. Ok, so a few might die. Sad, but we don't ban alcohol because some choose to drink themselves to death.

Paternalism

Our lives are over-regulated. The nanny-state and nanny-authorities should get off our backs and let us decide how we wish to lead our lives. Every adult should be free to decide whether they want to wear a car seat belt or not, whether they want to overeat or drink, and whether or not they want to take performance-enhancing drugs.

I guarantee this will not be providing the best sport

So there we have it, the three options: maintain the status quo, tighten up, or relax and go with the flow. As I have already intimated, I expect that in 2050 we'll still be operating under Option One, wrestling with our consciences, writs and test tubes. Sadly, though, I guarantee this will not be providing the best sport.

II Into the Unknown . . .

9 The Games We Will Play . . .

C. 2080

This is the crystal ball section. Building on the information from the first part of the book, I will suggest where our major sports may be in around 75 years from now, focusing on 10 of them. This is a fun exercise, of course – but perhaps also useful in that it may help us decide which paths we want our sporting future to take.

Unless, like Nostradamus, one takes refuge behind a veil of ludicrous mysterious-ness, predicting the future is fraught with difficulties. We cannot tell what wonders technology will have dreamed up, nor what horrors. Equally uncertain is what the world's political, economic and environmental state will be as we near the end of the 21st century. For the purposes of this chapter, therefore, I have had to make four crude but necessary bands of assumption. First, that technology will continue to develop along existing lines. Second, that the international political situation will remain roughly as now. This means that world organisation will be based on the nation state, with power shared and disputed between national and international bodies; that some peoples will have a say in their own government while others will be without this dubious privilege; that we will somehow have avoided a conflagration on the scale of a Third World War.

We cannot tell what wonders technology will have dreamed up, nor what horrors

Third, that the global economic system will stay essentially the same. There will still be a wide gulf – perhaps even wider than today – between the developed and the developing nations, and, despite periods of recession and dislocation brought about by overpopulation, shortage of resources and environmental change, the standards of living in the developed world will not have fallen much below those enjoyed today.

Sydney's Telstra Stadium. As TV coverage becomes more sophisticated, may it be necessary to pay spectators to fill such venues?

Fourth, that climate change will have continued at the level currently predicted by moderates. In other words, although by 2080 the mean global temperature may have risen by 3°C, the situation will be under control and further rise expected to be minimal.

Tele-games

Because élite sport is where the most significant changes are likely to be seen, it is at Cup Finals, Olympic Games and World Championships that our time machine will land, not on humble village greens – or 'browns' as they will probably be by then. We will also avoid what might be termed 'silly' options that would lead to sport becoming akin to *Jeux Sans Frontières*. This does not mean, however, that sports will stay much as they are or that they will retain their current popularity ranking.

Technology's biggest sporting impact over the last 75 years has not been on the games themselves but on our ability to broadcast them way beyond the place where they are happening. Of the many important effects this has had, I here offer just three and speculate on how they may develop.

One

Many professional sporting bodies are funded as much by fees from the broadcast media as from gate receipts. As travel costs increase, this trend will continue. Indeed, it may be possible that stadiums themselves will become redundant because spectators will be virtually rather than physically present. Or will we have to pay crowds with cash or other incentives to attend in order to provide a match atmosphere for the viewers sitting comfortably back home?

We can take for granted the rapid development of virtual games presented within multi-modal sensory helmets, etc. Over time, the experience they offer may well become so intoxicating that actual physical exercise, with all its attendant hassle and discomfort, will become ever more unfashionable. Indeed, may not today's obesity epidemic among the young be a sign that the process has already started?

Two

Sports have been obliged to adapt to suit their paymasters. While American football and baseball have done this for years, it is beginning to come in on this side of the pond with, for example, football referees waiting for TV clearance before starting a game and the extended half-times in rugby. Again, this change will be maintained. The French already show advertisements during a rugby game and it is but a short step between this and having carefully arranged commercial breaks in matches. In today's game, for example, plenty of time is lost while players walk to a line-out. Why not formalise this situation as a commercial break? Football will be more resistant – until it sees the size of the cheque. Thus, it will be only a matter of time before Premier League matches kick off at 9 a.m. to suit the hundreds of millions gathered around their screens in India and China. In such circumstances, we may well find English early-risers earning £20 by going to a football match and bawling their heads off before the TV cameras. Lens-fodder or fans?

Three

New, media-orientated sports have emerged. Apart from novelty-type events such as Gladiators, the best known are 'professional' wrestling and the newer, no-holds-barred Ultimate Fighting Championship (UFC). The latter may well represent an important strand of future development. Let me explain.

Technology has been widely employed to make sporting activity safer. The most obvious example is motorsport, especially F1, where fatal accidents are now rare. Although less dramatic, safety technology's impact has been important in other areas, too. Mouthguards have saved countless teeth and gums, elaborate headguards protect amateur boxers and many rugby players, and hockey goalies and American Football players now resemble more closely characters from *Star Wars* than athletes.

Perfect surfaces, padded players, falling injury rates . . . isn't it all getting a bit anodyne? Don't we want something a bit edgier, a bit less predictable, even a bit more violent? This may well become a trend in future sport – a sort of reverse-technology producing 'green' cricket wickets where the ball does unpredictable things, golf courses with unfair fairways and, most likely of all, genuinely dangerous sports.

To see what UFC is all about, try:
http://www.ufc.com

Welcome to the world of cage fighting, the blood-and-guts amalgam of boxing and wrestling of which America's UFC is currently a leading exponent. As anyone who has watched this barbaric sport live or on screen must admit, the morality of such 'entertainment' is pretty dubious. On the other hand, it is only cashing in on the instinct that makes us crane our necks as we pass an accident on the highway and the fact that the 'highlights' of a motor race will always show a smash, prefer-

Why else were **public** executions so **popular**?

ably one in which cars somersault like gymnasts over the track. Shaming though it may be, we have to admit that many human beings like watching violence. Why else were public executions so popular?

Safety first – does our current obsession with safety, personified in this super-padded field hockey goalie, detract from the animal thrill of sporting contest?

Blood lust – the Ultimate Fighting Championship seeks to restore to the sporting world some of the more basic appeal lost in the age of health and safety.

Cage fighting carries uncanny overtones of the movie *Rollerball* (Norman Jewison, 1975) which depicted an ultra-violent sport in a world controlled by giant corporations.

Sporting Spectacular

The developments mentioned above boil down to one thing: the continued blurring of the divide between the sporting and the entertainment industries. Undoubtedly, as long as our economies hold up, this will develop further over the coming years. In pessimistic mood, it is tempting to draw parallels with the declining Roman Empire, when the masses were kept happy with 'bread and circuses'. As our Western civilisation declines, to be replaced by something more vigorous, so our leaders will feed us with increasingly freakish entertainment masquerading as sport.

> The tendency towards the promotion of 'tabloid values' in sport was excellently analysed by Richard Williams in a *Guardian* article (11 December 2007) that labelled England the 'land of hype and glory'.

We in Britain had a glimpse of this when the NFL, with all its ballyhoo and razzmatazz, came to London in the autumn of 2007. So far our home-grown product has made only lukewarm efforts to emulate such transatlantic shows: the best we can do is usually a bit of banal singing, shivering dancing girls with frozen smiles and fireworks that leave the first minutes of a match invisible behind a pall of smoke. But these are early days. Acts will get slicker and the trivia that sand-

Hotpants and candyfloss: like it or loathe it, the future of top level sport lies with the global entertainment industry.

The acceptable face of technology: an athlete being measured on a force plate, Exeter University

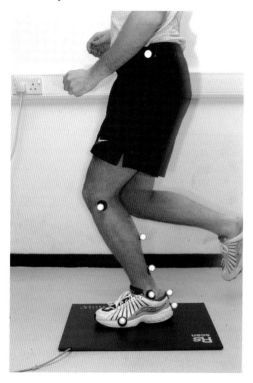

wiches the game will become thicker and thicker until the match itself becomes indistinguishable from the sugary spin of candyfloss surrounding it.

Heroes in the **public eye** yet in reality no more than **puppets** of the **media moguls** who pull the gilded strings

Packaged games of all sorts – football, rugby, cricket, tennis – will become increasingly fragmented, allowing time for analysis of fiendishly complex game plans, toilet breaks, meal interludes and commercial promotion. The players themselves, designed, even created or recreated in player farms for a required sporting role, will be a breed apart: heroes in the public eye yet in reality no more than puppets of the media moguls who pull the gilded strings.

Good Technology

None of the above is inevitable. Technology is our tool, doing only what we direct it to do. There is every possibility that, rather than separating the élite from the rest, technology may do the opposite. Cheap yet high-quality balls, rackets, boots, bats and other items may enable enthusiastic amateurs to raise their game to new heights. Artificial pitches are cheaper to maintain than real ones, making them an attractive alternative for the developing world.

There is every possibility, too, that technology will be employed to solve the very problems it has created. Take the drugs issue, for example. The crude 'sample' will soon be a thing of the past. Within 50 years it will be possible to monitor athletes electronically using an implanted chip and remotely recording on a central database every significant change in their body chemistry. Too much too fast, and they're out. Would this be an unfair intrusion into their personal privacy? No, not if they were seeking to win fame and fortune from the public. And if they resent the chip under the skin, there's one simple answer – back to the 9–5 job.

Within 50 years it will be **possible** to monitor athletes electronically using an **implanted chip** and remotely recording on a central database every significant **change in their body chemistry**

The sensible deployment of technology will make fallible human judgement redundant, too. Professional sport will be refereed by computer programs capable of ruling on all basic issues, such as offside in football, forward passes in rugby and LBW in cricket. The more sophisticated software will also be able to handle issues of foul play, although a live referee will be needed to defuse flare-ups and control abusive language. Scary? Why, all that is happening is the replacement of a flawed judgement system with a better model. Elementary technological development.

Backlash

Wikipedia offers a neat introduction to the concept of street hockey:
http://en.wikipedia.org/wiki/Road_hockey

Finally, there is the possibility of a popular backlash against the high-tech world of media-driven super sport. New environments may breed different low-tech sports, street hockey being a good example. Fed up with overpriced, faceless superclubs, fans may turn back to their vastly cheaper, more 'real' local alternatives where the goalie has a hangover, the pitch slopes alarmingly towards the duck pond and the stand is no more than a few pallets nicked from the nearby builder's yard.

Here, with its camaraderie and humour, valour and cowardice spiced with an outrageous element of chance, sport rediscovers its roots as an essentially human recreation undertaken primarily for amusement – for no more than a bit of fun.

Review of Sporting Technology, 2080

Football – The 209th FA Cup Final

The sections of the media devoted to sport begin their build-up to the 2080 FA Cup Final a week before it kicks off. Programmes include hour-long documentaries on each player. The day before the match features a full-length, computer-generated match (the Virtual Cup Final or 'VCF') based on information gathered throughout the season. The multi-gigabyte input includes the playing surface, the time of day, the behaviour of the crowd, and the temperaments, talents, personalities, and recent experiences of players and managers. The graphics are of such quality that the recreation is indistinguishable from an actual game.

The day before the match features a full-length, **computer-generated match** (the Virtual Cup Final) based on information gathered **throughout** the season

This is the fourth year in which the VCF has been shown before the real one. On each occasion, the winning team has been predicted correctly, although the margin of victory has not – thanks to subtle programming, the VCF produces more goals and is generally agreed to be a better game. Viewing figures for this year's VCF are only marginally less than those for the flesh-and-blood match played the next day. This trend is causing problems from bookmakers, although most have made good their losses by taking bets on the VCF (of course!). The FA is worried, too. With virtual games distinguishable from real ones only by their higher entertainment value, pundits are widely predicting the death of professional football.

The real Cup Final lasts 3 hours, with play broken up into 10-minute bursts interspersed with commercials and analysis. It is played in Wembley3, the high-tech eco-friendly stadium that in 2052 replaced the 'new' Wembley Stadium of 2007. That white elephant construction – just about the last to be designed and built in the age of energy profligacy – featured no means of creating its own power, no in-seat screens, did not have a fully closable roof and even boasted (if that is the right word) a playing surface of real grass! Wembley3, like all of today's stadia, is multi-sport and eco-neutral. The perfect playing surface is, of course, synthetic.

The players in both teams, with a single exception, come from one of the schools of excellence that are responsible for producing most of our top-class players. The exception is the Manchester goalie, Charlie 'Catchall' Grimshaw, whose parents insisted that he attend normal schooling before moving to professional football aged 18. His colleagues had all been selected to be footballers by the age of 10.

The public has come to see the élite players as 'robots', devoid of personality

Although rumours persist that genetic manipulation – long outlawed by FIFA – was employed in the young players' early lives, even in their conception, this has been consistently denied by their parents. Once at the school of excellence, however, genetic medicine is employed both to heal injuries and to strengthen bodies so that injury is less likely to occur. It has, for example, made serious ankle and knee injuries a thing of the past. The sport is clean, too: professional footballers, like most top-level sportsmen and women, are subject to highly effective Continual Electronic Monitoring (CEM) for banned performance-enhancing substances and practices.

Diet and routine are carefully planned and monitored so that all players remain at peak fitness throughout the season. This has led to a variety of problems. The public has come to see the élite players as 'robots', devoid of personality. To some extent this is the fault of the clubs for relying heavily upon professional psychologists to keep their players on the straight and narrow. Accusations of 'brainwashing' are not uncommon and rumours of secret chemical 'enhancement' persist.

The dilemma of the clubs, caught between control and respect for individual freedoms, becomes painfully obvious when one of their players 'freaks out', as happens from time to time, and indulges – often all too publicly – in an orgy of prohibited activity. We all remember how, earlier in the year, images of London's leading striker eating red meat and drinking beer in a smart restaurant made the headlines on our wallscreens.

Images of London's **leading** striker eating **red meat** and **drinking beer in a smart restaurant** made the **headlines** on our wallscreens

There is nothing unusual in the strips worn by the two finalists. Both Manchester's red and London's blue are in the same ultra-light, temperature-maintaining and piezoelectrically self-padding material. The images and text displayed on the panelled backs and fronts of the shirts vary with what is happening on the pitch. While the game is in progress, so as not to act as a distraction, just names and simple statistics are displayed. During the intervals and after a goal has been scored, the panels carry a variety of messages from the sponsors.

Footwear is much more interesting because there are players on both sides who prefer playing in bare feet. As little as 20 years ago, this was all the rage. Medics had made players' feet so strong and the soles so tough that wearing boots appeared redundant. Any advantage footwear might have brought in terms of grip (hardly necessary on the latest synthetic surfaces) was far outweighed by the increased skill levels achieved by being able to 'feel' the ball against the bare skin.

There are players on **both sides** who prefer **playing in bare feet**

This changed with the invention of the 'skinboot' that fits like a glove and, while maintaining the barefoot feel, gives greater purchase on the ball. Booted players insist that they can kick a swerving ball better than the barefoot brigade, while the latter claim that they pass more accurately and dribble more skilfully. Both sets of players, booted and barefoot, demonstrate the full range of skills in the match, so the jury remains out. It might be significant, however, that London's winning goal is scored from a free kick taken by a player – Algy Mundola – wearing his famous golden skinboots.

Basic decisions – **balls** crossing the line, offside and so on – **are unchallengeable** because they are **always correctly** made

It is difficult to believe that back at the beginning of the century there was almost as much interest in the human figure of the match referee as in the players. Mind you, when one watches old film and sees some of the horrendous mistakes they made, it is hardly surprising they were figures of controversy.

Wembley3, like all our top stadia, has the latest techref technology built in. During the Cup Final, cameras track every player's movements, from the blink of an eye to a trip, and feed these digitally to a program that interprets them according to the rules of the game and the position of the ball and other players. Decisions are conveyed to the players and the crowd via the electronic bleeper that has replaced the old-fashioned whistle, followed by explanations on loudspeaker and video screen.

> The bleeper attached to the electronic refereeing system delivers a different sound for each offence: a single blast when the ball goes out of play, for example, two for a free kick, three for a penalty, etc.

The technology is such that the judgements on foul play and diving, the two most controversial issues, are generally correct. Even so, a stadium referee with the power to overrule the techref is always on hand. He intervenes only once during the Cup Final and then only to uphold the techref's ruling after a digital replay. Basic decisions – balls crossing the line, offside and so on – are unchallengeable because they are always correctly made.

The Cup Final's **enviable record** remains intact: we have now had **43** successive games without once hearing the **shrill blast of a whistle blown** by a human referee

Strangely, perhaps, there is still a pitch referee during the Cup Final. His tasks are fourfold: enforcing the techref's decisions, defusing moments of heated temper, penalising bad language and – heaven forbid! – being prepared to take over the refereeing job in the event of a system failure. Fortunately he is not called upon to do this. The Cup Final's enviable record remains intact: we have now had 43 successive games without once hearing the shrill blast of a whistle blown by a human referee.

> Incidentally, robots have all but replaced the on-pitch medical team, too. Injuries are attended by a human doctor but diagnosis is made by robot and badly injured players are carried off on robotic stretchers.

The 2080 Olympics

As has been the case for 14 years now, during 2080 we have the opportunity to enjoy three Olympic Games: the Original Olympics, the Real Olympics and the Megalympics. The Olympic Games first split in the 2020s when a group of media entrepreneurs came to the decision that anti-doping regulations had made the event so insipid that it was no longer worth watching. So the test-free Megalympics was born and has been going strong ever since. The organisation from which it split renamed itself the Original Olympics.

> As long ago as 2007, the French Irmes organisation had worked out that un-enhanced human performance would reach its peak in the middle of the 21st century and that there would be no more world records after 2060.[1]

[1] Widely reported, for example *Sunday Times*, 23 December 2007.

During 2080 we have the opportunity to enjoy **three Olympic Games**: the Original **Olympics**, the Real **Olympics** and the Megalympics

The Real Olympics, which offers only track and field events and swimming, also grew out of disillusionment with the original product. Its proposed solution, however, was radically different from that of the Megalympics. Saying it was determined to give all competitors an equal opportunity for success, the Real Olympics Committee accepted the same testing regime as the Original Olympics but went further by insisting that their athletes perform in conditions mirroring those of ancient Greek Olympics.

These included bans on all technological gadgetry, such as timing devices, starting guns and photographic equipment at the finish. More controversially, it stipulated that athletes of both genders compete stark naked. The ostensible reason for this was to eliminate the advantages arising from more expensive shoes and other kit. Critics were quick to pooh-pooh this suggestion, saying that its true purpose was simply to win TV audiences. This it certainly does, although not in the UCSA (United Central States of America, established as an independent nation in the aftermath of the Great Californian Earthquake, 2031) or some of the stricter Muslim states.

Track and Field

The three Olympic stadia are not dissimilar to Wembley3, although that used for the Real Olympics was constructed by digging down into the ground rather than piling steel and concrete above it. This follows the design pioneered by the stadium built for the 2012 London Olympics. All three sites are energy-neutral and competitors are required to journey there by surface transport rather than by air. Overseas visitors who do the same are offered discounted tickets. Ticketing is completely electronic, admission being by instant iris recognition – spectators passing through the turnstiles are required to glance for 1 second towards a digital video screen. Paper tickets went out of use over 50 years ago.

The Original Olympics and Megalympics use a similar synthetic track surface. However, to improve performance times and increase the chance of record-breaking, the Megalympic engineers have made their track far more springy than permitted at more conventional games. Both meetings repeat their track surfaces on the long-jump and high-jump approaches. In the Real Olympics, all track and field events take place on grass. The only grass evident at the other two games is ornamental.

All **three** sites are energy-neutral and competitors **are required to journey there** by surface transport rather than **by air**

The real difference between the Games is in the physical appearance of the athletes. Those in the Original and Real Olympics retain the sort of physiques that have been the norm for the last century or so, although, for obvious reasons, this is more apparent with Real competitors than with those at the Original Games. The CEM program is so efficient that today's athletes, especially the sprinters, appear more 'normal' than many of those who took to the track 75 years ago. Looking back, I am amazed that sheer common sense did not drive officials to develop better tests for the substances that the overdeveloped monsters were clearly taking.

Which brings us to this year's Megalympics.

It would be wrong, as some have done, to describe the official policy of the Mega-lympics as 'anything goes'. Entry qualifications state quite clearly that participating athletes may use only those measures to enhance performance that have been sanctioned by the International Megalympics Regulation Committee. Before com-peting, athletes must swear an oath, in public, and sign a statement stating that they will abide by the rules of the Games. However, since there is no testing and the wording of the oath states that they must not *knowingly* indulge in unsanctioned practices, the safeguard is all but worthless. Athletes have simply to state that they were engaging in practices that their coach assured them were legitimate, and hey presto! they are not guilty because they did not know of their offence.

The most famous case in which the 'not knowingly' clause was used to exonerate an athlete accused of using unsanctioned performance-enhancing techniques was that of 100 m runner Emma 'LeopardLegs' King. The first woman to break the 9-second barrier, King successfully claimed that her legs' abnormal length and musculature were the result of genetic modifications made before birth – obviously, therefore, without her knowledge.

Seemingly unaffected by the barrage of criticism they always receive from sports purists, certain faith leaders and human rights activists, the Megalympics have always been a huge commercial success. This year was no exception. Conse-quently, although cold-shouldered by Britain, France, Germany, Japan and the ESA (the Eastern States of America, which also came into being after the California earthquake of 2031), there has never been a shortage of willing host nations. Brazil, China and Australia have all hosted the Megalympics on two separate occasions.

SportCorp recently issued figures suggesting that during the Megalympics fortnight two out of every three inhabitants of the planet – some six billion people

– watched at least a part of a single event. This staggering success is explained by four factors: slick presentation, guaranteed close competition and record-breaking, and the very real possibility of tragedy. The latter, explains SportCorp's Bill Jiechi, is the very essence of good drama, just as you find in Shakespeare.

As befits a product that grew out of the entertainment business rather than sporting competition, the Megalympics package is slicker and more glitzy than any other in the sporting calendar. Take the presentation of the athletes before an event, for instance. An individual's appearance is preceded by a short film of their life and experience, ending with a personal appeal for support in the ordeal that lies ahead. Competitors are carefully packaged with identifiable panto-type characterisation such as valiant underdog, foul villain, gutsy hero, remarkable granny, etc. As music plays and the arena is lit up with a brilliant display of laser beams and holograms, one by one they are raised into the centre of the stadium on an hydraulic platform and introduced to the cheering crowd.

Thrilling competition and record-breaking are ensured by the lengths individuals and their coaching staff go to in order to take home the coveted platinum medal and the multimillion yuan prize. Unlike the other two Olympic Games, the Megalympics is organised on a 'stable' basis, with each of the eight stables (Africa, Asia, China, Europe, India-Pakistan-Bangladesh, Middle East, North America and South America) allowed to enter three athletes for each event. Each stable receives handsome grants from SportCorp to recruit, train and select its athletes.

The precise details of what goes on in the secure training camps are open to conjecture. They are based, it is said, on the camps used by the East Germans and Chinese in times gone by. Those who enter do so willingly but must agree to abide by very strict rules that govern every aspect of their behaviour. The regime has been likened to that of a mediaeval monastery or nunnery, except that inmates devote their lives to sport rather than God. Their remuneration – far in excess of anything they might earn in the outside world – is paid to a relative, often a parent, or other nominated individual. It is easy to see why some parents, desperate for their son or daughter to gain entry to a stable, will go to almost any lengths, including genetic manipulation, to achieve this.

Camp training is both physical and mental. When athletes emerge they are so finely tuned that it is obvious just from their appearance what event they have been prepared for. As little as 50 years ago all would have been regarded as freaks. The sprinters are taut bundles of muscle, the distance runners boast legs that would not look amiss on an ostrich, the upper bodies of the throwers seem modelled on Michelangelo's figures, while it is not uncommon to find a high jumper towering to 8 ft (2.44 m) or more. All this is achieved, we are told, by legal GMH (Genetic Medical Enhancement), dietary supplements and a minutely con-trolled lifestyle.

Where possible, human error is eliminated from the presentation of the Games. Starting, measurement and judgement are handled by robots. As with the Cup Final, ticketing is entirely electronic. Athletes' movements are monitored elec-tronically, too, to ensure that they are at the right place at the right time, including at the elaborate victory ceremonies where the platinum, gold, silver and bronze medals are awarded.

No matter how they are measured, performances at the Megalympics are extraordinary, way beyond anything dreamed of at the beginning of the century. It is now common, for example, for all finalists in the 100 m to clock under 9 seconds, for high jumpers to clear 10 ft (3.05 m) and for the shot to be launched a staggering 98 ft (30 m) – and that's by the female competitors. Using slight adjustments to variables like the bounce afforded by the track, the organisers ensure that new records are set at each Games. Interestingly, too, the gap between male and female performance has steadily narrowed. In another 50 years, a SportCorp spokesperson suggested, it was likely that all events would be unisex.

Megalympic javelin throwing is conducted alongside the stadium rather than within it. This change was made after Marg Wei, the famous 1,500 m runner, was accidentally speared to death by a javelin launched from over 250 m away.

Then there is the issue of drama and tragedy. This is where the Megalympics are at their most controversial – and most alluring. To achieve the performances they do, athletes take considerable risks. Their bodies are virtually 'manufactured' to order – bones lengthened and strengthened, muscles bulked, hearts enlarged, etc. These human machines are then fuelled for optimum performance over a specific short period. The strains put on them by this one-off event are phenomenal and can have tragic consequences.

It is unheard of nowadays for a Megalympics athlete to compete at more than one Games. As their bodies can be prepared to optimum pitch only once, when the Games are over, retirement is the only option. Most do not live for more than another 10 years.

The 'explosion' can leave nearby officials and members of the crowd splattered with blood

Ligament and tendon rupture is the most common injury. This occurs when an athlete's muscle power is simply too great for the frame within which it operates. The bones of jumpers, pole-vaulters and hurdlers regularly fracture mid-event. More terrifying (or stunning, according to one's point of view) is what has become known as Exploding Heart Syndrome (EHS). This is total cardiac collapse at the moment of maximum exertion, during a sprint, for instance, or while launching a javelin. The 'explosion' can leave nearby officials and members of the crowd splattered with blood. Despite the best efforts of the human and robotic doctors, the incidents are invariably fatal. When criticised for allowing such apparent barbarity, SportCorp points out that the athletes are adults who have chosen of their own free will to train and compete in the manner they do. In the words of SportCorp boss Abdullah Nedje, 'We offer sport at the cutting edge. Too sharp for you? OK, try the Originals – maybe that milk-and-water stuff turns you on!'

Ghastly though the physical injuries sustained at the Megalympics can be, the Games' opponents are more concerned about the psychological damage they inflict. Many athletes find it difficult to reintegrate into the normal world once their camp life is over. After years of intensive conditioning, probably aided by selected drug therapies, some athletes lose all sense of who they are and what the purpose of their life is. The suicide rate in the camps is said to be well above that of the outside. Despite all the careful preparation, the stress of the Games themselves can sometimes bring an athlete to the point of total collapse. This appears to have been what happened to the Australian vaulter Greg Digby, who had been prepared by the Asian stable. He went missing the night before the final of the 2080 men's pole vault and has not been seen since.

Many athletes find it **difficult to reintegrate** into the **normal** world once their camp life is over

The Digby case is just one example among many. The path to that platinum pinnacle is strewn with thousands of broken minds and bodies. Unbridled technology brings us spectacular viewing and earns billions for the Megalympics' organisers and victors. But at what price to our humanity?

Tennis

Tennis is played only at the Original Olympics. It was tried at the Megalympics but failed to attract large enough audiences, despite ball-scorching serves and 15-minute rallies. The modern professional game remains essentially the same as it was at the start of the century, subsequent technological improvements having been counteracted by changes in regulation.

All professional tennis is now played on standard acrylic surfaces after the last grass court was dug up 50 years ago. Interestingly, it was not the speed or uneven bounce on worn courts that were the final undoing of grass, but water. By the later 2020s, when the worldwide water shortage had become acute, the waste of water on sports surfaces was felt to be morally reprehensible and so all grass courts were relaid in synthetic material. Traditional-minded Wimbledon experimented with a grass look-alike for a few years before switching to a plastic hard court surface similar to that used at this year's Olympics.

> Sports businesses were aware of the water problem in 2007, when attempts were being made to develop a salt-tolerant grass capable of being irrigated with seawater.

Like most sports, tennis subscribes to the CEM program that prevents top players from employing the performance-enhancing activities deemed unacceptable by the ITF. The players, therefore, though magnificent physical specimens and tremendously fit and powerful, still look normal and have all the expected human strengths and frailties.

At the request of the **media**, the top **tennis tournaments** are now **held indoors**

The rackets they wield are masterpieces of technological ingenuity. Their overall dimensions are the same as those used in the past, but synthetic stringing and power-sprung frames deliver about 50% more power. They are also vibration-free and feather-light. The ITF has counteracted the effect of increased player strength and better racket technology by lowering the pressure within the balls and slightly increasing their circumference. This has led to spin and placement dominating the modern game rather than sheer speed and power.

At the request of the media, the top tennis tournaments are now held indoors where the lighting is consistent, play guaranteed and a more dynamic crowd atmosphere generated. All lines and the net are observed by digital equipment that has made line judges and the umpire redundant, although, as in football, a human referee is retained to control the players' behaviour. A recent Japanese experiment with a talking rule-enforcement robot named Agatha was not a success. European Star Mary Umbagli said a reprimand from Agatha was 'like being told off by an 85-year-old schoolteacher.'

Cycling

Cycling features in both the Original Olympics and Megalympics. As offered by the former, it has changed little over the years. Although machines are lighter and cyclists more powerful, the UCI has made it a priority to see that the essence of the sport remains unchanged. Having suffered a serious loss of credibility follow-ing wave after wave of drug scandals at the turn of the century, cycling was one of the first sports to adopt CEM for performance-enhancing activities. As far as we can tell, the sport is now among the cleanest in the world. It is also, claims SportCorp, one of the dullest.

Megalympics cycling is raw, red-blooded and dangerous. The streamlined, hydrau-lic-driven, ultra-lightweight racing machines look more like toboggans than

The ground-breaking lotus superbike only scratched the surface of where cycle technology might go if the sport were deregulated.

traditional bikes – immediately the regulations were relaxed to allow anything on two wheels that was driven by human power, designers brought the rider down from the seated position in order to cut wind resistance. Streamlined faring was added at the same time. Not long afterwards, the chain was made obsolete by more efficient fluid drives. Much of this technology had been pioneered by the so-called 'recumbent' bikes of the 20th century.

There is a useful article on recumbents at:
http://en.wikipedia.org/wiki/Recumbent_bicycle

Like the track and field athletes, Megalympic cyclists look strangely distorted. Their chests bulge above waspish waists that swell to legs like pistons on an old-fashioned steam railway engine. Such is the pressure to win, collisions are quite common, especially as the Megalympic bike is built for pace rather than stability. A crash at over 100 mph (160 km/h), the speed at which the bikes can travel, can be very nasty indeed. Fortunately, although cyclists rarely return to normal life after a stint at the Megalympics, cases of EHS among cyclists are rare.

Megalympics cycling **is raw**, **red**-**blooded** and dangerous

Because the possibility of rain makes racing more exciting, all Megalympic cycling is held out of doors. At the insistence of SportCorp, which dubbed the conventional velodrome 'suitable only for those with superhuman boredom thresholds – and dogs chasing their own tails', the new 1 km tracks feature steep hills, straights and bends like an old motor racing circuit. As many as two dozen cycles may take part in a single race, with cyclists operating in teams. Deliberately crashing into a member of an opposing team is not officially permitted, but each race features at least 1 pile-up as the result of suspiciously reckless driving.

Swimming

All three Olympics include swimming in their programme. The Real is most aesthetically pleasing, the Megalympic the most awe-inspiring and the Original the nearest to the traditional sport.

Swimming in the Real Olympic Games takes place in natural baths – a lake or suitable stretch of coast – adapted to the purpose. The lanes are marked with rope and the swimmers start from a simple wooden deck. If all this seems a bit too rustic, readers should watch the 100 m freestyle from the 2080 Scandinavian Olympics. The sight of eight perfectly honed athletes diving into the crystal clear waters of Sweden's breathtakingly beautiful Lake Siljan just as the sun rises over the surrounding mountains is as memorable as anything offered by the Games' more aggressive rivals.

Original Olympic swimming takes place in purpose-built baths whose contents are automatically and instantly stilled so that no swimmer is affected by another's turbulence. All adjudication is electronic. The competitors' spray-on, friction-free suits cover the entire body, including the head, leaving only the smallest apertures for nose, eyes and mouth. Now that CEM keeps the sport clean, new world records are almost unheard of and emphasis is on racing and medal winning rather than times.

Webbed feet alone are said to increase a freestyle swimmer's speed by at least 20%

For several years now, Megalympic swimming has been dominated by what the media call the Web Controversy. This is nothing to do with the first man to swim the English Channel, but revolves around the extent to which modern medicine should be allowed to enhance the sporting physique.

It is a well-known fact that a number of babies are born each year – about 1 in 2,250 – with syndactyly. This is the medical term for having webbing between the toes, or two or more toes fused together – a condition said to have been exhibited by Joseph Stalin. It also applies to a similar condition affecting the hands. The advantages it brings swimmers are obvious: webbed feet alone are said to increase a freestyle swimmer's speed by at least 20%. So, once the Megalympic Committee had scrapped most of the previous restrictions on performance enhancement, medical scientists were quick to create syndactyly by artificial means.

Digit-linking surgery was performed on babies who then grew up with a condition indistinguishable from that of syndactyly. At the same time, the gene responsible

Syndactyly, the 'web-foot' syndrome at the heart of a major uproar in the 2076 Megalympics.

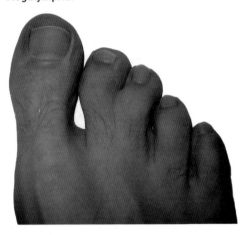

REPRINTED FROM HTTP://COMMONS.WIKIMEDIA.ORG/WIKI/IMAGE: SYNDACTILY_FEET.JPG

for syndactyly was used to 'manufacture' future swimming champions in the womb and, by genetic modification, in later life. The ethics of such processes hit the headlines with the case of Tamsin Wang, daughter of Original Olympic swimmer Chi-Chi Wang. Tamsin's 2076 Megalympic 100 m backstroke victory in a time of 42.26 seconds broke the previous world record by more than 2 seconds and earned her the SportCorp 'Champion of Champions' medal.

A process that will inevitably lead to **even grosser distortions** of the **human** body than seen at present

Tamsin, dubbed 'Duck Girl' by the popular media because of the pronounced webbing between her remarkably long toes and fingers, is now banned from all competitive swimming. Currently recuperating in an exclusive psychiatric hospital in Switzerland, she is said to want her syndactyly reversed by surgery. Her mother, on the other hand, insists that Tamsin's condition is not the result of genetic engineering but simply a 1 in 10 million chance of nature that in the past would have been rectified by post-natal surgery. The girl has every right, therefore, to compete in the Megalympics, if not in the Original Olympic Games. The case is now working its way through the convoluted Chinese court system and will almost certainly end up before the International Court on Human Rights.

Keen to continue offering record-breaking performances in every Games, the Megalympic Committee's current ruling is that 'natural' syndactyly affecting hands or feet is permitted, but not where both sets of digits are affected. On these grounds it has declared Tamsin's world record to be invalid. In making its ruling, however, it has in effect given the green light to further experimentation with hand or foot webbing, a process that will inevitably lead to even grosser distortions of the human body than seen at present.

The twin hulls of the ROCAT are a good example of positive technological innovation.

Both the Original Olympics and the Megalympics hold rowing competitions featuring both single- and double-hulled boats equipped with the moving riggers that have replaced the old-fashioned sliding seats.

Hockey

Field hockey, like tennis, is seen only in the Original Olympics. The Megalympics experimented with it for a few years but found it too quick for satisfactory TV coverage and, after some rules changes designed to 'liven it up', too dangerous even for their tastes.

The game that remains is clean, quick and popular with players if not equally so with spectators. The ball and sticks have changed hardly at all, except that wooden sticks are now seen only on clubhouse walls and, from the 2030s, balls were made a little softer to slow the game down. Self-stiffening materials have replaced much of the old bulky padding and add to the safety of every player. At Olympic level, all adjudication is electronic but this is too expensive for implementation at club grounds. The CEM program keeps the élite sport clean.

The **game that remains** is **clean**, quick and **popular** with players if not **equally so** with spectators

The most important technological development over the last 50 years has been the invention of the odd-named 'dry water-based pitch'. This appeared after several years of research to find a material that replicated the characteristics of the traditional water-based pitch, but without the need for watering. The answer the technicians eventually came up with was a sand-filled surface featuring plastic fibres that offered little resistance when impacted upon lightly – i.e. when the ball passes over them – yet increased their resistance in proportion to the force acting upon them. This solved the problem of players slipping about all over the place, which was an unfortunate characteristic of the early non-watered pitches.

Boxing, which apart from the introduction of the electronic Target Master points scoring system has remained largely unchanged over the last 150 years, takes place only in the Original Olympics. A far more brutal version of the sport was withdrawn from the Megalympics after the death of one third of all competitors in the 2068 Games.

The Paralympics

After about a century of existence, the Paralympics were held for the last time in 2060. The decision was fraught with controversy. For many years there had been disagreement over the extent to which technology might be allowed to help disabled athletes. The situation remained just about under control as long as the technological assistance was limited to items such as prostheses and wheelchairs. But when athletes registered as disabled appeared with what seemed to be whole new limbs and repaired spines, the situation got out of control.

Tragically, the Games were cancelled through lack of interest

Eventually an agreement was reached that redefined disability and ruled out athletes who had, to all intents and purposes, been made whole again by stem cell medicine.[2] Over time, this led to a significant drop in the number of disabled athletes entering the Paralympics. Those from developed nations who might have competed in the past had now been cured, while those from developing nations could afford neither stem cell therapy nor the cost of training and travelling to the Games. As a result, tragically, the Games were cancelled through lack of interest.

Other Non-Olympic Sports

Golf

Few sports have suffered from technology's outrageous slings and arrows to the same extent as golf. We can now determine three distinct phases. During the first, which lasted from the beginning of the century to around 2025, golfing authorities around the world struggled to control the technology that was forcing such rapid changes on their sport. More powerful clubs were threatening to make ancient and respected courses redundant, there was growing evidence that top players were using banned substances to increase their power, certain courses became so perfect that an air of predictability came over the games played on them, and the proliferation of virtual golf threatened to undermine the outdoor game entirely. And all this was happening at a time when the environmental lobby was attacking the sport for wasting water, despoiling the natural environment and keeping land out of agricultural production.

The second phase of golf's recent history, which began in the later 2020s and ended only with the Reconciliation Agreement signed in 2063, saw the game fragment in a manner reminiscent of the Olympic Games. Golf Unlimited espoused all technology that made its game more sensational, leading to longer courses, huge, fantastically shaped clubs, robot caddies and pumped-up players. At the other end of the spectrum, traditional golf consolidated its strict regulation of players, clubs

---

[2] See Section I, Chapter 7.

and courses. Its professional players were controlled by the CEM program and club power was reduced. At the same time, course lengthening and watering were banned, as was the construction of new courses. In time, traditional golf courses began to look like those of 150 years ago, with much of the old unpredictability. A growing number of players and viewers found this refreshingly entertaining.

Virtual golf lay somewhere between these two forms of the game. Inside a specially constructed dome, players could choose their course and which type of golf they wished to play, traditional or Unlimited. Wearing a lightweight virtual golf helmet, indoor golfers experienced every aspect of a real game, except that they did not have to walk the course. (Actually, some domes featured moving walkways to replicate even that aspect of the experience.) The virtual golfing world came to include wind, rain, poor lies, bunkers and even birdsong. And every dome had its 19th hole where players could repair after an exhausting morning on the links!

The third phase is where we are today. By 2062, Golf Unlimited was collapsing under its own weight. Club technology had reached a plateau and, with the organisation no longer able to guarantee a year-on-year improvement, public interest dwindled. Pressure from the environmental lobby persuaded many countries, led by Scotland, to ban Unlimited's highly commercial version of the sport. As revenues dried up, so did the supply of players willing to risk their lives (literally) by signing up for the performance-enhancement training that Golf Unlimited demanded.

The resulting Reconciliation Agreement was really a victory for the traditional game, now known as 'Standard Golf'. Players are CEM monitored, courses are no longer than they were 75 years ago and all but a few have had their fairways and greens laid with synthetic turf in order to guarantee a fine playing surface without the need for watering. The compromise over club technology has resulted in drivers capable of sending a ball over 350 yd (320 m) but the club head's reduced size and trampoline effect mean such distances are possible only with a perfectly struck shot. In another measure to keep scores near the par mark, professional golfers are limited to a bag of seven clubs chosen before each round. Wheeled and walking robot caddies carry the bags and offer technical advice over distance and club selection.

All but a few have had their **fairways** and **greens** laid with synthetic turf in order **to guarantee a fine playing surface** without the **need** for watering

Nowadays, all virtual golf domes that take their business seriously offer only Standard Golf. Their recreation of the golf course is so precise that most professionals now prefer indoor practice facilities, away from the distraction of the media and spectators, to the real thing outdoors. Virtual tournaments are growing in popularity, too, with some major ones broadcast internationally. Only this year

Inside a modern golf dome. Over time, video and projection technology will make the indoor experience virtually indistinguisable from the outdoor.

©ISTOCKPHOTO.COM/JGARERI

the world's leading professional golfer, Tiger Woods IV, signed a contract to play in three virtual tournaments as well as his usual round of open-air ones. There have even been discussions about making the Ryder Cup a virtual affair in 2085.

Rugby

Technology has had only a very light impact on the way rugby is played. The biggest change in the game has been one of structure. Just as it had lain behind the 19th century division of the game into two codes, so economics brought the two together again. By the 2020s, professional rugby league was finding it increasingly hard to keep going and so had little choice but to accept the IRB's overtures. Thus League was absorbed into Union to form the single sport of rugby.

Today **no one** would dream of **taking to the pitch** without first pulling on their **piezoelectric headguard**

By this time, technology had already brought about the reduction in Union team numbers from 15 to 13, where it stands today.[3] The change was needed because players had become so quick and strong that defence dominated attack, leading to a proliferation of dull, low-scoring matches. Interestingly, when rugby accepted CEM monitoring and performance-enhancing practices were finally rooted out, it chose to retain the 13-man team despite player size and speed falling back slightly.

[3] BBC Rugby Correspondent Ian Robertson believes that a reduction to 14 (removing no. 8) would be more likely so Union was not thought to be aping its rival, League.

Technology is also responsible for the modern kit. The lightweight self-padding material of the shirts and shorts is similar to that worn by footballers. No professional rugby player has yet followed the football fashion for playing in bare feet, although the modern skinboot is worn even by bulky forwards. Looking back at old pictures, it is amazing to see so many players bareheaded. Today no one would dream of taking to the pitch without first pulling on their piezoelectric headguard. Non-slip gloves, so much a feature of the 2030s and '40s, are today no longer permitted.

> Like FIFA, the IRB has outlawed the use of electronic game plans while a match is still in progress. The present regulations came into being to prevent coaches directing games like chess from behind their computer screens.

For much the same reasons as other sports, rugby abandoned grass pitches long ago. Electronic refereeing, though, was much slower to catch on. It was not a question of reactionary 'old farts' unwilling to espouse technology – rugby was way ahead of football in allowing digital replay to determine whether or not a try had been scored – but of cost and technical difficulties. When a dozen or more players were crushed together in a set scrum, ruck or maul, cameras found it extremely tricky to tell precisely who was doing what to whom. Human referees had the same problem, but were able to analyse the situation better by using a combination of sound and sight, and by drawing on extensive experience gained from having been in similar situations before. In other words, the human referee did the job better simply because he was human.

Despite this, calls for more electronic adjudication grew and a version of the football techref was introduced for clear-cut issues such as touch, forward passes, and whether kicks at goal were successful. The equipment was expensive, however, and found its way to international matches only slowly. Ireland, the last of the home unions to adopt it, did not do so until 2041.

The human referee **did the job better** simply because he was **human**

Twenty-one years later, the problem of refereeing every aspect of a rugby game by electronics was finally solved. Universally used for internationals today, 'Dark Art' technology involves spraying each player with an inert yet distinctive tincture before the game. This is linked to a digital identifier that tracks players individually, even working out where they are when all but a small part of them is hidden from view. This is something that the best human referees are unable to do. When integrated with techref technology, Dark Art manages a game far better than its human counterpart and its use has led to a marked decrease in foul play. Nevertheless, as with several other sports, a human referee still patrols the pitch to handle matters of language and temper.

Many regard the Dark Art refereeing technology as somewhat primitive, especially the need to spray players before each game. It is hoped that before long it will be replaced by the high-sensitivity pigment identification technique currently being developed by the University of Exeter.

Modern technology also has had impacts upon rugby training, stadiums and the treatment of injury. In a manner similar to football players, although somewhat less rigorously applied, coaches closely regulate the diet, sleep and exercise of rugby players in their charge. As in all sport, stem cell therapy enables players to overcome the most serious injuries and thus to extend their playing careers way beyond what was previously possible. At the last World Cup, for example, the Welsh team had five members over the age of 40, and the Argentinean hooker, Fernando Silva, actually celebrated his 50th birthday on the eve of his team's victory over Russia in the final.

Rugby stadiums are identical to those already covered in the section on the 2080 football Cup Final at the beginning of this chapter. As with football, the stadium-based game is under threat from virtual versions of the sport.

Cricket

Way back in 2007, the England cricket captain of the time, Michael Vaughan, was pleading, 'Common sense has to prevail . . . You've got the technology, let's use it.'[4] He was right, of course, and step by step the ICC agreed to extend the use of technology for decision-making to the point where it took over completely. This is where we are today, a position no one even dreams of questioning.

The authorities' principal objection to extending technological decision-making was the fact that the human umpire was there, on the pitch, hearing and seeing things at ground level. They could get the 'feel' of a situation – judging the tone in a player's voice when they appealed, for example – in a way remote technology never could. All this changed when the RoboUmp came on the scene.

One of the principal problems with the early RoboUmps was their inability to take evasive action when a ball was struck in their direction. The result was not only damaged cricket balls but smashed circuitry worth thousands of yuan!

The modern robotic umpire – still marketed under the old name 'RoboUmp' – has developed through 14 generations since its first appearance all those years ago.

[4] Speaking to BBC Sport, 9 December 2007.

The newest version is not only superbly nimble and blessed with perfect hearing and sight, but it also makes irreproachable decisions on the most complex of matters. Its precision over LBW and catches, issues that had previously brought umpires and players close to blows, has added immeasurably to the game's credibility. To cap it all, with splendid irony, RoboUmp XIV will sometimes refer questionable catches in the deep and doubtful boundaries to its electronic cousin under the stands!

At first RoboUmp took to the field in the company of a human umpire, who stood at square leg and dealt with matters like drinks intervals that were beyond the robot's ken. Even this is now considered unnecessary and before every test match we have become accustomed to seeing two sleek, white-coated machines glide effortlessly to the middle to the accompaniment of polite applause. This year, the robots in service at Lords for an unusual daytime game even sported rather dashing white sunhats.

Mechanical umpires do not rule on questions of unsporting behaviour – their 'brains' are far too objective to understand such esoteric concepts – but they pick up everything said and done on the field and relay it to the human umpire in the pavilion for a decision. It is surely only a matter of time before speech recognition is sufficiently advanced for RoboUmps to deal with these matters unaided? After that, it won't be long before its children are taking the field alongside our own . . .

> In common with all other sports, real cricket faces serious competition from the various virtual versions of the game currently available.

Other than umpiring, over the course of this century technology has altered cricket in a host of other ways. The pitches, stumps and bails are now synthetic, for example, and all major grounds enclosed – how much less exciting would the game be without the modern 'hit the roof for six' law? The old 'test match', a game that might last as long as five whole days (but no nights) and which some regarded as inordinately tedious, died out in the 2020s. By this time, floodlit limited-overs games, such as early versions of Twenty20, had all but taken over. Wooden bats – who remembers those gloriously handcrafted masterpieces? – were phased out of the professional game in 2037. The unpredictable cow-skin (leather) ball followed 3 years later.

Today's spectators have every possible piece of information instantly available on their personal and seat monitors

The modern, vibration-free bat, moulded from carbonised plastic, has several advantages over the old wooden implements. It is cheaper, for a start, allowing cricketers all over the world to play with the best equipment, and its weight is easily adjusted to suit individual tastes and needs. More important than either of these is its power. Tests suggest that the modern bat will drive a ball 50% further than the very best wooden equivalent. Technology has not just come to the aid of the batter, however. The latest cricket balls are specifically designed to swing prodigiously in the air throughout an innings. The traditional seam is retained, although it is no longer a necessary part of the construction. As the modern version of the raised join is slightly more pronounced than on the old leather balls, spinners and seam bowlers are afforded a better grip and the ball moves more sharply off the pitch.

Finally, there is the matter of information. Cricket has always been a game of statistics and, in accordance with this tradition, today's spectators have every possible piece of information instantly available on their personal and seat monitors, as well as on the larger ground screens. Averages are updated with each ball, as are matters such as over rates, strike rates, the speed of each delivery, the angle of its bounce, and the degree of swerve or turn off the pitch.

Winter Sports

By 2020, winter sports were struggling to survive internationally. Rising temperatures and climate change drove activities higher and higher up the mountains and further towards the poles. At the same time, economic recession and international agreements on aviation reduction led to a dramatic fall in the numbers taking traditional winter holidays. After massive public protest by the environmental lobby had caused the cancellation of the 2054 Antarctic Games, the Winter Olympics were suspended indefinitely. They are not expected to reopen until the middle of the 22nd century at the earliest.

After massive public **protest** by the **environmental** lobby had caused the **cancellation of the 2054 Antarctic Games**, the **Winter Olympics** were suspended indefinitely

Motorsport

With the replacement of the internal combustion engine by electric power, motorsport lost much of its appeal. The last old-fashioned Grand Prix was held in Dubai in 2029. Electric vehicle racing remains popular, but the cost of airfreight means that global competition is impractical. The European Electric Grand Prix (EEGP) attracts about 25,000 spectators annually.

And Beyond All That . . .

After 2080, the picture becomes increasingly blurred. The future of technology in sport depends on a multitude of imponderables: will we blow ourselves up or, equally crass, pollute our planet to such an extent that it is no longer able to sustain human life? Or might we have mastered space travel, ushering in an age of World Cups and sports invented for weightless athletes?

Who knows? It is fairly safe to assume, though, that as long as human beings something like ourselves continue to exist, so will sport. The form it takes is up to us. As technology leaps ahead, presenting thrilling new opportunities and terrifying threats in equal measure, the real challenge lies in finding a workable balance between what we can do and what we ought to do, between regulation and healthy competition. Ideally the former should serve the latter, but this balance can be struck only when we are clear in our own minds what sport is all about, exactly what it is *for*. That is the question underlying our final chapter, which is where we now turn.

It is **fairly safe to assume**, though, that as long as human **beings** something like **ourselves** continue to exist, **so will sport**

10 Is Technology Improving Sport?

Interviewer: 'Do you prefer grass or artificial turf, sir?'

Tug McGraw, famous major league baseball pitcher: 'I don't know. I never smoked Astroturf.'

Change

Let's get two things straight at the outset. First, technology is changing sport. It always has done, from the moment toehold groves were inserted into the start of the 'stade' in ancient Olympia, to the introduction of floodlights in stadiums in the

St Luke's Campus, Exeter University, the heart of one of Britain's leading centres of sports research.

©EXETER UNIVERSITY

1920s and fibreglass poles for vaulters in 1956. The big change in recent decades has been the range of technology available to sport and the speed of its development. It is not dissimilar to the impact of war or the space race upon their relevant technologies: as the pressure – even need – for success piled up, so the pace of change increased.

Second, and related to the first point, sport itself is changing. Essentially, this is not new, either. Again, what is new is the rate and scale of change. Over the last 20 years, sport has become much more than entertainment. It is now an industry, a major one, too. In 2007, sport and leisure accounted for over 4% of the UK's GDP (compared with agriculture's 1%), providing an estimated 2.5 million jobs and one in four of all new ones. Consumers spent around £12 billion per annum on sport and sport-related activities.

In the post-Marxist world, all commerce is by definition competitive. Thus the sporting competition between individuals and teams is underpinned by competition between their backers – regional, national and international. The rewards for success and the penalties for failure are monstrously greater than ever before. Tiny issues – a penalty awarded or not – can become major incidents. Scientists, engineers, technicians, trainers and coaches strive to find that special something to give their athletes a slight edge, the minute difference between 1st and 2nd, gold and silver. That non-essential yet vital 1%, as Sir Clive Woodward, manager of England's successful 2003 rugby team, put it.

So sport is changing and technology is closely involved in that change. The changes are great, but just how great? And are they sufficiently momentous to destroy the very essence of sport itself?

So, ladies and gentlemen of the jury, let's hear what the two sides have to say for themselves. I call upon the prosecution to state their case.

The Case for the Prosecution

Better sport?

Is technology improving sport? Well, at the level of raw statistics, yes, of course it is. Improvements in training, recovery, diet, performance analysis, clothing, equipment and surfaces . . . a multitude of technological factors combine to make sport more dramatic and statistically superior year on year.

Medical student Roger Bannister breaking the 4-minute mile barrier, 1957.

It took almost a century to knock 36 seconds off the world mile record in order to get it down to under 4 minutes. Since then, it has fallen another 17 seconds in 45 years.

Selected mile records, 1865 to the present day:

Time	Athlete	Country	Year
4:36.5	Richard Webster	England	1865
4:29.0	William Chinnery	England	1868
4:18.2	Fred Bacon	Scotland	1894
4:12.6	Norman Taber	United States	1915
4:09.2	Jules Ladoumegue	France	1931
4:07.6	Jack Lovelock	New Zealand	1933
4:01.4	Gunder Hägg	Sweden	1945
3:59.4	Roger Bannister	England	1954
3:54.5	Herb Elliott	Australia	1958
3:51.3	Jim Ryun	United States	1966
3:47.33	Sebastian Coe	England	1981
3:46.31	Steve Cram	England	1985
3:43.13	Hicham El Guerrouj	Morocco	1999

Today's times and distances in track and field are better than ever before, boats travel faster, sleighs and skiers slide at greater speed, soccer balls swerve more, rugby players collide with greater impact, tennis players serve harder, golfers hit the ball further, hockey is quicker, pace bowlers are supposedly pacier . . . everywhere one turns, records tumble and pundits wisely proclaim that no player or team from the past would stand a chance against their modern equivalent.

True. But is the sport they play really any better? At this stage, stepping gingerly into the proverbial minefield, we need to define 'sport'. Interestingly, all definitions contain certain keywords: 'game', 'recreation', 'amusement' and 'fun'. So I suggest that sport may be defined as a recreation, invariably involving physical activity, which is undertaken primarily for fun. 'Better' sport, therefore, is presumably that which offers more recreation and is more fun. This has very little to do with breaking records. Moreover, sport is essentially about those participating, not those watching.

Play up, play up . . . Beyond the NFL, beyond the hype of the professional game, thousands of amateurs play and watch American football for the sheer exuberant joy of it.

The contention of what follows is that technology's impact on sport has been to play the major role in redefining it, bringing in a poisonous commercial influence that distorts not just at the top level but seeps down to the municipal golf course and local school yard. There never was 'pure' sport, but what passes by that name today at the élite level is so impure, so polluted that it should be renamed altogether.

Batting on the beach – fundamentally sport is about participants having fun. Without that, the whole exercise becomes meaningless.

There **never was 'pure' sport**, but what passes by that name today at the élite level is **so impure, so polluted** that it should be renamed altogether

Double Whammy

Technology's damaging impact on sport has been twofold, direct and indirect. The latter first.

Indirect Damage

The commercialisation of sport is nothing new. One reason why the ancient Olympics lost their lustre was the influence of Roman money, and the famous chariot races of the Circus Maximus – more about betting, political prizes and pleasing the baying hordes in the stadium than fair competition – were an ugly forerunner of much that we see today. During the 19th century, technology in the form of mass public transport enabled this process to go a step further. As crowds grew, sport became less about the enjoyment of the players than about entertaining the viewers. Radio, film, TV and the internet completed the process.

Thus transport and communication technology undermined sport's recreational function, transforming it into something akin to a circus, a cinema or even a shopping trip – match or mall? As Dr Simon Hewson, noted sport enthusiast and psychologist, has observed, sport is being reduced to 'a set of high-tech spectaculars with most of the world as spectators – i.e. just a branch of the entertainment and celebrity industries.'[1]

[1] In conversation with the author, June 2007.

Smiles are all too often associated **not** with participation, **only with triumph**

In this brave new world, victory is more important than performance, viewing figures outweigh player satisfaction, and the bottom line is a truer indication of success than the goal line or the crease. So what? The very fact that billions around the world absorb sport vicariously through aerials and wires surely demonstrates that this form of recreational fun is what they want?

Maybe, but don't call it sport.

Moreover, I suggest that this sport-derived entertainment is probably more harmful than it at first seems. It pollutes true sport (recreational fun) by lauding individuals, such as drug-taking sprinters, and cheating practices, like diving for penalties in football. Anyone who has watched or refereed youth sport will have seen how the characteristics of the superstars – worthy and unworthy – are indiscriminately emulated by the young. It is fashionable to mock the 'Corinthian spirit', the idea that ultimately what matters is playing not winning. Yet, for the great majority of sportsmen and women, taking part is precisely what should matter most: taking exercise, meeting friends, letting off steam, having *fun*!

One reason why, in the West, governments and other bodies are finding it so hard to get more young people to play sport is precisely because, in the so-called 'sport' they know best, smiles are all too often associated not with participation, only with triumph. Besides, because sport is largely linked in their minds with the top-level performances they see on TV, they are inclined to reject it at an early age as something beyond them. And the gap that this leaves can always be filled with another piece of technology, the Xbox, PlayStation or GameCube . . . Why play poor football in the local park when you can be a premiership manager on your console?

Is that all there is? Technology threatens to turn all sport into a matter of hand-eye co-ordination.

©ISTOCKPHOTO.COM/DESTONIAN

There is a broader moral question, too. The great issues of the modern world – climate change, nuclear proliferation, terrorism, the chasm between the haves and have-nots – all require human co-operation on an unprecedented scale. In this situation, large-scale activities that promote aggression over tolerance and ruthlessness over fair play are counterproductive, even immoral. Significantly, we remember how British and German troops on the Western Front climbed out of their trenches to play football against each other on Christmas Day 1914 – but we do not recall the score. That, surely, is what sport is all about.

Direct Damage

The most obvious direct damage that technology is doing to sport is one that I have frequently pointed out in the preceding pages: the need for massive technological input in order to be able to compete at the highest level has made world-class sport a prerogative of the developed nations and often of the relatively well-heeled within those nations. Essentially, the more money you have, the more medals and cups you win. In 2004, only 4 of the world's 10 most populous nations were among the top 10 Olympic medal winners.

The sporting dominance of wealthy, industrialised nations is well illustrated by the following tables:

Top 10 Olympic medal winners, 2004[2]		Top 10 by population (billions)	
USA	103	China	1.32
Russia	92	India	1.12
China	63	USA	0.30
Australia	49	Indonesia	0.23
Germany	48	Brazil	0.19
Japan	37	Pakistan	0.16
France	33	Bangladesh	0.15
Italy	32	Russia	0.14
South Korea	30	Nigeria	0.13
UK	30	Japan	0.12

To a certain extent, this depends on the sport. 'Expensive' sports such as rowing, sailing, skiing, tennis, hockey, golf and airborne activities are all dominated by developed nations. In sports requiring less kit, such as boxing and football, there is more opportunity for athletes from developing nations to make it to the top. Nevertheless, no African nation has ever reached the semi-final of the football world cup, and sportsmen and women from less well-off countries invariably end

[2] Ranked according to number of gold medals. This information is taken from http://simon.forsyth.net/olympics.html

up living, training and conducting their sport away from home. The Senegalese footballer El Hadji Diouf and the athlete Wilson Kipketer, who swapped his Kenyan nationality for Danish, are good examples of this phenomenon.

> **❝ I love to see** every decision right, but it just doesn't **happen**. That's life. ❞

Boxing, the most elemental sport, remains one of the few in which pure talent, guts and determination are still sufficient to get an athlete to the top.

Going one step further, one might ask whether competitive activities heavily dependent upon technology rather than human endeavour and skill really are still sports? This has always been a debating point with motor sports and, to a lesser extent, with other machine-based competition such as cycling. But if, as the cup and medal tables seem to suggest, just about all sports are technology-dependent at the top level, then can any of it really be described as sport?

A further problem that technology creates, albeit in an attempt to solve other difficulties, is the undermining of officials. It has been a universal law of all sporting contest that the judge's decision is final and competitors must learn to accept bad decisions as they do defeat, with good grace. This traditional attitude was recently summed up by the great West Indian fast bowler Michael Holding: 'I love to see every decision right, but it just doesn't happen. That's life.'[3]

[3] Talking on Sky TV, 29 July 2007.

Then along come gismos like digital replay and Hawkeye – and bang goes the ref's authority as the sole arbiter of fact. 'That's life' is no longer enough – like spoilt children we demand the impossible: perfect accuracy. Millions can now see an offside that has been missed by the referee's assistant, the penalty awarded that was not, the dirty business in the scrum, the 'not out' that was patently LBW, the lob called 'out' that in fact just nicked the base line . . . and it's even worse when players are allowed to appeal. As we noted in Chapter 3, permitting appeals is a confession that officials are fallible. We have always known they are, but sport works only if all concerned accept the convention that they are not. Who but a masochistic peacock would volunteer to be an official in such circumstances?

As in other areas, technology's undermining of the authority of officials has a knock-on effect. It is now regarded as acceptable for otherwise excellent com-mentators, such as BBC Radio 5 Live's Alan Green, to join in the slagging off of officials. Inevitably, this corrosion of respect seeps down to other levels of sport, ending up influencing kids in the playground. And then it becomes mixed with a lack of respect for law and order in general. On the pitch or the TV in the afternoon, on the street by nightfall. Small wonder it is increasingly hard to find volunteers willing to officiate at sporting occasions. Don't blame the ref – save your brickbats for the replay.

'Drugs are very much a part of professional sports today, but . . . golf is the only sport where the players aren't penalized for being on grass.'
– Bob Hope

The gravest threat to true sport comes from chemical and biological technology. This was covered in Chapter 8, so all that is needed here is a brief summary of the perils at hand. Drugs enhance performance, allowing 'dirty' athletes to perform better than they might otherwise do. This negates a basic sporting principle: competition on a level playing field (or changing ends at half-time on sloping ones![4]). To make the situation worse, the drug manufacturers and pushers are generally one step ahead of the underfunded authorities, making detection uncertain, even unlikely. In such circumstances, it is surely impossible that technology enhances sport.

Watch the world's fastest bowler, Pakistan's Shoaib Akhtar, on http://www. youtube.com/watch?v=VW_Bhhh11DI

Now consider: in 2006, Akhtar was given a 2-year ban from competitive cricket for testing positive for the banned steroid nandrolone . . .

Sadly, drug-taking athletes at all levels appear prepared to risk not just the disgrace of being uncovered but serious ill health and even death. Testing, some argue, serves only to create a still more dangerous situation because 'athletes are now using shorter-acting, more toxic forms of . . . drugs to avoid detection.'[5] If you don't believe the situation is serious, just do an internet search for 'steroids'. You too can be bigger and more powerful, and all for just a few bucks. Great. But what's the real price?

Over 50% of American males aged 11 to 17 chose as their physical ideal an image attainable only by using steroids.[6]

[4] Never more necessary than when playing rugby at Redruth, with its famous 'Hellfire Corner'.
[5] Robert Voy, one-time chief medical officer of US Olympic Committee, cited by David Owen in *FT Magazine* 3/4 February 2007.
[6] Cited on http://www.drugstory.org/pdfs/musclemadness2.pdf

335

is technology improving sport?

In Conclusion

Ladies and gentlemen of the jury, I have laid before you overwhelming evidence that, far from improving sport, technology is actually damaging it. Higher, further, faster does not necessarily mean better, because improvements are often achieved not by effort or talent but by external factors such as equipment and chemicals.

To date, the corrosive effect has been reserved largely to sport at the top, professional level. Yet there is plenty of evidence of its adverse impact on other levels. Manifestations may be obsession with sporting image – "But getting those boots means I'll play better, mum!" – or attitudes mimicked from TV – "You blind? Course it was an effing penalty!" – or redress to dubious performance-enhancing

The US lightweight 4 at the 2003 World Championships showing the teamwork, dedication, skill and guts that sport, ultimately, is all about.

substances – 'SOPHISTICATED NEW ANABOLIC STACK will launch GIGANTIC increase of testosterone for power and endurance.'

But getting those boots means I'll play better, mum!

More alarming is the fact that the sport revolution is probably only just beginning. Over the coming century, it is likely that the technology-driven merger of sport with entertainment will proceed apace. Gene doping and genetic engineering will be almost impossible to counteract, making even-handed competition well-nigh impossible. Together these changes will make the 2080 sporting scene (and perhaps the athletes themselves) almost unrecognisable in our eyes. Is this really the way we want to go?

▌▌ SOPHISTICATED NEW ANABOLIC STACK will launch GIGANTIC increase of testosterone for power and endurance ▐▐

For almost a century, ever since the amateur Corinthian ethos of the Victorian era was blamed for the slaughter of the Flanders trenches, we have been pouring scorn on attitudes exemplified in the famous line, 'Play up! Play up! And play the game!' Now there is an edge of uncertainty to our mockery. Have we lost something? Is it possible that those unbelievably naïve and earnest Victorians understood something about sport that we have lost – what it is really all about?

Vitae Lampada ('Lamp of Life')

There's a breathless hush in the close to-night
Ten to make and the match to win
A bumping pitch and a blinding light,
An hour to play, and the last man in.
And it's not for the sake of a ribboned coat.
Or the selfish hope of a season's fame,
But his captain's hand on his shoulder smote
"Play up! Play up! And play the game!"

The sand of the desert is sodden red-
Red with the wreck of the square that broke
The Gatling's jammed and the colonel dead,
And the regiment blind with dust and smoke.
The river of death has brimmed its banks,
And England's far and Honor a name,
But the voice of a schoolboy rallies the ranks-
"Play up! Play up! And play the game!"

Sir Henry Newbolt, 1897

The Case for the Defence

Playing to Win

Before we go any further, let's knock on the head the ridiculous notion that playing sport is about something other than winning. The very essence of any game is competition, about playing to win – take away that and it's not a game any more, just a meaningless exercise. Even the old romantic Newbolt recognised as much in the second line of his *Vitae Lampada* (above). However, we may permit one small rider: in some sports, marathon running for example, the competition for most athletes is with themselves and the group around them, not necessarily with the race leaders. Nevertheless, it's still a race, still a competition.

If **anyone** tells you **it's fun to lose, don't** believe **them**

So there is no point in blaming technology because sportsmen and women seek a competitive edge. Being human, they want to win. Asking them to eschew technology to help them do this would be like asking Paula Radcliffe to train less so others had a chance of catching her. Sport is by its very nature cut-throat, with or without technology. If anyone tells you it's fun to lose, don't believe them.

As I am writing this, from time to time I flick across to the BBC website to see how England are getting on in their 1st test match against Sri Lanka. Everyone agrees that it's a great game, especially now Bell and Prior are showing a bit of backbone . . . but in the end, from an England point of view, that won't matter one flying bail if they lose. It will be a disaster.[7] 'It is about winning and not about being pretty.'[8]

[7] Which they did – and it was!
[8] Sir Clive Woodward on Sky Sports, 19 October 2007.

Rising Standards

For a top-rate sporting event – for example, the 1973 Barbarians v All Blacks match, Liverpool's victory in the 2005 European Cup or England's defeat of Australia at Headingley, 1981 – two ingredients are needed: excitement and quality. The former, that magic factor, is impossible to engineer or even predict; but technology has placed the latter very much in our own hands.

That try (Barbarians 1973) can be seen on YouTube: http://www.youtube.com/watch?v=AwCbG4I0QyA

Technology's impact on sporting quality has been threefold:

First, through better training, surfaces, equipment and all the other technical matters discussed earlier in the book, technology has allowed standards to rise across the board, especially in sports that have become wholly professional. This is not necessarily best reflected in new world records and the like, but in the performances of the also-rans. A good example is afforded by the famous Dream Mile that features in the annual ExxonMobil Bislett Games, Oslo. In 2007, all 13 finishers came in under the 4-minute mark that 50 years previously had seemed so magical.

The full results of the 2007 Dream Mile held at Oslo's ExxonMobile Bislett Games are as follows[9]:

Athlete	Nat	Time
KAOUCH, Adil	MAR	3:51.14
CHOGE, Augustine	KEN	3:51.62
BADDELEY, Andy	GBR	3:51.95
KOMEN, Daniel Kipchirchir	KEN	3:52.19
ALI, Bilal Mansour	BRN	3:52.35
CASADO, Arturo	ESP	3:52.38
GALLARDO, Sergio	ESP	3:52.85
SIMOTWO, Suleiman	KEN	3:53.08
MOTTRAM, Craig	AUS	3:54.57
KIPCHIRCHIR, Alex	KEN	3:55.96
SONGOK, Isaac	KEN	3:56.17
BOUKENSA, Tarek	ALG	3:56.37
IGUIDER, Abdelaati	MAR	3:59.79

These times make an interesting comparison with the world mile record times given at the beginning of this section.

Does this mean technology has improved sport? Well, I suggest that only devoted parents, fanatical fans and the hopelessly perverse prefer error-strewn, low-quality sport over that in which passes are made, putts holed, serves go in and times are excellent. Why else are crowds and audiences for world-class events always higher than for those of second tier events? No, the higher the quality, the more enjoyable the sport.

[9] From http://www.bislettgames.com/2007/results/re0140040.html

Second, technology provides the background against which good sport can flourish – improved pitches, tracks, shoes, clothing, skis, rackets and the like. Geniuses such as Maradona and Best cannot (yet) be produced at will, but technology can give them conditions in which their talents can be best displayed. One really does wonder whether a 21st-century star like Manchester United's Ronaldo would have coped on 1960s winter pitches, ankle-deep in mud?

Third, by growing the paying audience from a few hundred to many millions, communications technology has enabled the professionalisation that in turn is responsible for raising sporting standards. From radio, TV and the internet comes much of the revenue that improves pitches, builds gyms, hires expert coaches and allows sportsmen and women to train full-time. At the time of writing, the English Premier League is set to earn £900 million a season for TV rights. It is worth remembering this before we rush to complain about the number of broadcast games: TV money helps directly and indirectly to raise sporting standards, not just furnish the stars with their Bentleys.

Moreover, there is little evidence – perhaps with the exception of test cricket in some parts of the world – that televising games reduces the numbers travelling to see games live. In fact, it looks as if TV acts as a bait. Viewers see the screened product and, if they like it, go for the real thing. The top matches of the leading Premier League teams are frequently broadcast, yet Old Trafford, Anfield, the Emirates and Stamford Bridge are invariably sold out. The situation is similar with rugby union, which only recently turned professional. International, cup and league games are widely available on TV, yet crowds turn up in ever-increasing numbers.

TV money helps **directly** and indirectly **to raise sporting standards**, not just **furnish** the stars with their **Bentleys**

> In 2006, Rugby Union Premiership crowds averaged 10,000 per game for the first time. Only a few years earlier, a club like Newcastle Falcons was lucky if spectator numbers reached four figures.

For the fantastic array of excellent sport available 24 hours a day, thank you technology.

Spreading the Word

That top-class sport is now wholly international is due to developments in communications and transport technology. An Olympic Games in China or a football world cup in South Africa? Both would have been inconceivable before the age of cheap flights and radio/TV. So would competitions like the Tri-nations rugby tournament, the modern test cricket itinerary and the UEFA Champions League with mid-week games played from Glasgow to Jerusalem. This matters because it raises standards, helps break down barriers between nations and adds variety and the spice of international rivalry to sport.

More Fun, Different Fun

Technology has given birth to a whole calendar-full of new sports. From the 19th century's cycling and motorsport to the snowboarding and paragliding of today, the entire sporting picture has become brighter and richer as new opportunities have arisen. Skating is no longer reserved for the winter months nor tennis for the summer, and floodlighting has revolutionised the times games can be played.

New varieties of sport – the immensely popular Twenty20 cricket, for example – owe their existence to technology.

As well as improving the standard of what's happening on the pitch, technology has improved the whole match-day experience. Think better sound systems, wireless links to the ref, simultaneous large-screen coverage and replays, more detailed scoreboards, more comfortable and better laid-out stadiums, improved transport to and from grounds, greater security with video surveillance . . . No, only romantics seriously wish away the benefits of modern-day technology.

Furthermore, there are the benefits of technology-aided judgement. Although these do not yet extend to football, they do include photo finishes, precise timing, video replay, light meters, Hawkeye and all the other gadgetry that help to cut down acrimonious controversy. Also, as noted elsewhere, referring a judgment to some form of replay adds a new and exciting element to the match-day experience.

Well-Regulated

Most sports administrators believe that any potential threat to sport posed by 'cheating' technology is nullified by controls exercised by the national and international bodies overseeing individual sports. The classic example is the ICU's intervention to outlaw the high-tech superbikes that threatened to take over the sport and put it beyond the pocket of ordinary cyclists (see Chapter 4).

Other sports have regulatory systems of their own. The extent of padding permitted beneath shirts worn by players in the Rugby World Cup 2007, for instance, was strictly limited by the IRB to avoid the 'body armour' appearance of the NFL and consequent injuries caused by collisions between players who felt unrealistically secure. Rowing has outlawed sliding riggers, cricket does not allow electronic communication between players and coaches during play, and the dimensions, weights and composition of all sporting bats, racquets and balls are precisely specified. The performances of track and field athletes are regulated by a basket-ful of controls ranging from track bounce to javelin weight, from the composition of a vaulting pole to dietary supplements.

Which brings us to the big question: performance-enhancing substances. We have heard a good deal of scaremongering. For example, it has been suggested that, in the light of alarming yet unsubstantiated rumours and the number of high profile cases of drug abuse that come to light, the battle against drugs in sport is being lost. So let's reconsider the evidence.

One. It's important to bear in mind that a positive drug test is a story – a negative one is not. It is always in the interest of the media to make things appear worse than they really are because that way they attract more viewers and readers. As an example, take the clean slate reported for the 2007 Rugby World Cup: the story was tucked away at the bottom of the sports' pages and websites. Now, had Brian Habana or Lawrence Dallaglio tested positive, that would have been news!

Two. As far as we can tell, the drug problem is concentrated mainly in a few power/endurance sports: cycling, athletics, weightlifting, swimming. In those where style, skill and technique are pre-eminent – football, cricket, golf, rugby, tennis, etc. – drug abuse is rarely detected. This is hardly surprising. We are a very long way from the point when popping a pill will turn my two left feet into the twinkle toes of a Pelé. So to claim that sport as a whole is riddled with drugs is a gross exaggeration. The majority of sports and competitors seem to be largely unaffected.

Three. Testing may not be perfect, but the stream of offenders being caught for drug abuse shows that the system is working. If masking or getting away with taking performance-enhancing substances were so easy, why are so many caught? Just plain dumb? I doubt it.

Four. It is not necessarily so great a problem if the cheats are one step ahead of the testers because, as long as the testing regime is robust, they will eventually be collared. Besides, if we adopt an anti-drugs policy such as that suggested at the end of Chapter 7 (the Anti-Doping Tax), the problem can be managed effectively.

The immeasurable majesty of sport: Brazilian superstar Pelé in in his prime.

To conclude, sport at the serious level is sufficiently well controlled to negate the detrimental effects of new technology. In the end, it is all a question of self-inter-est. The administrators of a sport are also its guardians. Their aim is to maintain its distinctive qualities, its integrity and its competitiveness by striking a fair and realistic balance between innovation and preservation. Moreover, it is not in their interest to have too wide a technology gap between the top and bottom, the pro-fessionals and the occasional participants. Sports change, of course, and technol-ogy is often behind that change, but it happens within what is generally a well-regulated environment.

Carry on Sporting

For all the ballyhoo, technological innovation has made precious little difference to sport below the élite level.

Technology **may sharpen the cutting edge** but at the blunt end **things remain as charmingly crude** as they ever **were**

Sunday morning footie players in the park might sport flashier boots and the ball they play with may be lighter than the leather cannon balls of yore, but the game remains essentially that of the last 125 years. The same goes for just about all other sports: I ski just as badly on composite skis as I did on the old wooden ones on which I learned. Technology may sharpen the cutting edge but at the blunt end things remain as charmingly crude as they ever were.

Go with the Flow

We have now reached the last point in our defence of the happy marriage between sport and technology: change brought in by technological development is inevitable, so there is no point in fighting against it. Better to harness it for the good it can bring, as we mostly do now, rather than bemoan the loss of a vague Corinthian spirit in a mythical bygone age of innocence when sport was sport and not the plaything of equally mythical evil scientists.

The Verdict

Weighing the evidence, **there can** be little reasonable doubt that sport in general has benefited enormously from technological development. The range and scope of activities has grown and at the top end, standards of performance have risen sharply. Competitions are less insular and officiating and judgement are generally more accurate. Sporting occasions are better presented and can be enjoyed by millions unable to witness them in person.

Yet our verdict is not unanimous. A small but passionate minority have serious reservations.

What are these anxieties that hover so darkly, spoiling an otherwise rosy picture? They are, in no particular order, a worry that sport may become a mere vehicle for technology and all its attendant commercial interests; that the cost of sporting technology widens an already ugly chasm between rich and poor; that another gap is growing between sport at the élite level and the grass-roots activities of the majority; that drugs and, far more seriously, genetic manipulation may eventually make a mockery of the entire sporting scene.

Therefore, while accepting that technology is innocent and should be free to resume life with its sporting partner, we impose the following four conditions:

Condition One

A suitable international body – the IOC or even the UN – must draw up and make readily available an authoritative and universally acceptable statement setting out (i) what sport is for, and (ii) the values and principles of sporting participation and achievement. All leading athletes and officials must make a public commitment to uphold these ideals.

Condition Two

Professional sport accepts its responsibilities by committing itself to maintaining strong ties with the amateur echelons through funding, personal links and the dispersal of technology.

Condition Three

The developed world's sports clubs, their governing associations and the technological enterprises with whom they work, including private companies and universities, agree to close the technology gap by producing cheaper, more practical technologies which can be readily shared worldwide.

If computers can be provided to developing nations at reasonable prices, why not all the technological paraphernalia of modern sport, from boots and balls to analysis programs?

Condition Four

The governing bodies of all sports are to agree (a) to a precise definition of 'natural' and 'human' achievement; (b) to a fixed levy on all sport's revenue streams for the purpose of funding an all-powerful international watchdog and testing organisation whose task is to see that every sportsman and woman is clean of doping and genetic tampering; and (c) to impose a life ban from

Winner of the celebrated Tour de France on seven consecutive occasions, US cycling superstar Lance Armstrong was constantly under suspicion of drug-taking. Until such issues can be decided definitively, an ugly stain on top-level sport will remain.

competitive sport on all those found to have contravened doping and genetic tampering regulations.

If these conditions are agreed and adhered to, the future of sport as we know it is assured. If they are not, the outlook is at best uncertain. Top-level competition may well continue its sad transformation into just another branch of Hollywood, with all its dubious values and tawdry practices. What price then the nightmare scenario of our Megalympics, where manufactured humanoids compete like Meccano monsters, devoid of conscience, heart and soul?

'O brave new world that has such people in it!'
– William Shakespeare, The Tempest

Index